# Structuring European Private Equity

# Structuring European Private Equity

Edited by
Iggy Bassi and Jeremy Grant

EUROMONEY BOOKS

Published by
Euromoney Institutional Investor Plc
Nestor House, Playhouse Yard
London EC4V 5EX
United Kingdom

Tel: +44 (0) 20 7779 8999 or USA +1 800 437 9997
Fax: +44 (0) 20 7779 8300
www.euromoneybooks.com
E-mail:hotline@euromoneyplc.com



ISBN 1 84374 262 4



Printed by TJ International, Padstow, Cornwall

# Contents

# Foreword

The competitive dynamics of the European private equity market are changing rapidly. The unique confluence of low interest rates, availability of significant leverage finance and greater adoption of private equity has created enormous interest in the region and record amounts of capital have been committed to funds, with corresponding attractive returns for investors. The size and growth of the private equity market in recent years has meant it has become a permanent feature on the financial landscape. With success and relatively low barriers to entry comes an inevitable normalisation of investment returns in the mid to long term. By all accounts, the maturing of the private equity market coincides with a capital over-supply, which may lead to some disruption down the road. At this stage of any maturing industry, innovative players will seek to craft strategies to ensure sustainable long-term yields. As the private equity market matures, delivering upper quartile returns will rely more on the ingenuity and innovation of fund managers.

A simple structure-conduct-performance analysis of the private equity market highlights an expected long-term trend towards declining investment returns. Furthermore, the resilience of economic tenets governing demand and supply laws means an inevitable rise in target asset prices in the short term. The current capital supply-side imbalance has eroded many of the traditional asymmetrical advantages which private equity funds once relied upon for premium returns. The efficacy of the 'auction' process has shifted the balance of power towards sellers of assets. Predictably, many private equity stakeholders have lowered their overall returns expectations in the mid to long term. At the same time, there is a growing gulf in the performance between upper quartile and median funds, as witnessed by the ever increasing IRR spreads. Lower expected returns and widening IRR spreads will undoubtedly sharpen the investors' approach to selecting the fund manager, which is still the single most important determinant of upper quartile returns.

As with many other industries, 'excess capacity' will cause market disequilibrium and bring about a certain level of disruption. As the private equity industry enters the next phase of maturity, it presents threats and opportunities for limited partners, general partners, and new potential participants such as hedge funds. Innovative funds will seize the opportunity and recalibrate their competitive positioning to ensure they are able to sustain premium returns. Funds unable to significantly differentiate their strategy are unlikely to enjoy above-average returns, forcing their investors to re-allocate to other funds or asset classes. It is worth remembering that investors expect a meaningful risk-adjusted premium over the public markets to justify the illiquidity of private equity investing, and as history demonstrates, only a minority of private equity funds beat the public markets.

The success and maturity of private equity in Europe presents significant opportunities for European private and public enterprises. The cumulative effect of global competition, deregulation and demographic shifts calls for a heightened sense of 'industrial renewal'. Although not a panacea, private equity provides enterprises with an opportunity to improve their competitive positioning and renew capital structures by realigning shareholder interests.

The senior management teams of mid and large cap public companies increasingly embrace private equity solutions to introduce much needed transformation programs in a private environment and seek high personal rewards not traditionally available through European public companies. Generally, private equity funds have a short-to-mid term view and are not constrained by the need to integrate acquired assets into an existing operation, thus making it easier to transform companies and divest non-core or underperforming assets.

As the adoption of private equity increases, so to do the expectations and confidence levels of enterprises seeking to partner with funds. Sellers motivated by maximising financial returns behave in a predictable manner and are keen to play off bids from competing PE funds in what is best described as the e-Bay model of private equity investing. The global over-supply of capital has caused intense rivalry among funds, leading some to focus on operational improvements of their acquired companies as many traditional financial advantages have been competed away. The need to create this 'transformation' imperative inside portfolio companies has caused many funds to differentiate their endowment of human assets by hiring experienced operational executives, or seek advantages by forming alliances with consulting firms. Others will seek to focus on certain industry sectors or focus on proprietary 'upstream' advantages to pre-empt the auction process. Blended or hybrid models of private equity and hedge funds are also likely to grow to offer investors risk-adjusted returns and liquidity solutions.

Another important area for Europe is the ability to effectively fund its innovation, which lies at the heart of its long-term ability to compete. Although there has been renewed interest in the European venture capital market in 2005, it still confronts its perennial challenge of having an innovation advantage but a commercialisation disadvantage. Transferring successful aspects of the US and Israeli venture model may help overcome this predicament, however, European VC funds need to recognise the venture market has gone global. The authors rightfully point out there is a necessity at both ends of European private equity (buyouts and venture) to transition from being a local 'supplier' of capital towards a global 'service provider'. Both buyout and VC funds will be increasingly reliant upon an 'active' ownership model to create above market returns for investors.

This book is an important and timely contribution in understanding the changing dynamics for private equity stakeholders as the industry continues to mature, especially within the European context. It covers pertinent topics such as the adoption of private equity by enterprises, performance measurement, corporate governance and the need to create value beyond financial engineering. The book balances the views of limited partners, fund managers and intermediary channels. There are also important contributions highlighting the application of the private equity model in new areas, namely the non-profit sectors and also the penetration of private equity in the transition economies of Eastern Europe. The insights of the contributions will be very useful to both private equity practitioners and investors in European private equity.

Mark B. Fuller
Chairman and CEO of Monitor Group
April, 2006

# Author biographies

## About the editors

**Iggy Bassi**

Iggy Bassi specialises in private equity at The Monitor Group, a leading strategy consulting and investment advisory firm. He is currently developing focused private equity funds for the European market, where he plays a key role in the strategy, structuring and fundraising process. Over the last 10 years he has been actively involved in Europe's high growth sectors through entrepreneurial ventures, operations and strategy consulting. He started his career in M&A at Jefferies-Broadview. Iggy holds a masters degree in management studies from the Judge Business School, Cambridge University, where he was awarded the Economic & Social Research Council scholarship. He is currently an advisor to FiNoble, an India-focused investment advisory firm.

**Jeremy Grant**

Jeremy Grant is on academic sabbatical based at the Graduate Institute of International Studies in Geneva and the London School of Economics. He holds a law degree from the LSE, and MSc degrees in Management and International Relations from the same institution. His research focuses on corporate governance, M&A, takeover defences and anti-trust regulation of mergers. He has worked for JP Morgan in corporate finance and equity research. He is also co-author *Corporate Governance in the US and Europe*, and author and editor of *European Takeovers: The Art of Acquisition*, published by Euromoney Books.

## About the contributors

**Carsten Bienz**

Carsten Bienz is an Assistant Professor in Finance at the Norwegian School of Economics and Business Administration. He is also a Research Associate at the Financial Markets Group, London School of Economics, where he spent a year as a Post-Doctoral Scholar. Carsten is affiliated as a researcher with the Center for Financial Studies in Frankfurt. He holds a PhD in Finance from Goethe University in Frankfurt and an MSc from University of Tübingen. His current research interests include corporate finance, especially venture capital and private equity.

**Stephanie Biggs**

Stephanie Biggs is a solicitor in the private equity group at SJ Berwin LLP. She specialises in alternative investment funds and has acted for fund managers in relation to the establishment and operation of private equity funds, real estate funds and hedge funds. She also has experience in the field of financial services law, and has advised fund managers on the application of the UK regulatory regime to their businesses. Stephanie graduated from the University of Reading with a first class law degree, and is currently studying for a postgraduate diploma in financial services law and regulation.

**Jonathan Blake**

Jonathan Blake, Head of Private Equity at SJ Berwin LLP, specialises in advising private equity and venture capital fund managers in Europe and elsewhere on the structuring of private equity and venture capital funds, management companies and carried interest incentive arrangements. He also advises private equity funds, investing institutions and management teams on management buyouts, venture and development capital investments and related taxation issues. As former Chairman of the Tax and Legal Committee of the EVCA, he produced and edited several publications on venture capital related matters across Europe. In April 2004, he was admitted to the BVCA 'Hall of Fame' in recognition of his contribution to the private equity industry over the past two decades. In April 2005, Jonathan was named global lawyer of the year for Private Funds by *The International Who's Who of Business Lawyers*.

**Dmitry Bosky**

Dmitry Bosky is Managing Partner with Berkeley Capital Partners. Prior to that, he served on the boards of a number of Russian regional venture funds of the EBRD, advising on the strategy for such funds. He spent 10 years at Security Pacific Venture Capital Group and was appointed Managing Director for Europe in 1987, with responsibility for building a portfolio of investments in a broad range of industries and across all stages of company development. He studied Operations Research, Finance and Accounting and graduated Phi Beta Kappa from the University of California, Berkeley, and holds an MBA from Harvard Business School.

**David Patrick Eich**

David Patrick Eich represents some of the largest private equity funds in their most complex leveraged buyouts and other sophisticated transactions in the United States, Europe and Asia. Dual qualified in the U.S. as an attorney and in the U.K. as a solicitor, he has closed many deals around the world from his offices in Chicago, London and Munich since 1994. He is a founding sponsor of the London Business School Private Equity Institute and a member of its Global Advisory Board. He also lectures on private equity annually to classes in the LBS M.B.A. degree program. David graduated from Harvard University magna cum laude in 1988 and Columbia Law School with Honours from the Parker Program in International and Foreign Law in 1992.

**André Frei**

André Frei, CFA, is Head of the Risk & Quantitative Management team at Partners Group, where he oversees the risk and quantitative management for the firm's hedge fund and private equity investments. He has authored several quantitative private equity research publications.

Together with Michael Studer, he has developed the latest generation of Partners Group's private equity commitment and cash flow models - used for commitment steering and cash flow management of Partners Group's private equity mandates and securitised private equity products. He holds a master's degree in mathematics from the Swiss Federal Institute of Technology (ETH) in Zurich, Switzerland, with a specialisation in finance and insurance mathematics.

**Sylvia Gansser-Potts**

Sylvia Gansser-Potts, Senior Banker at the EBRD, has been focusing on its fund-of-funds activities for six years. Her responsibilities include investments in new funds as well as the management of a portfolio of funds. She serves on the advisory boards of several funds investing in central Europe and Russia, as well as on the investment committees of certain funds. Sylvia joined EBRD in 1992, involved in direct investments and lending initially in the Balkans, followed by an emphasis on financial institutions. Prior to the EBRD, Sylvia worked for Swiss Bank (now UBS) in Switzerland and Japan. She is a graduate of Paris University, and holds an MBA from INSEAD in France.

**Didier Guennoc**

Didier Guennoc is EVCA's Chief Economist, advising on areas such as professional standards and the analysis of returns generated by the private equity asset class. Didier joined Origo Management in March 2005. His areas of expertise include investor relations and the asset allocation strategy of limited partners. He helps general partners in assessing and improving their investor relations and also advises limited partners in designing their allocation strategy and monitoring their environment and portfolio. Didier holds a PhD in business and administration from the University Robert Schuman, Strasbourg. He is also a member of the Advisory Board of the Center for Entrepreneurial and Financial Studies at the Technische Universität München, Germany.

**Matthew H. Hurlock**

Matthew H. Hurlock is a resident partner in the London office of Kirkland & Ellis International LLP. Matthew regularly advises private equity funds in connection with leveraged acquisitions and other complex transactions in Europe and the United States. Matthew also advises general partners and limited partners in connection with private equity fund formations, including some of the largest funds currently active in Europe. Prior to entering private practice Matthew worked at the World Bank in Washington, D.C. and the European Bank for Reconstruction and Development in London. Matthew graduated magna cum laude from Princeton University in 1988 and from Columbia Law School in 1993, where he was Notes and Comments Editor for the *Columbia Law Review*.

**Rob John**

Rob John FRSA trained as an organic chemist, completing his doctorate at Oxford University, followed by research posts in the USA, Switzerland and Ethiopia. He then spent 15 years managing refugee and international development programmes throughout

Africa and Asia. In 2000, he directed a UK-based 'venture philanthropy' fund, and since 2005 has been a freelance consultant and Fellow of the Skoll Centre for Social Entrepreneurship at the Saïd Business School, Oxford University. He is currently adviser to the European Venture Philanthropy Association, and consults on venture philanthropy and social entrepreneurship.

**Vesa Jormakka**
Vesa Jormakka has been heading Argo Global Capital's operations in Europe since 2000. Prior to joining Argo, he was a Partner and one of the founding members of Mustang Ventures, the corporate venture capital arm of Siemens AG Information & Communication Group, now part of Siemens Venture Capital. Vesa has also been in charge of the global M&A and partnering activities of the Networking Systems business unit for Siemens AG in Munich. From 1988 to 1997, he held various engineering, sales and general management positions for Siemens in Germany, the UK and Finland in the data networking, defence electronics and mobile communications divisions. Vesa's experience also includes the implementation and introduction of the first GSM network in Europe.

**Tom Kirchmaier**
Dr Tom Kirchmaier is lecturer in Strategy at the Manchester Business School and Fellow of the Financial Markets Group, London School of Economics. He also holds a PhD and MSc from LSE. His research interests include corporate governance, M&A and corporate restructuring. He teaches corporate governance and strategy to students and business executives, and publishes in this area both academically and in the business media, such as the *Financial Times* and the *Wall Street Journal Europe*. He works regularly as a consultant for a number of global firms including the Volkswagen Group, the DaimlerChrysler Group and Oracle.

**David Latter**
David Latter is a Principal at Apax Partners in London, where he is a member of the Technology and Telecoms Group. He joined Apax in 1998 and has worked across a range of telecoms, technology and financial services investments. He previously worked at Schroders investment bank. David's transactions at Apax have included Global Refund, Best International, Moneybox Corporation, Inmarsat, Intelsat and Travelex. David graduated with a first class honours degree in psychology from University College London and also holds an MPhil in management studies from Cambridge University.

**Oliver Markl**
Oliver Mark is a London-based Principal at Monitor Clipper Partners, a mid-market buyout fund with US$1.5bn under management. Before joining Monitor Clipper Partners in November 1998, Oliver was a Vice President in JPMorgan's Structured Products department in London, and prior to that in the firm's M&A department in Paris. Oliver started his professional career as an M&A analyst at JPMorgan in 1990 after obtaining a master of science from the Ecole Polytechnique in Paris.

**Christophe Nicolas**

Christophe Nicolas joined Greenpark Capital in 2004 and is now a senior member of their investment and management committees. He is responsible for sourcing and executing secondary transactions which offer early liquidity to global investors in portfolios of direct private equity investments and in private equity funds. Prior to this, Christophe spent over three years at global private equity firm Permira, sourcing and executing leveraged buyout investments in Europe in the media, leisure and business services industries and spent five years as principal at Broadview (now Jefferies), a London-based merchant bank. Christophe started his career in investment banking at Goldman Sachs in London and BNP in Hong Kong. He holds an MBA from Ecole Supérieure de Commerce de Paris.

**Shashank Singh**

Shashank Singh is part of Apax Partners' Tech & Telecoms team in London, focusing on investments in the telecoms sector, including fixed and wireless service providers. His investments include TIM Hellas, Q-Telecom, Bezeq, Synetrix and Damovo Group. Shashank is also part of Apax's Asia Group, with particular focus on India. Prior to Apax, Shashank was a strategy consultant with Monitor Company in London, focusing on telecoms and high-tech. Shashank has an MBA from Harvard Business School, from which he graduated as a Baker Scholar, a first class degree in economics from Cambridge and a BA (Honours) with distinction from Delhi University.

**Joe Sovran**

Joe Sovran is a Partner at Capvent, jointly managing the strategy, sourcing, due diligence and monitoring of its international private equity programme, which seeks the best risk-adjusted investments worldwide across all sizes and styles of private equity. He sits on several fund advisory committees, and is also an international partner of Capvent India Private Equity. He previously worked on M&A, valuations and capital raising with Regent, a European investment bank specialising in the technology sector. He has also been an investor and manager of an entrepreneurial business, and was with Nortel and IBM. He also holds an MBA and a BSc in Engineering.

**Michael Studer**

Michael Studer, PhD, works within Partners Group's Risk & Quantitative Management team with responsibility for the risk and quantitative management of the firm's private equity investments. Together with André Frei, he developed the latest generation of Partners Group's private equity commitment and cash flow models, which are used for commitment steering and cash flow management of Partners Group's private equity mandates and securitised private equity products. Prior to joining Partners Group, Michael specialised in financial and insurance mathematics during his PhD studies at the Federal Institute of Technology, Zurich. In his thesis, he analysed analytical methods in market risk management. He has authored several quantitative private equity research publications.

# Introduction

This book focuses on the key developments of the European private equity market as it becomes a permanent feature of the European investment scene. Its evolution towards a professional and mature investment asset class will invariably impact strategies deployed and levels of governance, transparency and performance measurement, which may ultimately lead to a new equilibrium between reasonable disclosure and the need to retain the 'private' in private equity.

The role of private equity in the modern European economy is vital as the Continent faces significant challenges from globalisation, corporate restructuring and succession issues in many mid to large companies. Private equity investors have increasingly emerged to facilitate solutions to the dilemmas faced by corporate Europe. Increasingly, the gaze and pressure of surviving as a public company has made CEOs and managers more attuned to the possibilities of partnering with private equity players in order to achieve necessary transformation and realise significant value.

Going private can give senior management a breathing space from achieving short-term (quarterly or bi-annual) earnings targets, and allow them to focus on longer-term strategy. Moreover, senior management will often find that their compensation package will improve when the company is taken private, as their equity stake in the enterprise will usually increase substantially. In turn, this will strongly align management's interests with the fund's general partners and subdue the traditional principal agent problems faced by dispersed shareholders in public companies. The general partners also maintain a level of contractual governance over managers in their portfolio companies that extends far beyond that available to institutional investors in a listed firm. The general partners are also the direct enforcers of contractual governance terms, as they will maintain a significant presence on the boards of all of their portfolio companies – unlike the boards of public companies, which are populated by non-executive directors, elected by shareholders, but often with close ties to management. Chapter 5 by Carsten Bienz, Jeremy Grant and Thomas Kirchmaier examines private equity contractual corporate governance in depth.

Armed with ever greater fund sizes, private equity buyout funds are becoming agile players in acquiring business assets and re-orientating business strategy towards delivering value in a short to medium time horizon. Yet, private equity funds are a victim of their own success as more enter the market in the quest for higher returns, driven by a global liquidity surplus.

With increased competition, funds are responding by shifting their strategies away from the generalist model focusing on pure financial engineering, to become more specialised in relation to industry focus, deal size and geography. This in turn makes it easier to source industry or geographically focused deals, and for limited partners to identify the top performers in each class. As deals increase in both size and complexity at the top end of the spectrum, the need for specialisation will continue to grow. Two other emerging trends reinforce this point. First, the rise of larger club deals combining syndicates of private equity firms with industry partners. Often these facilitate the acquisition of larger publicly listed firms. Examples include the US$5bn purchase of MGM studios by a combination of Texas Pacific Group, Providence Equity Partners, Sony and Comcast, the US cable operator in 2005. In Europe, also in 2005, the Italian wireless service provider Wind was acquired by the Egyptian telecommunications company Orascom in partnership with a number of private equity players in a deal valued at €12.1bn. This trend and the acquisition strategy of combining private equity and industry partners is examined in more detail by David Latter and Shashank Singh of Apax Partners in Chapter 1.

Another emerging trend to engender advantage in an increasingly competitive market is the consultancy model – where funds are aligned with global consulting firms – such as Monitor Clipper Partners, allowing them to draw on industry-specific strategy consulting resources. Other funds have established captive or 'in house' consulting operations: for example, KKR with Capstone, facilitating transformation strategies. Oliver Markl of Monitor Clipper Partners discusses this perspective in Chapter 8 in more detail.

Despite these strategic shifts, which allow for creation of greater value for investors, the heightened competitive intensity of the private equity industry will undoubtedly have an impact on the expectations of returns in the next two to three years. The efficiency of pricing target firms through the auction process has led to an escalation of entry prices, thus ultimately driving down returns. This has the effect of forcing fund managers to seek more innovative deal sourcing strategies and more importantly it creates a 'transformation imperative' within target firms so value creation becomes a function of improving the target's operations and earnings, for which these emerging strategies cater.

Another area subject to shifts in its traditional parameters, again driven by the maturing of private equity as an asset class, and its professionalisation, is the performance measurement of the funds themselves. The industry has continued to develop innovative approaches to overcome hurdles such as illiquidity, lack of historical performance data and traditional scarcity of disclosure (all of which are more pronounced in Europe than the US), and provide effective and comparable performance measurements for limited partners. Didier Guennoc of the European Venture Capital Association, in Chapter 9, critiques current measurement methodologies and argues that, because of such flaws, limited partners' due diligence in relation to potential fund investments and the general partners is an increasingly vital element for achieving outperformance.

The private equity market itself is also providing solutions to these issues – for example, Chapter 7, by Christophe Nicolas, examines the market for limited partners to trade fund positions in secondary deals – which ultimately increases the liquidity of private equity portfolios – while funds of funds provide another more liquid avenue for exposure to the market.

At the other end of the buyout spectrum lies the European venture capital industry, which has begun to show signs of recovery following the collapse of the technology bubble in early 2000. It is entering the new investment cycle with a greater recognition that it needs to incorporate several successful and transferable dimensions from other high-return venture capital markets, such as the US and Israeli market. Improving market reach and organisational capabilities will be key strategies in the new investment cycle leading to greater probability of success.

Paradoxically, both venture capital and buyout firms are recognising that they need to transition from being a *'supplier'* of capital towards being a global *'service provider'*. The former because of systemic weakness in the European venture model, and the latter because of its own success through capital over-supply and accompanying asset inflation. Put simply, above-market private equity returns, whether in buyouts or venture capital, will be increasingly reliant on creating value through a successful 'hands-on' operational model, rather than through financial engineering.

The book is split into four parts. Part I explores the current market dynamics in the private equity market. Chapter 1, by David Latter and Shashank Singh, highlights the relationship possibilities between private equity and industry and how a fund can help corporates achieve specific objectives. This is supported through a series of short case studies. Chapter 2, by Iggy Bassi and Vesa Jormakka, explores the current dynamics of the European venture capital market and highlights which aspects of the venture capital model European funds can apply from the US model. This is especially relevant as the competitive landscape and the effects of globalisation will widen the gap between weak- and strong-performing funds.

Part II focuses on the fund structures and the question of corporate governance in private equity-owned firms. Chapter 3, by Jonathan Blake, examines changes in current fund structures in relation to the agreed general partner and limited partner terms – while Chapter 4, by Matthew Hurlock and David Eich, looks at the nature and current boundaries of the traditional limited partnership fund structure. Chapter 5, by Carsten Bienz, Jeremy Grant and Thomas Kirchmaier, explores the governance relationship between a fund's general partners, and the management of portfolio firms.

Part III explores investment strategies and the key area of investment performance. Chapter 6, by Joe Sovran, examines the increasing role and influence of the fund-of-funds channel, highlighting the benefits for limited partners considering entering or increasing their exposure to private equity investing. Chapter 7, by Christophe Nicolas, deals with the question of 'Where next for the secondaries market?', highlighting the rise and growing sophistication and use of the secondary market for private equity funds and limited partners. With increasing asset inflation and concerns of lower expected returns in private equity, Chapter 8, by Oliver Markl, examines how private equity funds can create value beyond financial engineering through examining how operations and strategic decisions can be improved. Chapter 9, by Didier Guennoc, analyses in detail the issue of private equity returns versus public market return, which is a key and persistent issue for investors allocating to private equity. The promise of private equity has been to deliver a risk-adjusted premium over public equities; however, with heightened levels of commitments to private equity, higher competitive intensity and asset inflation, average private equity returns will fall. However, there is a widening gap between the IRR performance of top quartile funds and median funds, hence the manager selection choices are critical for investors. Related to Chapter 9, Chapter 10, by André Frei and Michael Studer, examines the performance measurement of private equity funds, utilising empirical analysis to assess performance methodologies and the implications for interpreting outcomes.

Part IV deals with the new frontiers of private equity, namely in new geographies and sectors. Chapter 11, by Sylvia Gansser-Potts and Dmitry Bosky, explores the rise of private equity investing in eastern Europe. Since the collapse of the Berlin Wall, private equity allocations and returns have increased steadily across the region. The chapter highlights the key clusters of countries in the region and highlights Europe's largest emerging economy – Russia. Finally, Chapter 12, by Rob John, is devoted to how the principles of private equity are increasingly applied to yield social returns. The chapter explores the rise of venture philanthropy with cases studies of some pioneering work in this field initiated by professionals from the private equity community.

# Part I

# The market

Chapter 1

# 'Partnering with the large caps': The private equity opportunity for industry

David Latter and Shashank Singh
*Apax Partners Limited*

This chapter considers the changing interaction between private equity and industry in the modern economy. The evolution of the private equity industry over the last 30 years has led to ever-more sophisticated transaction dynamics and structures. It is argued that plain vanilla financial engineering has increasingly made way for a new breed of transaction, where partnership with industry has become the key driver. This trend is considered by reference to a number of case examples demonstrating this evolved model of private equity.

## The new model for private equity

The year 2005 was a landmark for the private equity industry. A slew of jumbo deals on both sides of the Atlantic culminated with the announcement in November of the largest private equity transaction since KKR's 1989 acquisition of RJR Nabisco for US$31bn. A consortium of private equity funds advised by Apax Partners, Blackstone, KKR, Permira and Providence announced a €12bn transaction to acquire Tele Danmark (TDC), Denmark's national telecommunications carrier. Some commentators saw this as marking the return to the 1989 era of leveraged mega-deals, perhaps implying the same inevitable consequences of those excesses. Yet the reality is that, apart from the relative sizes of the transactions, these deals have little in common with their predecessors.

The RJR Nabisco deal was a sign of its times: very high leverage, returns driven through simple financial engineering and a hostile takeover of a company offering 'low-hanging fruit' in the form of outrageous corporate excess. Stories are legendary of US$300m spent on developing smokeless cigarettes, the 'RJR Air Force' with 36 pilots for 10 corporate jets, along with corporate apartments in New York and corporate boxes at Madison Square Garden. All the excesses came under control after the buyout. Leverage in these types of transactions could be 90 per cent of the purchase price or more, which served the twin purpose of supercharging equity returns and imposing discipline on management teams. Holding periods were long with the key driver of value being the pay-down of senior debt: for example a study of 38 buyouts conducted by KKR between 1977 and 1989 suggests a median holding period of 7.6 years.[1]

Despite the parallels in terms of size, the TDC transaction is much more representative of the evolved model of private equity prevalent since the 1990s. The attributes of this new model typically include:

- a higher equity contribution, typically in the range of 20–30 per cent of the purchase price;
- purchase of companies in cooperation with management, with hostile takeovers being a rarity; and
- private equity governance being a cornerstone of the strategy of the industry, in particular the increasing importance of 'hands-on' investors, operating partners, internal consulting arms and 100-day plans.

This evolution has been necessitated by both the increasing number of private equity funds that understand the pure financial engineering model and therefore have competed away 'simple' returns, and the fact that industry itself is much more savvy and competitive today than it was in the old era.

A regional comparison of the private equity industry shows that the European sector (especially outside the United Kingdom) has historically been slower to develop than its counterpart in the United States. However, this has changed, and the current decade has seen a step-change both in the total amount of private equity investment in Europe and in the role played by buyout investments in this total. Exhibit 1.1 shows the absolute amount of capital invested by European private equity since 1986. The graph demonstrates that, after the boom in start-up and expansion capital in the later 1990s and early 2000s, driven in part by the technology bubble, the growth of the European private equity market has been driven by buyout investments. As would be expected, private equity fund-raising in Europe shows a similar trend (see Exhibit 1.2).

There has been speculation for several years now that the weight of available private equity money would lead to fierce competition for a limited supply of assets, driving up prices and

Exhibit 1.1

**Private equity funding in Europe by stage of investment, 1986-2005**

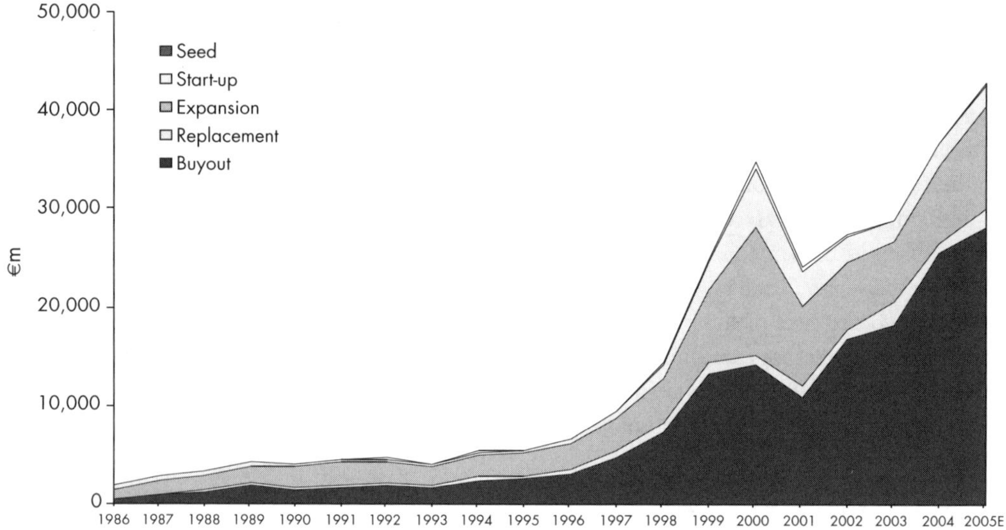


*Source*: EVCA Yearbooks, 1990-2004, EVCA March 2006 press release on 2005 activity.

Exhibit 1.2

**Annual private equity fundraising in Europe, 1986-2005**

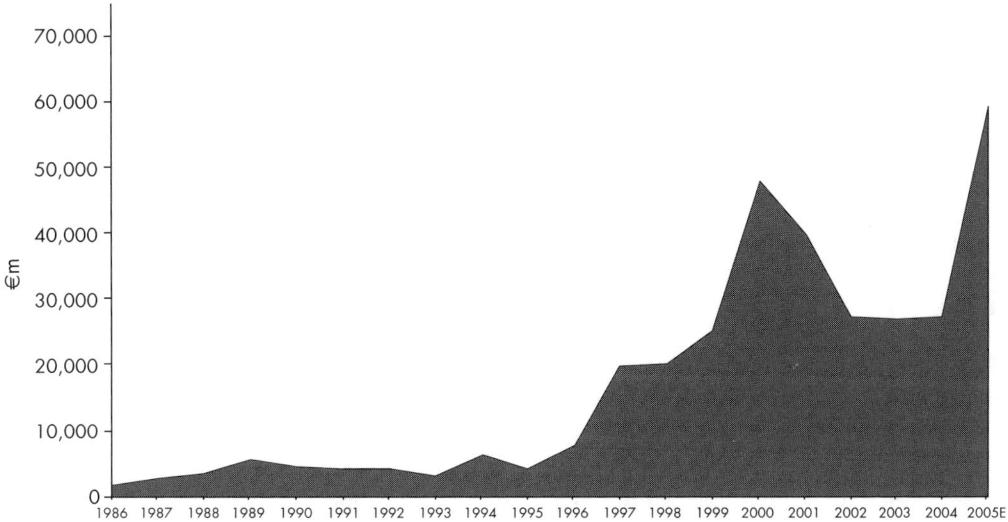


*Source*: EVCA Yearbooks, 1990-2004, EVCA March 2006 press release on 2005 activity.

leading to long-term reduced returns. While the market is undoubtedly competitive, private equity returns have in fact continued to outperform most other asset classes; 2005 was notable not only as a record investment year, but also a record year for successful exits and returns of cash to private equity funds. Part of the reason for this may be that, in practice, the supply of assets has increased as much as the demand. The era of mega-funds has opened up a new range of possibilities: four- or five-way consortia to consummate transactions previously out of reach for private equity; increased numbers of public-to-private transactions; proprietary transactions; and industry partnerships brought about through now well-established networks with industry. This is demonstrated by, for instance, the increasing volumes of public-to-private transactions in Europe, in terms of both total value and number of transactions, the growth of which has actually outpaced that of total private equity and also buyouts (see Exhibit 1.3).

Meanwhile, the public equity markets are becoming more complicated to deal with. Public companies suffer from a number of constraints, including:

- an emphasis on quarterly analyst calls, leading to a focus on the achievement of short-term financial goals;
- greater requirements for public disclosure;
- a focus on accounting-based earnings rather than fundamental cash flow;
- impact of a number of corporate scandals, which has resulted in an increased burden from regulations such as Sarbanes-Oxley; and
- fragmented shareholder bases, some with complicated shareholders such as activist hedge funds, making shareholder decision-making a decentralised and sometimes arduous process.

Exhibit 1.3

**Value and number of public-to-private transactions in Europe, 1995-2005**

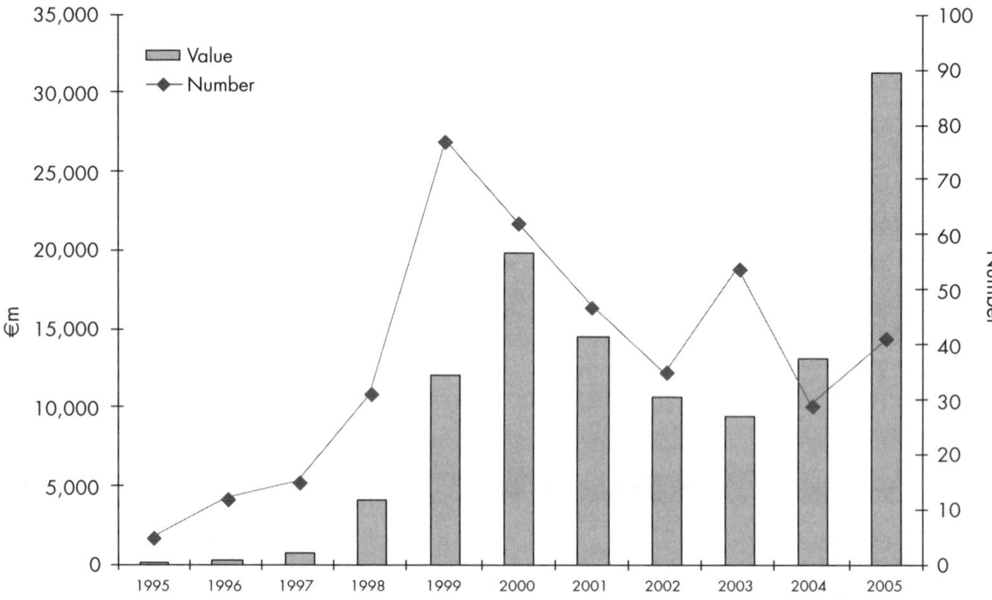


*Source*: CMBOR European MBO Review.

These constraints would suggest that the public markets are becoming less effective governance vehicles for many companies, especially companies in need of turnaround or radical changes in strategy.

With imaginative financial engineering now a given, real outperformance in private equity will be driven by industry expertise and successful partnerships with industry in order to identify and price the best assets, and then to work with the investee companies to maximise performance, and not just below the EBITDA line (earnings before interest, taxes, depreciation and amortisation) of the profit and loss account. Such partnerships can take many forms, including partnership with management, with shareholders, with corporates and with governments. We present in this chapter a number of examples of investments by funds advised by Apax Partners that reflect this model of partnership with industry.

The first case describes a partnership with a listed company, Phillips-Van Heusen, to facilitate acquisitions in a time of weak stock market conditions. The second, Inmarsat, is an example of how early partnerships with shareholders can be critical to facilitating complex transactions. TIM Hellas, the third case study, demonstrates how private equity can partner with corporates to create exit solutions for non-core businesses under demanding conditions. Finally, Bezeq provides an example of how private equity can successfully address the very different requirements of a government partner. All the cases are representative of the new, evolved model of private equity investment.

## Case study 1: Partnering with management – Phillips-Van Heusen's acquisition of Calvin Klein

Phillips-Van Heusen (PVH) is a US clothing manufacturer and distributor with particular strength in the area of men's shirts, with brands such as DKNY, Kenneth Cole, Geoffrey Beene and Van Heusen. In this segment they lead the department store market with a share of 40 per cent, and are also the market leaders in factory outlets with over 700 outlet locations carrying the brands of IZOD, Van Heusen, Bass and Geoffrey Beene. The multi-brand strategy in all business sectors is based on a mutually utilised and highly efficient infrastructure that has yielded a steady rise in earnings per share over a number of years.

With the existing body of experience at PVH in the integration and further development of brands, as well as the established infrastructure, further significant growth in sales and profits seemed possible through the acquisition of another strong brand name. For some time therefore, PVH together with Apax had been searching for a suitable addition to its portfolio of brands. After examining several acquisition options, PVH and the Apax Funds chose Calvin Klein as a brand with an excellent global position and a strong potential for further growth.

With a purchase price of US$430m, PVH was unable to finance the acquisition of Calvin Klein on its own, and the US public markets in early 2003 were not particularly receptive to an acquisition on this scale, which would have led to substantial dilution. While maintaining strict confidentiality, the challenge for Apax was to find a financing structure that did not necessitate an increase in capital through the stock market and at the same time did not burden PVH with excessive loans.

The transaction structure, in addition, had to fulfil three central prerequisites.

1. It had to be transparent enough to meet the requirements of a company listed on the stock market.
2. The complementary strengths of both companies had to be merged in such a manner so as to achieve maximum synergy.
3. The financing had to provide for an exit route for the Apax Funds in order to realise their investment after several years of successful collaboration.

The Apax Funds and PVH finally decided on a structure that allowed PVH to consummate the acquisition with only minor resort to bank loans. The Apax Funds invested US$375m into the project. US$250m of this amount was made available as a convertible loan, which could be converted at a rate of US$14 into preferred PVH stock. This convertible loan carried an accrued interest rate of 8 per cent, with no cash disbursement of interest during the term of the loan. Critically, in order to facilitate a speedy transaction, the Apax Funds also furnished an additional US$125m in the form of a bridge loan. The convertible nature of the instruments was crucial for Apax's exit planning, providing ultimate liquidity in a public stock without the need for a complex exit process.

The acquisition demonstrates how enterprises can successfully consummate new acquisitions by partnering with private equity, even in a time of weaker capital markets.

*(Continued)*

In addition, this kind of partnership guarantees speed of execution and absolute discretion prior to the transaction, which is of critical importance. On a more general level, the transaction is a good example of the critical role that private equity can now play in international industry consolidation, beyond the traditional buyout model.

The strengths of both companies complement each other ideally in the new enterprise (see Exhibit 1.4): PVH now owns an additional, world renowned, positively engaged brand capable of being expanded. Within PVH, this brand can not only be handled with efficiency via the existing infrastructure and distribution structure but can also be expanded considerably. The management, for example, has plans to introduce a Calvin Klein sportswear collection for men and women, in addition to the already existing line of Calvin Klein shirts, and they want to launch their own Calvin Klein factory outlets. Furthermore, PVH profits from the potential Calvin Klein Inc. brings to the table: Calvin Klein possesses significant know-how in the area of licensing, which in turn can be applied to the expansion of the already existing PVH brands.

Exhibit 1.4

**Comparing PVH and Calvin Klein pre-acquisition**

| **Phillips-Van Heusen** (US$14bn in sales) | **Calvin Klein** (US$1.7bn in external sales) |
|---|---|
| Leading position in shirts and sportswear (contact with the trade) | No sportswear collection |
| Leading factory outlet entrepreneur | Outlets offer potential for improvement and growth |
| Efficient processes | Partially inefficient processes |
| Excellent infrastructure | High overhead |
| Little internationalisation | Internationally known designer Lifestyle brand |
| Licensing of some brands at early stage | Great international licensing know-how |

*Source:* Author's own

The transaction completed in February 2003. The Apax Funds continue to advise PVH in their growth strategy, and appointed three supervisory board members for this purpose.

## Case study 2: Partnering with shareholders – Inmarsat

Inmarsat is the leading global provider of mobile satellite services to the maritime, land and aeronautical sectors via a fleet of 11 owned satellites. Inmarsat wholesales voice and data principally on an on-demand basis through a global network of distribution partners. Apax Partners and Permira led the US$1.5bn buyout of the company in 2003, together with institutional shareholders including Telenor and Lockheed Martin, who rolled over part of their existing shareholdings into the new company.

*(Continued)*

Inmarsat was founded in 1979 as an inter-governmental organisation, originally the International Maritime Organisation, to provide infrastructure for maritime communications. The company launched its first generation of satellites in the early 1990s, and began wholesaling services via its governmental owner-distributors. In 1999 the company underwent a privatisation as a precursor to an eventual IPO, and the former governmental owners – in most cases via national post, telephone and telegraph administrations (PTTs) – became shareholders of the new company.

The new corporate structure facilitated a limited number of divestitures and acquisitions by certain shareholders, but by and large the overlap between the shareholder base and the customer base remained substantial when Apax and Permira came to evaluate the opportunity (initially independently) in mid-2002. At that time the company had been undergoing preparatory works for an IPO, but had not proceeded due to weak stock market conditions. A private equity buyout of the company presented an alternative, but there were two key obstacles: (i) a challenging LBO cashflow profile as the company was in the midst of a large capital expenditure programme for a visionary Broadband concept and (ii) the highly fragmented base of 94 shareholders with widely divergent interests, Apax and Permira's deep sector expertise in technology and telecommunications made them well positioned for this transaction, but general private equity interest in the opportunity was extremely limited and the auction quickly reduced to Apax/Permira and one other competing private equity consortium. The divergence of interests of the shareholder base at that time can be demonstrated by the positions of just the six largest shareholders (see Exhibit 1.5).

Exhibit 1.5

**Analysis of Inmarsat's top six shareholders**

| Shareholder | Ownership (%) | Distributor | Selling shareholder |
|---|---|---|---|
| Telenor | 15 | Yes | No |
| Lockheed Martin | 14 | No | No |
| KDDI | 8 | Yes | No |
| Xantic (KPN) | 6 | Yes | Yes |
| France Telecom | 5 | Yes | Yes |
| Deutsche Telekom | 4 | No | Yes |

*Source:* Author's own

This was to be an auction process where success was dictated as much by the bidders' partnering abilities as by the price. To secure the deal, Apax and Permira undertook multiparty discussions with the different shareholders to determine their needs and devise a solution that would work under the 'one size fits all' constraints of the UK Takeover Panel. The situation was further complicated as the company's five-year price-governing contract with its key distributors was up for renewal in 2004, creating further uncertainty for distributor shareholders. The complexity and interdependencies of the situation were such

*(Continued)*

that the potential solution became dubbed (internally) by the private equity houses as the 'Rubik's cube'.

In December 2003, some 18 months after Apax and Permira had first begun looking at the opportunity, the board recommended the US$1.5bn Apax/Permira offer. Critically, irrevocable undertakings were obtained from three of the larger shareholders. The offer was structured as a scheme of arrangement and, importantly, included a 'rollover' option whereby shareholders could elect to reinvest a portion of their proceeds from the transaction to maintain a shareholding in the new levered entity up to the same percentage they had held in the old company. The aggregate limit of the reinvestment was limited to 43.3 per cent, thereby ensuring Apax/Permira control of the new entity after taking into account the 5.7 per cent of equity reserved for management. There was a high take-up of the rollover alternative, which, at 42.5 per cent, was just inside the cap.

Board seats were granted to shareholders owning over 10 per cent of the new company, and thus Telenor and Lockheed Martin appointed board representatives alongside Apax and Permira. Apax and Permira have since worked collaboratively with their institutional partners on the board through a busy period at the company. This has seen the conclusion of a new distribution contract, the appointment of new CEO, Andy Sukawaty, and CFO, Rick Medlock, a detailed strategic review of the company leading to both cost initiatives and the building of a new business development team, three successive US debt offerings and the launch of the first of a new generation of satellites. The company has delivered a solid financial performance, and the numerous growth initiatives have led to a substantial re-rating of the company's growth prospects. This was reflected in the heavily oversubscribed IPO of the company on the London Stock Exchange completed in May 2005. Since the IPO, Apax and Permira have continued to work collaboratively with their institutional partners, co-ordinating with Telenor and Lockheed Martin in the subsequent sell-down of their public holdings.

### Case study 3: Partnering with corporates – TIM Hellas

TIM Hellas is the third-largest mobile telephony operator in Greece with about 2.4 million subscribers and just over 20 per cent market share, offering voice and data services in an increasingly saturated Greek market.

TIM Hellas was founded in 1992 as the first mobile operator in Greece – STET – and began operations in 1993. The original shareholders of the business were Telecom Italia Mobile (TIM) with 74 per cent, Verizon of the United States with 21 per cent and a local Greek insurance company, Interamerican Group, with 5 per cent. In 1998 the company, then known as STET Hellas, listed its shares on Nasdaq and Euronext, with Interamerican exiting on the stock market and TIM purchasing Verizon's shares. Thus, TIM came to own 81 per cent of TIM Hellas, and rebranded the company in 2004.

Despite being the first entrant to the market, TIM Hellas had steadily lost market share and position, first to Vodafone-Panafon, which entered the market in 1994, and then to Cosmote, owned by the fixed-line incumbent OTE, which only entered the market in 1998 but was aggressive in its pursuit of market share. TIM Hellas had initially been hampered by

*(Continued)*

having two trade owners with competing objectives for the company. By the time that TIM had taken sole ownership in 2002, however, market leadership had already been lost by TIM Hellas, which then could only play catch-up in Greece with its larger and better-funded rivals.

Meanwhile, many changes were afoot at TIM in Italy. Telecom Italia (TI), TIM's parent company, was acquired in 2001 by Pirelli, the tyre and cable company run by Marco Tronchetti Provera. The TI/TIM acquisitions were structured through a series of complex cross-shareholdings, which included the Benetton family as shareholders, and were financed through a large debt package in Pirelli. After taking over as chairman, Tronchetti began to focus on rationalising TI/TIM's holdings across the world in order to increase business focus and to pay down some of the significant mountain of acquisition debt. This included several high-profile exits such as Seat Pagine Gialle, the yellow pages business in Italy sold in 2003 to a consortium of private equity investors for €5.65bn. In addition, Tronchetti decided to refocus TIM on its home market of Italy and certain major emerging markets such as Turkey and Brazil, where TIM had substantial subsidiaries that would also drive future earnings growth. A number of smaller, more marginal mobile operators in other countries were identified for sale, including its subsidiaries in Peru (sold in 2004 to America Movil), Chile (sold in January 2005) and Venezuela (sold in 2005 to Telvenco). Proceeds from these various asset sales were used to pay down debt.

In December 2004 Tronchetti announced the merger between TI and TIM, when TI announced that it would acquire the 44 per cent of TIM it did not already own in a cash and shares deal worth €20bn, including €12bn in fresh debt, which brought net debt to €44bn. It was critical at the same time for the company's credit rating to stay the same, and so Tronchetti needed to search for new sources of cash from within TI and TIM's various holdings.

It was at this point that a consortium consisting of Apax Partners and Texas Pacific Group approached TIM in late 2004 with an expression of interest in TIM Hellas. TIM did not have the time or management focus to conduct a full-fledged private equity auction process, especially since it was managing exits in Chile and Venezuela concurrently.

The consortium recognised the key concerns of TIM – speed and certainty of completion. Therefore, instead of going through the normal process of multiple offer rounds, TIM set its reservation price for TIM Hellas and entered into six weeks of exclusivity with the consortium in late January 2005. The consortium then conducted its due diligence with a view to confirming that this price was achievable. Apax had considerable experience in the telecommunications sector in Europe, including in mobile operators, and the consortium was confident that a turnaround was possible in the performance of the company, despite a number of initially concerning operating metrics.

Finally, at the end of the exclusivity period in April 2005 the consortium agreed to acquire TIM Hellas for €1.6bn, and the transaction was completed in June 2005. Subsequent to the acquisition, the consortium has worked on completing the management team at TIM Hellas with capable Greek managers from within the industry, on ensuring a rapid turnaround in performance at the company and on the acquisition of Q-Telecom, the fourth and smallest mobile operator in Greece.

*(Continued)*

While PVH demonstrated an example of private equity teaming up with industry in the matter of acquisitions, TIM Hellas demonstrates how private equity can partner with corporates to create exit solutions for unwanted businesses and provide immediate liquidity, often to very demanding time schedules.

## Case study 4: Partnering with government – Bezeq

Bezeq is the incumbent telecommunications operator in Israel, providing a complete range of telecommunications services to the market, including fixed line, broadband, mobile telephony, data communications and satellite TV. In October 2005, Apax Partners, in consortium with Saban Capital Group (SCG) and a local entrepreneur, Mori Arkin, acquired 30 per cent of Bezeq from the Israeli government as part of a privatisation process for €813m, financed through a combination of equity, senior debt and mezzanine debt. In addition, the consortium also acquired an option to acquire the Israeli government's remaining stake of 10.7 per cent over the next four years as part of a pre-agreed formula, with 4.7 per cent going towards an employee option pool. This acquisition of shares also carries with it control of Bezeq.

Bezeq was created in 1984 when it was separated from the Ministry of Communications. From then until it was acquired by the consortium, Bezeq had functioned as a separate entity, but always under government control. Until 1994 Bezeq was the sole provider of telecommunications services in Israel, but since then the market has been progressively deregulated and competition has been introduced in various sectors, the last of which was fixed-line telephony in 2004.

The Israeli government has been progressively reducing its holding in Bezeq since 1989, with major divestitures of state holdings taking place in 1991, 1998 and 2003. This process, however, has not been without its problems. In 1999, a local Israeli businessman, Gad Zeevi, acquired from Cable & Wireless a 20 per cent stake in Bezeq for US$630m, which was financed through a combination of equity and debt through a special purpose vehicle (SPV) known as Zeevi Holdings Limited. The debt was raised from a consortium of Israeli banks, and relied on the payment of dividends by Bezeq in order to pay interest and debt amortisation. However, due to his inability to control Bezeq's dividend stream, Zeevi was unable to service the debt, and in 2002 the bank consortium enforced its pledge over the shares. As a result, prior to the acquisition of the consortium's stake in Bezeq in 2005, the company's shareholder structure was as follows: Israeli government (46.4 per cent); free float on the Tel Aviv Stock Exchange (35.8 per cent); and receivership with the banks of Zeevi's stake (17.8 per cent).

The process of purchasing control of Bezeq was highly unusual and complex. First, the Israeli government had twice previously entered into processes to privatise Bezeq fully, but both times decided to not follow through due to political reasons. As a result, when the current privatisation process was begun in August 2004, there was a considerable risk that it might once again end with no result were there to be unfavourable political developments along the way. This was notwithstanding the fact that Ariel Sharon's government

*(Continued)*

was committed to the process of privatising major government-owned companies, including the El Al airline, the major Israeli banks and, of course, Bezeq. The consortium, therefore, had to become comfortable with the uncertainties of the process.

Secondly, Israeli law does not allow debt push-down to the operating company as is typical in most leveraged buyouts. As a consequence, the consortium had to develop a unique transaction structure, whereby the shares would be acquired by an SPV, which would be dependent on dividends being up-streamed into the structure in order to service debt. With no historical balance of retained earnings, dividends would be capped by annual net income, which is far more volatile than EBITDA. As financial investors, the consortium was able to develop a number of strategies to drive net income growth at Bezeq in order to mitigate the financing risk.

Thirdly, Bezeq is a strategic company in Israel, with several links to the security establishment. As a result, the government continues to exercise considerable influence and control on the ownership of Bezeq. As a result, regulatory approval is required before either a trade sale or exit on to the stock market. This clearly creates challenges for financial investors, who have a specific exit timeframe. Again, the consortium had to assess and become comfortable with this risk, which was somewhat mitigated by the fact that the company was already a publicly listed entity.

The consortium worked closely with the government in order to ensure that the latter's key concerns about the future of Bezeq were addressed, while also providing transaction certainty. At the same time, it required significant persistence and creativity on the part of the consortium to address some of the transaction issues that arose out of the unusual nature of this transaction. A satisfactory conclusion was reached in October 2005 when the consortium finally took control of Bezeq.

## Summary

This chapter has outlined the changing role of private equity in the modern economy. The old competitive advantages of financial engineering have eroded over time as the competitive intensity of the market has increased. Private equity firms must add value beyond the realms of financial engineering. To achieve this, private equity firms must migrate towards the partnership model, which can provide superior strategic insights in order to satisfy stakeholders, facilitate core growth and reduce risk through effective investment structuring. Industry and government are increasingly recognising the necessity of value-added private equity investors and the solutions they can offer in a variety of situations. Equally, competitive pressure, high entry multiples and interest rate uncertainty are compelling private equity firms to become active owners of their assets in order to create value.

---

[1] Baker, G. A. and G. Smith, *The New Financial Capitalists* (Cambridge: Cambridge University Press, 1998).

Chapter 2

# European venture capital: The path to maturity

Iggy Bassi
*Monitor Group*

Vesa Jormakka
*Argo Global Capital*

> 'A wise man will make more opportunities than he finds.'
> (Sir Francis Bacon: English author and philosopher (1561–1626))

This chapter outlines the dynamics within the European venture capital (VC) market in terms of sourcing deal flow, investing and exits, highlighting key emerging trends and challenges since 2000. It identifies how European funds can develop options to meet these challenges and raise the likelihood of improved investment performance. Through expanding market reach and improving organisational capability the European VC industry will continue transitioning from a local supplier of capital towards a global service provider.

### Scenario

Hans, a second generation German entrepreneur, convenes a board meeting with his investors in New York (Google, Infosys, Siemens AG and a Texan VC fund) to discuss the all-cash acquisition offer made by China's largest media company. The German-based company is also being wooed by investment banks for an initial public offering (IPO) in India. His company, Navigus AG, developed (in conjunction with intellectual property (IP) spun out of Siemens Defence Unit) an intelligent semantics search engine. Navigus has achieved trailing 12-month revenues of US$60m with an EBITDA (earnings before interest, tax, depreciation and amortisation) of US$14m and has operations in six countries with 170 employees representing 14 nationalities.

## Introduction

An unlikely situation today perhaps, but if current trends in global venture capital, emerging economy growth strategies and corporate innovation continue, such scenarios will be possible and probable in the coming years. The frontiers of the European venture market are changing fast, representing new challenges and opportunities for venture funds, investors and entrepreneurs. The key strategic challenge for European VC funds is to recognise the current wave of global market and geopolitical trends and position themselves in a timely and innovative manner to justify sustained limited partner interest and continue supporting entrepreneurship.

As the venture capital industry enters a new investment cycle, European VC funds are facing pressure to improve their overall performance as an investment asset class, which has persistently lagged behind other regions. Since the downturn in 2000, a confluence of a contracting market, limited exit opportunities and weak comparative returns have sharpened the focus of European VC funds towards delivering performance. The new investment cycle provides an opportunity for European VC funds to incorporate several successful and transferable dimensions from the US and Israeli markets, which could contribute to improved performance. There are two important and addressable dimensions to achieving this.

- *Extending market reach*, both geographic reach (by creating a greater global footprint to assist in portfolio growth and source deal flow) and enterprise reach (by exploring greater scope for collaboration with large enterprises and research institutes).
- *Enhancing organisational capability* to develop a 'blend' of internal VC skill sets, from operational and financial to technical and market know-how, ensuring value can be added and risks managed across all stages of the investment lifecycle.

These two key dimensions are particularly critical within Europe given the combined effects of consolidation and outsourcing. The former has reduced the universe of large addressable firms for early-stage companies to target, and the latter has diminished the amount of discretionary expenditure available to enterprises for new products and services.

## Current VC market

Many commentators viewed 2004–05 as turnaround years for the global VC industry, with increased fund raising, exits, valuations and new investments all showing positive signs of recovery, especially in the US market. The puncturing of the 'internet bubble' in 2001 left the entire VC industry depressed up to the latter half of 2004. The legacy of the period includes an estimated US$60bn[1] venture capital 'overhang', a reduction in the number of investors committed to the VC asset class and a halving of the number of VC funds. Undeterred by the 'overhang' and comforted by the overall reduction in the supply side (investors) and the demand side[2] (VC funds), limited partners regained their confidence in the asset class, committing €3.7bn (US$4.4bn)[3] in 2005 to over 30 European funds, an increase of 160 per cent on 2004's €1.4bn (US$1.68bn). This compares with €18.5bn (US$22.2bn) in 2005 for the US market. Furthermore, investors have re-calibrated their expectations of exit timing. Today, market expectations are 'normalising' to pre-bubble levels, where building a global business with substantial returns will take five to seven years and shortcuts to success have become an exception rather than the expectation.

The sentiments of Mark Heesen, President of NVCA, in the fourth quarter of 2005 perhaps capture best the current state of the VC market:[4]

> The VC industry has reached an echelon of maturity that brings with it a universal sense of prudence and discipline that will begin to impact decision making in 2006. The coming year will be characterised by less risk, less hype, and more intricacies

within investment sectors. There will not be another bubble as we simply do not have the liquidity to fund one, the exit market to fuel one, nor the 'tourists' to create one.

As the VC market emerges from the prolonged downturn, both limited partners and venture fund managers will ensure the new VC investment cycle will be characterised by greater maturity, notably in terms of greater due diligence of fund manager selection, risk-adjusted investment decisions and improved governance at both the fund and portfolio levels. In addition to this industry maturation, the VC industry is contending with powerful external market forces. Chief among them is the irreversibility of the globalisation of markets, knowledge, technology and capital. Pulitzer journalist Thomas Friedman contends the sum of integrative technology and reduced economic and political barriers has made the world increasingly 'flat',[5] which will necessarily disrupt economic innovation and social paradigms, and will invariably serve to dilute the traditional epicentres of innovation in Europe and the United States.

Furthermore, the new investment cycle may give rise to greater competitive pressures from powerful and well-financed non-VC players (such as Yahoo, eBay and Google), although their early investment preferences suggest they will co-invest with VCs. Also, it is conceivable that investment capital may flow into traditional innovation hotbeds from low-tech but high-growth regions seeking to attract the increasingly 'stateless entrepreneur' to leverage the regional 'cost and growth curve' advantages of countries such as India and China.

The effect of these forces and the higher expectations of investors will continue to redefine the frontiers of the VC industry away from the preserves of a 'cottage industry' towards greater maturity consistent with other asset classes such as buyouts. The diminishing returns of geographic proximity may eventually lead to a Darwinian selection process, leading to only the best performing VCs receiving funding and not necessarily at a national or regional level but rather globally. This will pose a challenge to many of the small and medium-sized national funds in Europe, who at a minimum require a pan-European or transatlantic presence to achieve scalability and international reach.

## Key industry trends

### Deal sourcing

The landscape for sourcing VC investment opportunities is changing. During the 1980s and much of the 1990s European venture capital was essentially a 'cottage' industry, which largely solved the capital scarcity problem – namely, providing financing solutions to high-risk companies unable to secure capital through the banking system. The pool of VC funds was much smaller, thus allowing for favourable pricing terms. The volume of firms seeking venture funding steadily increased as many countries embraced the doctrine of free markets, which spurred entrepreneurship and risk-taking, leading to a significant rise in entrepreneurs and new company formations. VCs played a critical role in successfully financing this risk, leading to high returns vis-à-vis other asset classes, which, coupled with relatively low barriers to entry, meant the supply of VC mushroomed in the 1990s. This ultimately led to a bubble, described at the time by John Doerr from Kleiner Perkins, the leading VC fund, as 'the single greatest legal creation of wealth in the history of the planet', which was swiftly followed by a significant and prolonged economic downturn.

Despite the excesses of the late 1990s, several key trends have prevailed. First, Europe continues to produce a stream of entrepreneurs seeking to commercialise their ideas and, secondly, there is a dominant logic prevailing inside firms and governments that innovation continues to be the engine of growth and competitive advantage. Simply put, innovation matters; entrepreneurs and organisations are becoming smarter at recognising its commercial value; and they are becoming savvy in how and when to finance innovation.

The net result is the European venture capital 'ecosystem' is maturing through experience, not just at the venture fund level, but at the firm and entrepreneur level. This follows the pattern that also occurred earlier in Silicon Valley, which pushed venture deal sourcing beyond the realms of just the market, towards a complex interplay between firms, research organisations and entrepreneurs, with some funds actually 'making ventures' – that is, finding entrepreneurs to commercialise ideas. As such, European VCs need to expand their market reach to secure deals and future investment optionality in more creative ways.

**The innovation imperative**

National and regional governments around the globe are increasingly recognising the value and necessity of fostering and commercialising innovation to boost their competitiveness. This 'innovation imperative' has resulted in the creation of new innovation hotbeds, outside the traditional US clusters in Silicon Valley and Route 128. Asian nations, keen to develop their own champions, are aggressively designing innovation and research ecosystems designed to compete globally. For example, China doubled the number of science and engineering doctoral students in five years to reach over 8000 in 2001 and in 2004 trebled the number of universities targeted for world-leading scientific research to reach 38.[6]

Europe, through its publicly funded universities, governments and enterprises, remains active[7] and very strong in producing leading edge 'breakthrough innovation' vis-à-vis its competitors (key areas include, for example, communication technologies, energy technology, enterprise software and biotech). Key regional technology VC clusters, such as Cambridge, Munich and Stockholm, continue to evolve in Europe with accompanying support ecosystems, providing economies of scale in both investment and human assets. The fundamentals are in place, but work remains to be done in the areas of early selection of promising ideas and focused commercialisation, as still too often success remains a result of coincidence instead of rigorous selection processes. The rules of engagement for commercial funding of university projects and access to research and intellectual property still vary across Europe, and greater cooperation between government-funded institutions and the private sector is required in order to fully realise the potential.

The European environment to create scaleable, high-quality innovation is currently very favourable through a growing entrepreneurial culture that is increasingly aided by new EU tax incentives and industrial policy schemes. The EU (through the Lisbon Objective[8]) has targeted R&D spending to be increased from the current 2 per cent of GDP to 3 per cent by 2010. All these initiatives should result in a considerable increase in R&D output from Europe and present opportunities for sustained venture capital collaboration and investing.

**The value of IP and research**

Organisations, both public and private, are recognising the value of their IP and proprietary research: as such, there is a greater drive to treat it as an asset with the potential for commercialisation. The collective endowment of public and private European intellectual property – both latent and active – is immense. The ability to effectively partner with research organisations and corporate R&D departments to 'explore and exploit' this IP will become an important source of advantage for VC funds. Extending the VC reach 'upstream' into the enterprise and research organisations will be an important aspect to securing access to innovation. Since 2001, approximately 70 per cent of large global enterprises have abandoned or significantly reduced their corporate venturing investment levels.[9] Many of them suffered from a loss of focus trying to navigate between lucrative short-term returns via the buoyant M&A and IPO markets, and long-term strategic objectives related to innovation and sustainable competitive edge. The market correction flushed out most corporate venturing programmes and only the few with a focused strategic approach survived.

If structured carefully, venture funds can provide a strategic gateway for enterprises to continue capturing the benefits of venturing and commercialising their IP without the traditional cost structure or the issues relating to the cyclicality of such corporate venturing programmes. Pioneer funds such as New Venture Partners[10] have made this their core investment thesis and have successfully secured significant commercialisation rights with firms such as British Telecom and Phillips.

Some enterprises and research organisations are actively seeking to share their IP in order to improve their yield on innovation through commercial partnerships. There are three notable recent examples.

- *Microsoft Intellectual Property Ventures*. Microsoft will work in partnership with VCs and entrepreneurs to license MSFT IP to early-stage companies, in exchange for equity positions in the portfolio companies. MSFT formed this initiative in conjunction with 10 VC funds plus several research universities (Stanford and Massachusetts Institute of Technology).
- *IBM Ventures in Collaboration*. IBM launched a new IP cross-licensing programme called IBM Ventures in Collaboration, which makes much of its patent portfolio accessible to early-stage start-ups funded by IBM's venture capital partner network.
- *Cambridge Venture Partners*. Cambridge University partnered in Europe with leading VC funds[11] to provide greater commercial opportunities for the university's research.

It is worth remembering that the core algorithms behind Google's search engine technology was the output of research undertaken at Stanford University. The decision to apply this research to solving a market problem was taken by the PhD researchers Larry Page and Sergey Brin, and was actively supported by Stanford University, who granted Google an exclusive licensing partnership until 2011[12] in exchange for equity, cash and royalties. As of January 2006, the estimated value of Stanford's capital gain exceeded US$350m. European VCs would be wise to extend the 'market boundaries' for seeking and cultivating investment opportunities with traditional research organisations and corporate R&D departments.

### Experienced and demanding entrepreneurs

Within Europe, a growing pool of second generation 'US-styled' entrepreneurs and managers has emerged with a proven record in creating world-class technology companies through dealing with the challenges of internationalisation and business partnership formation. Furthermore, there is a greater acceptance of human capital cross-over from the traditional business and scientific world into entrepreneurial ventures, although the rate of cross-over remains slow. Furthermore, unlike in the US market, very few European entrepreneurs migrate into the venture capital domain.

Through experience and market information, entrepreneurs have greater awareness of venture capital, termsheet literacy and control issues. Although seasoned entrepreneurs are becoming increasingly sophisticated in setting the terms of capital, it is often not their first priority. Seasoned entrepreneurs, recognising that their firms essentially behave like mini-multinationals, are demanding a greater hands-on approach from their VC investors, especially in the areas of international growth, access to leading enterprises and the development of partnerships and joint ventures. Venture commentator Martin Haemmig notes: 'The value added by international VCs helps build faster and more globally exposed start-up companies that lead to bigger and more competitive firms and thus potentially higher returns for VC funds if executed properly.'[13] In essence, like their portfolio companies, the venture capital business model needs to be global in order to compete, which in turn requires an enhanced general partner (GP) skill set.

Also, European VCs will need to migrate towards the 'Silicon Valley' model of venturing in terms of team formation – the GP skill set in the United States typically includes former entrepreneurs with business, operational and technical expertise. This formation significantly enhances the likelihood of successfully managing the process of fast growth and thus reducing the risk of failure. Arguably, it is the US venture funds in Europe who are accelerating the pace of change in the European venture market. Such funds, through differentiated GP skills, generally have greater capability in adding non-financial value to their portfolio companies such as international commercialisation, business development and initiating partnerships. Such competences are forming an integral part of the venture capital selection process for entrepreneurs seeking equity funding. Forming and maintaining such a skilled pool of experienced GPs is becoming an important issue for the European VC industry.

The overall opportunity in Europe is substantial, although it remains more geographically dispersed than in the large US VC clusters. To compete effectively and generate higher returns, many European venture funds have embarked upon and will continue to migrate towards creating a multi-regional presence – a pan-European VC community has been emerging since early 2000. Leading VC firms recognise that deal flow will have to be sourced on a pan-European basis and portfolio firms commercialised globally in order to succeed. In a nutshell, European venture funds need to transition towards becoming global service providers rather than local suppliers of capital.

## Investing and growth

### A shift to later-stage venture investing

There has been a marked shift towards later-stage investing across Europe (see Exhibit 2.1). During 2005, around half of all venture deals were considered to be late stage (according to VentureOne), driven in part by additional capital requirements in the light of weak exit markets. However, many venture funds comment on their strategy to only invest in companies where 'significant early-stage risk has been reduced' and with 'a minimum of €7–10m of revenues'. Some funds repositioned themselves as late-stage venture funds and others even as 'small buyout funds' that syndicate with traditional buyout funds to pursue larger deals.

Exhibit 2.1

**The gradual shift to late-stage ventures, 2000–05**

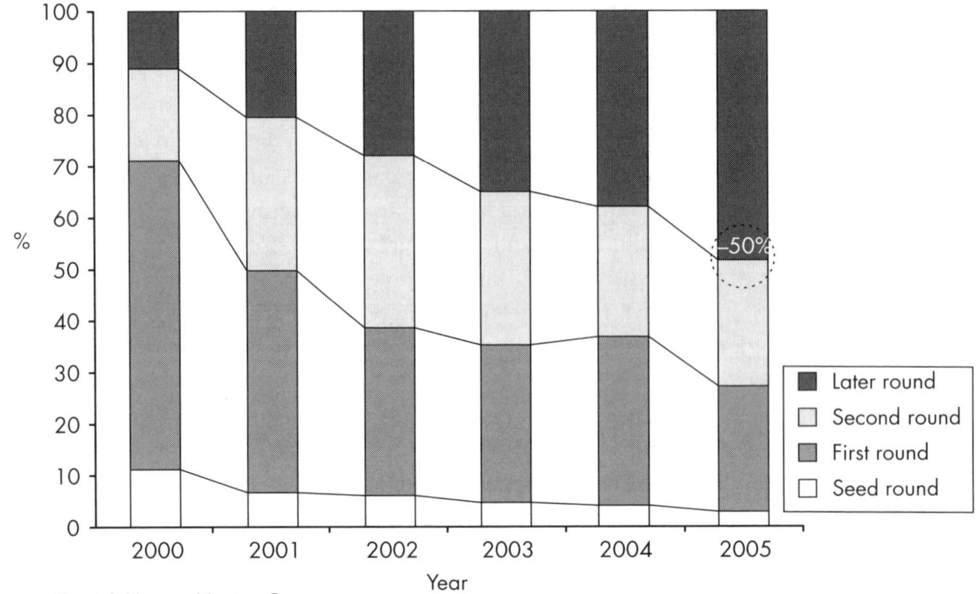


*Sources*: Ernst & Young; VentureOne.

While it is clear many VC funds sought to increase their investments in later-stage investing during the downturn (in both existing portfolio companies and new investments), due mainly to limited exit markets, such a marked 'strategic drift', if sustained, may have long-term consequences. Historically, the largest venture returns have accrued to those investors who have invested in the early stages of a company's life. The falling volume of European early-stage investments (hence stock of companies), may lead to a deficit of quality early-stage deals graduating to later-stage funding, thus creating pricing competition and entry barriers for the reduced pool of firms seeking follow-on funding: in essence, later-stage funds may lose the 'right to play'. The good news for early-stage companies in 2005 was that they received more capital than previously for their stage in life – recognition perhaps among European VCs they must close the funding disparity with US early-stage VC rounds where similar stage investment rounds are typically 30–40 per cent larger. The growth in late-stage venturing also reflects the growing industry consolidation in Europe and the United States, where new entrants require significantly more capital to 'play the game' with increasingly fewer corporate purchasers. An example is Cerimon Pharmaceuticals, which specialises in seeking FDA approval for drug compounds sourced from foreign countries; it raised US$70m first round funding, which, according to the CEO, will allow the firm to get only one compound approved.[14]

While it is important to leverage past experiences in making future investment decisions, it is also worth investing in a balanced portfolio including early, mid and later-stage venture deals. Furthermore, the strategic drift into buyouts may be short-lived as a sustainable fund strategy, as the competitive intensity of the European mid-cap private equity market will invariably expand the definition of what a 'mid-cap' fund is, leading some funds to focus on smaller buyouts and even transgress into late-stage VC. Limited partners should be mindful of such strategic drifts when assessing a fund's stated investment strategy with its core capabilities. Equally, they should be aware that consolidation effects of large industries will require venture funds to develop a deeper strategic understanding of an industry's value chain: some areas require much bigger bets to create champions, while others will require minimal capital to have a disruptive impact.

**The dynamic ecology of technology, markets and individuals**

The pace and the 'biological' nature of technological development are transforming entire industries and innovation patterns. The fusion[15] of disciplines such as IT, life sciences, media and biology, coupled with the ever morphing communication mediums such as the internet and wireless are creating whole new categories for innovation and investments, such as nanotechnology, biometrics, optoelectronics and radio-frequency security systems. Such developments mean firms live in a perpetual state of transformation. For instance, Cisco started life as an internet networking firm, but has successfully morphed into the related areas of IP telephony and wireless security solutions.

The patterns of innovation are also changing. Distributed innovation systems are emerging as new collaborative formats, which co-exist with traditionally centralised modes of innovation and product design. Perhaps the best and most disruptive example is the emergence of open source software (such as Linux). Such 'networks' are shifting the locus of innovation outside the boundaries of the firm – a pattern Erik von Hippel of MIT refers to as 'democratising innovation'. Many traditional blue chip firms are successfully adopting this dual approach, often referred to as 'open innovation'.[16] For example, Procter and Gamble augment their innovation search by utilising InnoCentive,[17] an online professional community with a global pool of over 80,000 scientists and researchers, which has radically reduced its research costs and raised its external-to-internal new product ratios. Firms like Google depended upon the power of open source software to launch and commercialise their search engines, and now over 100,000 Linux servers provide the infrastructure to conduct 1 billion search queries daily. Competitive survival will depend upon a sophisticated interplay of traditional innovation patterns and externally market-based innovation.

Technologies like the internet are empowering firms and also transferring power directly to individuals. The global connection of over a billion people to the internet is unprecedented in human and economic history, providing them with the tools for economic and social exchange, dissemination of ideas and collective activism: 'For the first time in human history, mass cooperation across time and space is suddenly economical.'[18] Howard Rheingold's book, *Smart Mobs: The Next Social Revolution*,[19] argues that the power of such 'peer-to-peer' collaboration may lead to a new economic order beyond the established conventions of the market and the firm.

The implications for venture capitalists of such fundamental shifts in innovation patterns, the power of individuals and collaborative networks are immense. The evolution patterns of innovation; the multiplier effects of the networked economies; and cross-pollination of technologies/processes will all continually morph to create new market ecologies and deconstruct existing industry value chains. For example, the success of Skype[20] illustrated how the nexus of new technology, peer-to-peer collaboration and networks can create value and challenge incumbents, in this case the telecoms industry. It received approximately US$24m in venture capital funding and was sold for US$4.1bn in 2005. Venture capitalists will need to better understand how these forces will affect their investment decisions in firms and sector choices where commercial success relies upon a high degree of sophisticated coordination across geographies and strategic partnerships. This task is made more difficult through the democratising effects of open source, which ensures proprietary positions are short-lived and increasingly beyond the control of a single firm.

**Greater focus on due diligence**

Investment decisions in the new investment cycle will be characterised by greater understanding of both the capabilities of the firm, its management and the market dynamics in which it competes. To achieve this, fund teams will need to conduct rigorous analysis of the market, industry purchasing patterns and budget cycles, industry value chain scenarios, disruption risks, cost dynamics and, crucially, the robustness of the business model vis-à-vis competitors, including claims to intellectual property.[21] Fundamentally, the products or services of portfolio firms should seek to enhance the competitive edge of their target business clients, either through differentiation or by creating a significant cost advantage. For consumer markets, firms should focus on a business model providing products or services that can be easily adopted on a mass scale and eventually monetised.

Some VC funds have formed strategic partnerships with enterprises to de-risk investment decisions and assist portfolio growth strategies. Argo Global Capital,[22] for example, which focuses on the global wireless industry, has partnered with over a dozen global wireless carriers in Europe, North America and Asia for its funds and actively solicits input from these 'operator partners' on issues such as likely adoption, service configuration and technology compatibility, as part of assessing the investment entry decision. Its portfolio companies are strategically positioned to access these global wireless carriers for business development and partnership opportunities.

The global dimension will play a larger role in shaping early investment decisions on market entry choices, partnerships, distributed R&D and human capital. Former European star performers like e-finance solutions provider Brokat AG focused on the smaller and less competitive region of Europe, only to be culled when powerful global players arrived. Although Europe is a large cumulative market, it is filled with national idiosyncrasies and high friction costs, which at times will be expensive in terms of time-to-market advantages. Accordingly, a crucial dimension of the investment decision is assessing the ability, desirability and cost of transplanting the target portfolio company for commercialisation to its most strategic market. The disconnect between the host market in which an innovation is developed and where it is commercialised will increase as the global regime for protecting intellectual property continues to improve. The success of Israeli's venture capital experience is testament to this innovation–commercialisation *disconnect*.

**Strategic selection of co-investors**

Investments, especially for early-stage, will be increasingly syndicated to share the risks and leverage the capabilities of other parties. A true pan-European syndication market is emerging and most of the firms already have experience in cross-border syndication.[23] As European portfolio companies seek global expansion, their VC investors, who have often adopted a national or a pan-European business model, may co-invest with VCs in target markets to gain a local presence. The economics of European venture funds[24] may not allow for an organic multi-regional presence and hence the need to partner with local investors. US-based funds in Europe actively market the ability to provide *access* to the US market as a way to convince entrepreneurs of their value. Martin Haemmig notes: 'In Israel, 26 per cent of all investment rounds on average included an American and 15 per cent a European VC investor, with a mean of two foreign investors in internationally syndicated deals. This is of crucial importance to Israeli start-ups, since foreign VC firms help finance their expensive expansion activity into foreign markets.'[25]

The attraction of the Asian market, notably countries such as India and China, will invariably mean some European funds developing transpacific expansion and co-investment partnerships. The cost advantage of the region is only one aspect for funds to consider; there is also the question of the huge growth potential within the region. Many US VC funds, leveraging the Chinese and Indian diaspora, have built a presence in the region in 2004–05, both organically or through partnerships; however, the actual amount of investment is likely to remain low at present. In the 2005 *Global venture capital investment report*, Gil Forer, Global Director of the Ernst & Young Venture Capital Advisory Group, has noted: 'Overall, the venture capital ecosystem in China is in its early days. The long journey to a mature ecosystem, such as Silicon Valley, has started. The road has tremendous opportunities but also numerous risks.'

Corporates remain attractive co-investment partners and they are more receptive in order to gain innovation advantages and leverage their own R&D investments. While many of the leading funds in Silicon Valley are focused on searching for the next big thing, they also stay 'connected' to the larger enterprises to evaluate product gaps, corporate development and the focus of R&D expenditures. Leading US funds actively assist start-ups in convincing larger enterprises to trial the latest innovation. European funds should also strengthen ties with larger enterprises, enabling them to both help their portfolio companies penetrate key customers and sharpen their investment decisions through better understanding corporate needs and emerging trends. This is particularly important within Europe where the twin effects of consolidation in major industries and the large-scale adoption of outsourcing has made it more difficult for start-ups to gain access to large, high-spending companies, especially in the financial services and pharmaceuticals sectors. Recognising these new realties, entrepreneurs and their investors need greater global partnering and alliance building capabilities to grow their businesses.

## Exits

### The recovery of exit markets

Quality exits showed signs of a comeback in 2004–05. Ultimately, it is only through exits where investors realise value and retain confidence in the investment class. Fortunately, high-profile exits in Europe since 2004 have significantly helped in restoring LP confidence in European ventures, especially the acquisition of exciting companies such as Skype, PartyGaming, Kelkoo, Jamba and Apax's successful realisation of Q-Cells in 2006, which returned 27 times its original investment within two years. The rapid growth of AIM[26] has also excited investors seeking to flush out ageing portfolio companies, although it is too

Exhibit 2.2

**European venture-backed IPOs, 2000–05**

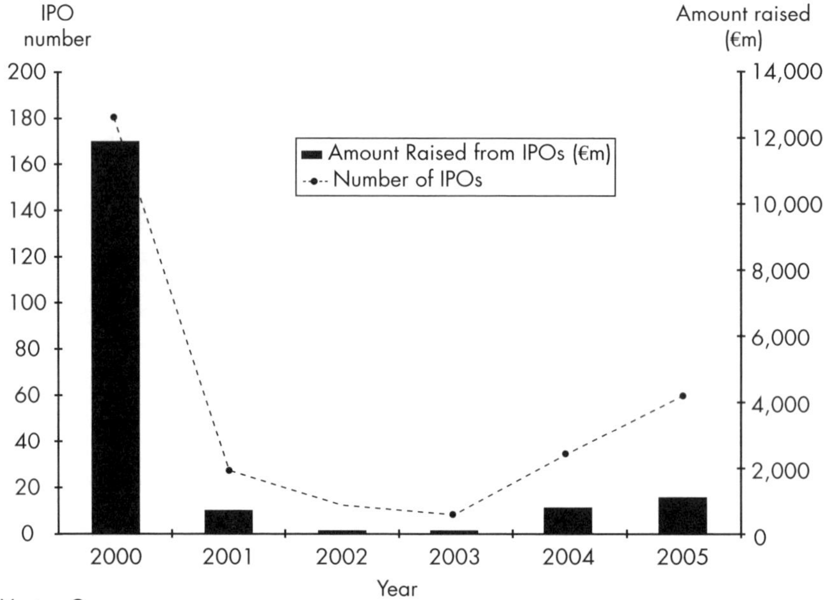


*Source*: VentureOne.

early to view this exchange as a significant source of exit value. Some entrepreneurs have opted to go directly on to AIM as a source of funding, bypassing the VC route, although it remains to be seen whether these firms can graduate to become world class companies.

In 2005, 60 venture-backed firms went public across European exchanges,[27] almost doubling the 35 firms in 2004, raising US$1.3bn, an increase of 50 per cent on 2004 (US$861m) (see Exhibit 2.2). In comparison, 41 VC-backed firms went public on US exchanges in 2005 (down 40 per cent), raising almost twice the amount raised by European firms at US$2.2bn. The median valuation of the US IPO was over three times greater (at US$167m) than the European VC-backed IPO (at US$51m). European M&A activity for VC-backed firms fell 16 per cent in 2005, although the average consideration per firm was up 26 per cent at €22.5m (US$27m). M&A volume was down marginally (6 per cent) in the United States to US$14.4bn, with an average consideration of US$91.5m, up from US$83.4m in 2004 for VC-backed firms.

While the global IPO markets are recovering, they still remain lack-lustre for growth companies seeking to raise capital. The overall hurdle for an IPO, especially on Nasdaq, has been raised significantly in recent years. The impact of Sarbanes-Oxley, especially on small to mid-sized companies has further impeded the volume of companies seeking a US listing, where 2005 IPO volume for VC-backed firms fell 40 per cent.[28] Today, only the boards of Europe's most successful companies assess Nasdaq listing as a viable alternative. An option that seemed to be obvious for everybody a few years ago has become a privilege of a few who have substantial business in the United States and the required scale.

The sustained weakness of the US IPO market may have a negative effect on the returns for the VC industry – much of the above market returns have historically been driven via the US IPO markets. Prolonged weakness in the IPO markets may necessitate longer holding periods of portfolio assets and higher investment rounds, thus forcing funds to focus their efforts on managing a larger pool of portfolio companies rather than relying on the two or three star performers out of every 10. European capital markets remain highly fragmented, despite renewed interest in creating centralised exchanges for high growth companies. Venture capital cannot fund most growth companies to profitability and market leadership; they have been reliant in the past on a much higher and sustained level of investment that only a public market[29] offers.

**Exit scenario planning**

Venture partners will need to consider more detailed scenarios for exit options prior to making investment decisions, and fostering relationships with large enterprises will undoubtedly help identify product/service gaps in the enterprise offering. Developing cooperative relationships with larger firms helps to build trust between the portfolio firm, the VC and the generally rigid enterprise. A good working relationship with one of the big players in a particular sector will also improve a VC's understanding of the entire market dynamics, thus further de-risking the investment decision.

Larger private equity players should also be viewed as potential partners for exit – with ever growing competitive intensity, escalating entry prices and unsustainable leverage for deals, private equity firms could provide excellent sources of liquidity for VC investors and growth capital to fund globally competitive firms. Some private equity funds, recognising the large funding requirements to build a market leader in the venture space, are seeking opportunities to acquire promising companies; for instance, in 2005 Warburg Pincus acquired the European firm Searchspace with a view to making it a market leader in enterprise software for the finance and banking industry.

## A note on limited partners

The landscape of the limited partner (LP) world is changing fast. There has been a widespread *institutionalisation* of the investor base in recent years through the effects of cross-border consolidation and as the sheer magnitude of capital apportioned to alternative investing rises. Also, the lessons of recent history have sharpened the asset allocation and due diligence policies of many LPs. The growth and role of funds of funds[30] will continue to reduce the large information asymmetries that once existed in selecting VC managers, helping the industry edge away from a cottage industry towards a professional asset class in Europe.[31]

European VC GPs are beginning to realise that fund-raising is becoming a professional and process-driven activity rather like other asset classes. The importance of funds of funds means 'having to confront the new realities of ruthless professionalism, committee decisions and global benchmarks'.[32] As LPs continue to deploy capital on a global basis, so they develop their understanding of the global venture market. Accordingly, a key dimension of LP due diligence that has emerged in recent years is the focus on a 'coherent global strategy' – there seems to be a shared view that 'Europe doesn't lack great young businesses – what it perhaps lacks is the ability to execute strategies on a global rather than national/regional basis.'[33] European portfolio firms, with the endorsement of their VCs, developed a bias towards commercialising regionally rather than addressing larger global markets or high-growth markets.[34] Limited partners increasingly have a bias towards European venture capitalists pursuing the 'Silicon Valley model with an Israel twist' – that is, accelerating the commercial rollout of the most innovative technology firms in its most strategic market.

Overall, there is a much higher burden of proof for European GPs to defend the robustness of their investment strategy and target fund size, and prove they have the requisite skill sets and capabilities to guide this to success. This is particularly relevant for many European VC funds that raised funds in 2000, as they now approach the end of the fund's investment cycle and management fees will be reduced. Negative returns, coupled with the reduced pool of LPs committed to European VC mean that it is unlikely that all funds will be successful at raising successor funds. Many expect the European VC industry to consolidate in the next 12–24 months (2006–7).

## Summary: Seizing the opportunity

Europe has been notoriously weak at IP and technology commercialisation compared with its competitors, notably the United States and Israel, and as a result has suffered weak returns. However, as the VC market emerges from the prolonged downturn, European funds have an excellent opportunity to adopt several transferable features from the US and Israeli model – namely improving market reach and the organisational capabilities of the GP across the lifecycle of the fund. Improving GP capabilities will enhance the competitive positioning of European funds (see Exhibit 2.3), which in turn increases the likelihood of improving the overall performance of VC investments.

Increasingly, European VC funds will need to create a multi-regional presence to contend with the unprecedented challenges caused through the effects of globalisation, new patterns of innovation and the rapid pace of technological change. Coupled with this, entrepreneurs recognise that commercial success requires a global stage and their criteria for selecting VC funds has moved well beyond negotiating the specifics of the termsheet. Seasoned entrepreneurs want value-adding partners to help them grow their business globally. LPs are also demanding differentiated skill sets and extended reach from VC funds to help commercialise the most promising European firms globally.

Venture commentator Martin Haemmig notes:[35]

> ... the emergence of truly international VC firms is proving a complementary source of capital for entrepreneurs to partner with a leading US or European firm. International VC firms are well placed to assess the competitive, market and growth challenges for new technology companies. Such firms can provide assistance that is both operational and international. ... Access to VC firms' partners and their network is key for start-ups. Strong VC firms have well established links to larger corporations to enable partnerships for distribution, for joint projects, or supplying critical technology components to provide a complete offering. Global corporations prefer collaborations with international VC firms since both understand global markets and may offer a single point of contact at the VC firm for global issues, which simplifies the working relationship for corporates.

Exhibit 2.3

**Sources of VC advantage and core capabilities**

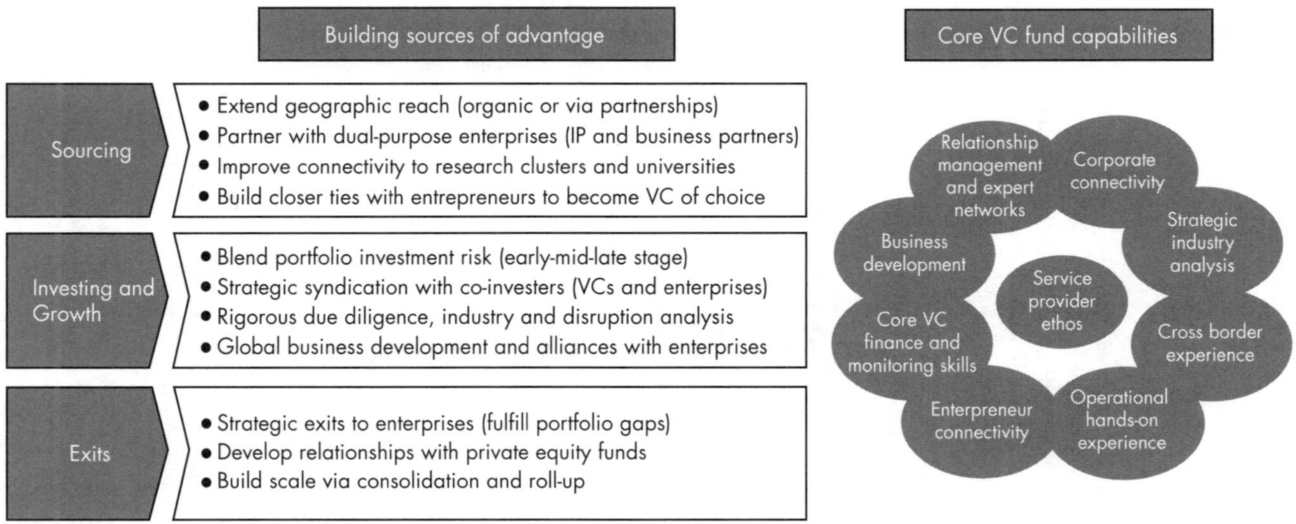


*Source*: Author's own.

As with most industries, European VC funds must innovate to remain competitive and relevant.

---

[1] Ernst & Young/Dow Jones VentureOne. The overhang represents limited partnership (LP) fund commitments in Europe, the United States and Israel. However, much of the global overhang derives from LP commitments in vintage years 1999–2002, where funds have reached or are close to reaching the average five-year investment period, thus relinquishing investors from further drawdowns (except for management fees and reserves for follow-on investments). In Europe, the overhang is around €10.5bn, of which approximately 50 per cent is embedded in vintage years 1999–2001.

[2] Ernst & Young/ VentureOne estimate a reduction in the number of VC funds in the US of circa 40 per cent and 50 per cent in Europe.

[3] VentureOne.

[4] National Venture Capital Association for the US venture industry (www.nvca.org).

[5] Thomas Friedman, *The World Is Flat* (New York: Farrar, Straus and Giroux, 2005).

[6] 'Is China the Next R&D Superpower?', by Dennis Normile, *Electronic Business*, July 2005.

[7] While Europe remains strong at R&D spending as measured by percentage of GDP (1.93 per cent in 2003), other regions maintain higher absolute levels of spending – for example, the United States at 2.7 per cent and Japan at 3.4 per cent. However, the growth rates in R&D spending are higher in countries such as China, which increased its spending 10 per cent annually from 1997 to 2002 compared with Europe's 0.7 per cent, which will mean Chinese R&D expenditure will surpass Europe by 2010 if current growth patterns continue (data from the European Commission 2005 and OECD).

[8] This is in addition to the significant research and development tax incentives increasingly offered to European technology firms. The EU's Framework 6 Programme (FP6) will be updated through FP7, which will see the creation of the European Research Council – which is modelled on the successful US National Science Foundation – to promote higher R&D spending.

[9] 'The Future of Corporate Venturing', *MIT Sloan Management Review*, Fall 2003, Vol. 45, No.1. According to the EVCA, corporate venturing in Europe decreased by 21 per cent in 2004.

[10] New Venture Partners was a spin-off from Lucent Technologies New Ventures Group in January 1997.

[11] Cambridge University has partnered with the following funds for this programme: 3i Group, Amadeus Capital Partners, Avlar BioVentures, IDG Ventures, Porton Capital and TTP Ventures.

[12] Google has negotiated with Stanford University a perpetual licence for the algorithms used for ranking web pages in search results, known as *PageRank*. The exclusivity period ends in 2011, whereby Stanford University has the right to license the underlying technology, or derivatives of it to third parties.

[13] 'Global Innovation: The Case for International Venture Capital Firms' (www.martinhaemmig.com, 2004).

[14] Big Deals: VC Deals Red Herring, 16 January 2006.

[15] The fusion of biology and economics is best captured by Christopher Meyer and Stan Davis in their book *It's Alive: The Coming Convergence of Information, Biology, and Business*, published by Crown Business, New York (2003).

[16] The term was coined by Professor Henry Chesborough of Harvard Business School in his influential book *Open Innovation: The New Imperative for Creating and Profiting from Technology* (New York: Harvard Business School Press, 2003).

[17] See www.innocentive.com.

[18] 'The Power of Us', *Business Week* (20 June 2005).

[19] Howard Rheingold, *Smart Mobs: The Next Social Revolution* (New York: Basic Books, 2003).

[20] Skype is an internet telephony company that was sold to eBay in 2005 for US$4.1bn. It represented one of the largest single European venture exits since 2000.

[21] The legal claim against RIM's (Research in Motion) hugely successful Blackberry handset highlights the need to secure intellectual property agreements early on in the product lifecycle.

[22] Formed in 1997, Argo Global Capital has US$450m under management with offices in Europe, Asia and North America. Its 'operator partners' include: France Telecom, Orange, SingTel and Deutsche Telekom. Argo's operator partners comprise approximately one-third of the fund's committed capital.

[23] Research suggests that around half of Europe's VC funds have either an office or partnership outside their host country ('After the Drought', *The Economist*, 1 April 2004).

[24] The median European VC fund size increased 245 per cent in 2005 to reach US$71m compared to 2004 at US$20.5m. This places the 2005 median fund size as the highest in the last six years. This may allow greater opportunity for improving the reach for European VCs. However, the median fund size in the United States remains significantly larger at US$200m in 2005 (source: VentureOne).

[25] 'Global Innovation: The Case for International Venture Capital Firms' (www.martinhaemmig.com, 2004).

[26] In 2005, 287 firms listed on London's Alternative Investment Market raising £3.4bn (up from 243 in 2004). Of the 2005 pool of companies, only 46 raised more than £20m, with the remainder averaging £5m.

[27] VentureOne databases for liquidity and VC data.

[28] Based on research with VC funds the *Venture Capital Journal* (2005) quoted Tim Draper, managing director of Draper Fisher Jurvetson: 'It costs a minimum of US$1m per year to comply with Sarbanes-Oxley, a real deterrent for small companies to go public. So they are waiting longer.' ('Is SOX to Blame for IPO Decline? What's Next?', November 2005.)

[29] The European Private Equity and Venture Capital Association (EVCA) promoted a high growth European stock market as one of its key policy goals in 2004–05.

[30] The fund-of-funds channel accounts for approximately 12 per cent of capital committed according to industry sources.

[31] Europe has also seen its first dedicated VC fund of funds through the formation of Mowbray Capital.

[32] Andy Thomson, 'Cheerleaders for Venture' (www.privateequityonline.com, 12 May 2005).

[33] Andy Thomson, 'Cheerleaders for Venture' (www.privateequityonline.com, 12 May 2005).

[34] For example, approximately 50 per cent of global sales in the technology market are between San Francisco and New York.

[35] 'Global Innovation: The Case for International Venture Capital Firms' (www.martinhaemmig.com, 2004)..

# Part II

# Fund structure and governance

Chapter 3

# Fund structures: New developments in general partner–limited partner terms

Jonathan Blake and Stephanie Biggs
*SJ Berwin LLP*

## Introduction

### A successful model

In the first five years of the new millennium, the private equity industry in Europe has enjoyed notable success. Private equity funds have raised, and invested, impressive amounts of funds from a growing range of investors. That investors have been happy to commit such significant amounts suggests that the industry has found a fund model that is broadly satisfactory, with general partner–limited partner (GP–LP) terms that work for both general partners and investors. Consequently, for many funds, the new millennium has not heralded a radical change in fund terms, but a honing and refining of earlier agreements.

Private equity is a rapidly maturing asset class, and current trends in fund terms reflect this. Although limited partnership agreements remain heavily negotiated and highly individual documents, it is possible to see certain 'market norms' developing. A degree of standardisation is most evident in relation to headline terms such as management fees and carried interest rates, although even these terms continue to differ depending on the individual circumstances of particular funds – the bespoke nature of private equity fund arrangements continues to be one of the industry's strengths.

### Focus on corporate governance

Many investors had their fingers burned in the dot-com crash of 2000, finding themselves locked into underperforming funds on disadvantageous terms. It is unsurprising then that prospective fund investors have been paying progressively closer attention to the terms on which they invest. Since 2000, law firms have seen a marked rise in requests from investors for a full legal review of fund terms as part of their pre-investment due diligence. What is more, a growing number of investors are not just looking at the headline terms, but are digging down into the detail of the limited partnership agreement.

Since the dot-com bubble burst, no-fault divorce has become common, giving investors an early way out of non-performing funds. Investors have also focused heavily on corporate governance issues, being particularly concerned to ensure that general partners do not have conflicting interests that might work against the interests of limited partners. For example, investors have become increasingly interested in third party fees – such as transaction fees, abort fees or monitoring fees – payable to general partners, and are more often asking general partners to share with the fund fees arising in connection with a fund's investments. This focus on conflicts is also reflected in the growing role of the investors' advisory committee; by 2005, it had become usual for funds to have an investor's advisory committee with a right to be consulted in conflict situations.

Another notable change is the growing demand for key executive clauses. It has become increasingly important for many investors to ensure that the investment executives who have been extensively evaluated and assessed during pre-investment due diligence are the people who will actually be managing the fund. At the turn of the millennium it was rare to find a key executive clause embedded in the fund documentation, but by 2005 it had become widely accepted.

Initially, pressure to improve the corporate governance of private equity funds came from investors. However, most general partners have been ready – even keen – to address corporate governance issues. This continues to be true, even though the recent fund-raising climate has favoured general partners. Private equity fund-raising enjoyed a bumper year in 2005; investor demand was so strong that top funds were oversubscribed, with general partners scaling back commitments and even turning investors away. Notwithstanding this, corporate governance issues have remained at the fore, demonstrating how the industry is coming of age.

## Economic terms

Over time, an economic model acceptable to both general partners and investors has developed, and there were no major changes in the economic terms of private equity funds in the five years to 2005. The headline management fee for buyout funds has been consistently within the 1.5 per cent to 2 per cent range, with fees for larger funds generally lower than those for smaller funds; venture fund management fees have generally remained between 2 per cent and 2.5 per cent. In relation to carried interest, a rate of 20 per cent has for some time been near-universal for both buyout and venture funds, at least in Europe.

More interestingly, even in a low interest rate environment, a preferred return of 8 per cent remains the norm for buyout funds. Rates of 6 per cent or 7 per cent are sometimes seen, but there does not yet seem to be significant pressure from general partners for investors to accept a hurdle that truly reflects current returns on risk-free investments – the original rationale for the 8 per cent rate. This is, of course, less true for venture funds, many of which continue to be hurdle-free.

Although headline terms have remained largely steady, there has been a subtle but noticeable change in the detailed provisions of limited partnership agreements, making current economic terms slightly more investor-friendly overall.

### Management fees

It is now more or less standard for limited partnership agreements to include a management fee step-down at the end of the investment period. During the investment period, the management fee is charged on total commitments – that is, the maximum amount that could potentially be drawn down from investors. At the end of the investment period, although the management fee percentage generally remains the same, it is often charged on a reduced amount. However, the basis for calculating this reduced amount varies from fund to fund; the reduced amount may be the total amount drawn down from investors ('capital employed') or it may be limited to the total amount drawn down for investment purposes ('no fees-on-fees'), and it may or may not include the acquisition cost of realised, written-off and/or written-down investments.

### Transaction fees

General partners are coming under increasing and sustained pressure from investors to share fees received in connection with fund investment activities. In the late 1990s, general partners might have expected to keep all transaction fees, investment-related fees (such as directors' fees or monitoring fees) and underwriting fees received in connection with investments made by their funds, after an offset against abort costs. Now such fees are more usually shared between the general partner and the fund, with the sharing ratio again varying from fund to fund. In a number of funds, the general partner's profit share is reduced by the entire amount of any fees received, meaning that investors and not the general partner effectively benefit from the entire amount of such fees.

Allowing general partners to retain transaction fees clearly gives rise to conflict of interest concerns, and the increasing pressure on general partners to share such fees in part reflects investors' increasing focus on corporate governance issues.

### Carried interest

There has been little change in carried interest terms since 2000. An increase in the headline carried interest rate never seemed likely for most funds. However, a number of observers thought that general partners might take advantage of high investor demand to seek to move from the usual European 'fund-as-a-whole' carried interest model (where an investor's total investment in the fund must be repaid before any carried interest is payable to the management team) to the 'deal-by-deal' model favoured in the United States (where carried interest is payable by reference to the performance of each separate investment, subject to losses on realised investments having been recouped and a clawback in the event that subsequent investments underperform). It can be difficult for general partners to incentivise junior investment executives if carried interest is not payable for several years, and the deal-by-deal model allows management teams to receive carried interest earlier in the life of the fund than the fund-as-a-whole model.

Investors have indicated that they have a degree of sympathy with general partners on this issue, understanding the need for management teams to remain motivated. However, many general partners seem to be happy with, or at least resigned to, the fund-as-a-whole approach at present, and only a few general partners have so far shown any enthusiasm for opening a debate with investors. It will be interesting to see if this changes in future.

## Corporate governance

Investors have been focusing increasingly on corporate governance issues when evaluating funds. Investors now expect limited partnership agreements to include investor protection provisions, such as key executive clauses and no-fault divorce mechanisms, and general partners are largely accepting of this. In addition, the majority of funds now have an investor's advisory committee, offering investors a forum in which to examine and comment on the operation and management of the fund.

## Advisory committees

The exact role of the investor's advisory committee differs from fund to fund, but it is fair to say that the role of the advisory committee has expanded over recent years. Most funds now have an advisory committee, and a number of large institutional investors routinely look for confirmation from the general partner that they will be allocated a seat on the advisory committee before they will invest.

For most funds, one of the main functions of the advisory committee is to review any conflicts of interest arising from time to time between the general partner or the management team and the fund or its investors, with the aim of ensuring that conflicts are resolved fairly. This may include, for example, reviewing the amount of any transaction fees received by the general partner in connection with investments made by the fund. Advisory committees are also commonly involved in reviewing investment valuations, although it will be interesting to see whether this role becomes less important to investors following the introduction of the *International Private Equity and Venture Capital Valuation Guidelines*, published by the British Venture Capital Association (BVCA), the European Private Equity and Venture Capital Association (EVCA) and the Association Française des Investisseurs en Capital (AFIC) in March 2005, which have been widely adopted by funds.

The advisory committee may also be a means for the general partner to report back to investors generally on the performance of the fund and its investments. In some funds, the general partner sees an advisory committee meeting as a useful opportunity to give detailed investor presentations and receive investor feedback. In other funds, particularly where the advisory committee consists of representatives of only a limited number of investors, the advisory committee function and the investor reporting function are kept separate.

When considering the remit of any advisory committee, it is important to note that investor advisory committees are exactly that – advisory bodies. Legal restrictions on limited partners taking part in the management of limited partnerships mean that the remit of an advisory committee will not include any power to take decisions regarding the management of the fund. Although investors will expect a general partner to listen to, and take account of, the views of the advisory committee in relation to certain matters, ultimately all decisions rest with the general partner, and the general partner is under no obligation to follow any advisory committee recommendations. It seems probable that this legal restriction will act as a natural brake on the expansion of the role of the advisory committee, allowing investors to be informed and consulted about fund management issues, while allowing general partners freedom to manage funds on a day-to-day basis.

## Key executives

Given the significant amount of time and effort that investors expend in due diligence, it is not surprising that they are increasingly looking for assurances that their investment will actually be managed by the management team who have been so carefully investigated. Many investors now expect general partners to have considered succession issues, and for there to be active and early debate about possible changes to the management team. General partners also need to demonstrate that their success is not dependent solely on one or two individuals; they are expected to show that their management teams have depth.

In consequence, key executive clauses have become very common, and the clauses themselves have become more rigorous. For older funds, an investor vote was usually needed to trigger a suspension of the fund's investment powers following a key executive departure. It is now more common for suspension of investment powers to be triggered automatically by such a departure, with an investor vote required to lift the suspension.

The trigger events themselves have also become more sophisticated, and a two-tier approach is often seen. Under this approach, a key executive clause could be triggered if, for example, any one senior member of the management team ceases to be actively involved in the management of the fund, or if any three junior team members depart. This requires general partners not only to keep the headline names, but also to maintain a team of sufficient depth. As key executive clauses have grown in popularity, many advisory committees have taken on the role of approving new 'key executives' as the composition of the management team changes over time.

### 'No-fault divorce'

Funds have almost always allowed investors to remove general partners for acts of default, such as fraud, gross negligence or wilful disregard for the general partner's obligations to the fund. However, a majority of limited partnership agreements now also include no-fault divorce clauses. These clauses permit investors, acting together, to remove a general partner where there is no identifiable fault (for example, where investors believe that a fund is underperforming), although the general partner is usually protected from removal for an initial one or two-year period. In Europe, it is standard for the general partner to receive compensation in the event of such removal, the amount generally being calculated by reference to the general partner's annual priority profit share (once or twice this amount being common).

## Freedom of information

### The right to know

Protecting the confidentiality of fund information and, in particular, portfolio company information is an area of growing importance to general partners. Generally speaking, general partners have an extremely open relationship with their investors. Limited partners typically undertake extensive due diligence before deciding to invest in a fund and, once invested, receive detailed reports from the general partner containing comprehensive performance information for both the fund and its portfolio companies. This transparency requires an understanding between general partners and limited partners that the information provided by the fund will be kept confidential. However, the open relationship between funds and their investors has come under pressure from the introduction of freedom of information legislation entitling members of the public to require investors who are public bodies to disclose information held by them.

European funds with US pension funds as investors have been grappling with freedom of information issues for some time. Notably, litigation in the United States forced CalPERS to disclose a significant amount of information about its private equity investments, and the internal rates of return and investment multiples of the funds in which it invests are now freely available on its website.

The coming into force of the UK's Freedom of Information Act in January 2005 put freedom of information issues firmly on the European agenda, and some believe that EU freedom of information legislation cannot be too far away.

## Striking a balance

The US legislation differs slightly from state to state, but has generally struck a balance between public interest and commercial sensitivity by requiring disclosure of fund-level information, but accepting that portfolio companies' financial information should remain confidential to protect their competitiveness (although the ongoing litigation involving the Ohio Bureau of Workers' Compensation suggests that the issue is not yet finally settled). The US position means that some European general partners have become more open to disclosure of fund performance information, but there is still significant sensitivity regarding the disclosure of management fees and carried interest rates, and an almost universal determination to protect portfolio company information.

## Dealing with the risk of disclosure

Uncertainty over the application of freedom of information legislation, which is relatively untested in Europe, has led to a change in fund terms. General partners are more conscious of confidentiality issues generally, and this has resulted in a strengthening of the confidentiality provisions applicable to all investors. In addition, some funds whose investors are subject to freedom of information laws have introduced specific terms to combat the risk of disclosure of sensitive information.

These terms vary from fund to fund. Some general partners reserve the right not to provide such investors with information, although it is not yet clear to what extent this right is being exercised in practice. Others are providing information in non-written form only, either at face-to-face meetings or through read-only websites, but this approach has received a mixed response from limited partners. Agreeing to keep no written records raises governance issues for some, and others are concerned at the quantity of information to be memorised, particularly where one individual is responsible for a large number of funds.

Perhaps the most effective term from a general partner's perspective is a requirement for investors to notify the fund if a disclosure request is received, and to work with the general partner to ensure that disclosure is limited to the minimum required by law. In order to make this administratively manageable, some investors are asking general partners in return to identify upfront any information that is commercially sensitive and for which disclosure should be resisted. Whichever approach is taken, it seems that general partners are relying on contractual protections against disclosure; only a small number of the very top funds have decided to exclude public bodies from investing altogether.

## Secondaries transactions

Although interests in private equity funds are fundamentally long-term, illiquid investments, there are signs of an active secondaries market developing. Both specialist secondary funds and certain funds of funds are in the business of acquiring investments from primary investors, and the number of secondaries transactions has increased noticeably. It is not yet clear whether, as a result, general partners are coming under pressure to relax the transfer restrictions contained in limited partnership agreements.

At present, a majority of general partners take the view that a private equity fund is a private club, and spend a significant amount of time building relationships with prospective and actual limited partners. Similarly, many limited partners like to know the identity of their fellow investors. The most common transfer restrictions, therefore, provide that limited partnership interests may not be transferred without the consent of the general partner, and that consent may be given or withheld in the general partner's absolute discretion. In many cases, general partners are exercising this discretion to refuse consent to transfers. To preserve the long-term nature of the GP–LP relationship, where consent is given, some general partners are making consent conditional on the prospective transferee agreeing to subscribe as a primary investor in the general partner's next fund.

Certain general partners will agree to transfer provisions under which consent to a transfer may be withheld by the general partner only if it is reasonable to do so. However, this is by no means universally accepted; many general partners take the view that it is their right to decide who their investors are, and they do not wish their reasons for refusing a transfer to be open to scrutiny or challenge.

It remains to be seen whether the secondaries market will continue to grow, and whether this, in turn, will lead to private equity fund investments becoming more freely transferable. At present, there does not seem to be significant pressure from investors for general partners to relax transfer restrictions, although some funds of funds are asking for, and receiving, permission to transfer investments between different funds of funds managed by the same manager. In addition, a few limited partners are thought to be using innovative methods such as total return swaps and other derivative instruments in an attempt to circumvent transfer restrictions, and so achieve virtual liquidity. However, it is not certain that these methods are effective, and general partners who become aware of such arrangements often seek to challenge them. Investors would be well advised, therefore, to continue to view their private equity fund investments as non-transferable, at least for the foreseeable future.

## Practical implications

In recent years, there have been no dramatic developments in GP–LP terms. Rather, fund terms have been subject to a process of continuing refinement as the private equity fund industry matures. However, the subtle developments that have taken place do have a number of practical implications for those who expect to be negotiating limited partnership agreements for new funds in the near future.

## For general partners

It seems likely that investors will continue to exert pressure on general partners in relation to fees, requiring general partners to look closely at their own business models. Fee structures for new funds are likely to be tighter than the fee structures for funds from earlier vintages, and it is less likely that general partners will be able to rely on transaction fee income to supplement management fees.

On the other hand, investor demand is high, with many funds comfortably reaching their target fund size. It may, therefore, be an opportune time for general partners raising new funds to consider testing the water by proposing more management-friendly carried interest models.

In addition, the developing secondaries market means that it would be advisable for general partners to consider their policies in relation to transfers. Investors are increasingly likely to ask for permission to transfer partnership interests. Although decisions will, of course, need to be made on a case-by-case basis, general partners will benefit from having evaluated the more general pros and cons in advance.

## For investors

Investors have been largely successful in convincing general partners that corporate governance issues matter. Investors can, therefore, expect to see more (although by no means all) funds coming to the market with provisions, such as no-fault divorce clauses, that might previously only have been included under pressure from investors.

The developing secondaries market also has implications for investors. For some investors, even those who are not secondaries market players, the prospect of increased liquidity in the market may be a good thing. However, others may dislike the prospect of new, unknown investors being admitted to mature funds, especially if a new investor has a sufficiently large interest to determine the outcome of those matters on which investors are entitled to vote.

Finally, it has been known for those running information services to go on fishing expeditions in search of fund information. Investors subject to freedom of information legislation should ensure that they are prepared for disclosure requests, as the UK legislation (in particular) gives public authorities only a short time in which to respond. It will be easier to deal with requests if a policy has been formulated, and discussed with general partners, in advance.

Chapter 4

# The limits of limited liability: How key jurisdictions differ

Matthew H. Hurlock and David Patrick Eich
*Kirkland & Ellis International LLP*[1]

## Introduction

The limited partnership is the most common form of investment vehicle for private equity funds. The benefits to both private equity sponsors and their investors of using a limited partnership include the limited partnership's fiscal transparency and the flexibility it provides for organising economic arrangements tailored to the specific goals of sponsors and their investors, such as, for the sponsors, the level of control the general partner has over the partnership, and, for the limited partners, their limited liability. There exists a natural tension, however, between the general partner and the limited partners over the degree of freedom the general partner should have to conduct and manage the business of the limited partnership. As the private equity asset class grows and becomes more mainstream, and investors invest ever larger amounts through limited partnerships, there is pressure to formalise and, in some cases, expand the role of limited partners in the conduct and management of the business of the limited partnership.

The risk of extending limited partner involvement in a limited partnership is, in general, that, if such involvement constitutes 'managing' the business of the limited partnership, then that limited partner may lose the limited liability protection provided under the applicable statute. The types of involvement that limited partners currently are seeking have been widely discussed. The purpose of this chapter is to consider the limited partnership laws in several of the jurisdictions most commonly used for private equity fund formations to determine whether and how clearly they demarcate the actions that limited partners may take with respect to the business of limited partnerships from those which could threaten a limited partner's limited liability.

The jurisdictions surveyed in this chapter include the State of Delaware, England, the Cayman Islands and the Channel Islands (Jersey and Guernsey). These jurisdictions are most commonly used by private equity funds and illustrate a range of potential limited partner involvement in the business of a limited partnership. The key differences concerning the limited partnership laws in the jurisdictions discussed in this chapter are summarised in Exhibit 4.1.

## Delaware

Of the jurisdictions reviewed in this chapter, the state of Delaware, with the Delaware Revised Uniform Limited Partnership Act (6 Del. C. §17-101 *et seq.*) (the 'Delaware RULPA'), provides the most comprehensive and protective standards regarding the actions a limited partner may take with respect to a limited partnership. The basic rule states:

> A limited partner is not liable for the obligations of a limited partnership unless he or she is also a general partner or, in addition to the exercise of the rights and powers of a limited partner, he or she participates in the control of the business. However, if the limited partner does participate in the control of the business, he or she is liable only to persons who transact business with the limited partnership reasonably believing, based upon the limited partner's conduct, that the limited partner is a general partner.[2]

As long as a limited partner does not breach this rule, the limited partner's liability to the partnership will not exceed the amount of its capital contribution. In determining whether a breach has occurred, the main question is what constitutes 'participat[ing] in the control of the business'. The Delaware RULPA provides an extensive and detailed list of 'safe harbours' for actions taken by a limited partner, none of which will be considered participating in the control of the business. This list includes, among others, a limited partner:

- serving as an agent or officer or employee of the partnership or its general partner;
- serving as a consultant or adviser to the general partner;
- lending to, guaranteeing debt of, or borrowing from a limited partnership or a general partner;
- serving on a committee of the limited partnership or the limited partners or partners;
- voting on any of the following matters:
  - the dissolution and winding up of the limited partnership;
  - the sale, pledge or other transfer of any asset of the limited partnership;
  - the incurrence, refinancing or payment of indebtedness by the limited partnership;
  - a change in the nature of the business;
  - the admission, removal or retention of a general partner or limited partner;
  - any transaction or other matter involving an actual or potential conflict of interest;
  - any amendment to the partnership agreement or certificate of limited partnership;
  - any merger or consolidation of the limited partnership;
  - the making of ... investments, including investments in property, whether real, personal or mixed, either directly or indirectly, by the limited partnership; or
  - such other matters as are stated in the partnership agreement or in any other agreement or in writing; or
- serving 'on the board of directors or a committee of, to consult with or advise, to be an officer, director, stockholder, partner, member, manager, trustee, agent or employee of, or to be a fiduciary or contractor for, any person in which the limited partnership has an interest or any person providing management, consulting, advisory, custody or other services or products for, to or on behalf of, or otherwise having a business or other relationship with, the limited partnership or a general partner of the limited partnership ...'.[3]

In addition to this extensive list of safe harbours, the Delaware RULPA permits limited partners to make decisions as to any 'other matters as are stated in the partnership agreement or in any other agreement in writing'.[4] Furthermore, the Delaware RULPA provides that, even if a limited partner does exercise powers beyond those explicitly permitted under the safe harbours, this does not necessarily 'constitute participation by him or her in the control of the business of the limited partnership'.[5] In particular, a person challenging the limited liability of a limited partner would have to establish that:

- the limited partner actually participated in the control of the business; and
- the third party transacted business with the limited partnership reasonably believing, based upon the limited partner's conduct, that the limited partner was a general partner.[6]

The Delaware RULPA thus sets a very high standard for establishing that a limited partner is conducting the business of a limited partnership. Given the 'reasonable belief' requirement described above, among other things, this standard is, in practice, a difficult one to meet, because the names of all general partners of a limited partnership are on file with the Secretary of State of Delaware.

As a result of the breadth and protectiveness of the Delaware RULPA provisions, there does not appear to have been extensive litigation with respect to their meaning. The terms of most limited partnership agreements, and, in particular, the typical participation rights requested by limited partners, such as certain approval rights or membership of an advisory board, fit squarely within the safe harbours permitted under the law. Thus, as a practical matter, limited partners are well protected by the Delaware RULPA from incurring by such activities liability in excess of their capital contributions.

## England

In contrast to the Delaware RULPA's exhaustive list of safe harbours for limited partners, English law reflects a more traditional notion of limited partnership, namely that, in exchange for limited liability, limited partners will remain essentially passive. The Limited Partnerships Act 1907 (the 'English LP Law') provides the legal foundation for limited partnerships under English law, but it has received infrequent judicial review, and there has been almost no further statutory activity since its inception.[7] Consequently, although the question of what a limited partner should do, or avoid doing, in order to retain its limited liability is fairly straightforward at either end of the spectrum of permissibility, the lack of judicial interpretation or material statutory evolution regarding the terms of the English LP Law has left a substantial grey area in the middle.

Under the English LP Law, each limited partnership will have: (a) at least one 'general partner' who will be 'liable for all debts and obligations of the firm'; and (b) 'limited partners' who must contribute capital (whether by way of cash or property) on joining the firm but who, following such contribution, will 'not be liable for the debts and obligations of the firm beyond the amount so contributed'.[8]

A limited partner's limited liability status may be lost, resulting in it being deemed to be (or treated as though it were) a general partner, in two scenarios, namely:

- if the limited partnership is not registered in accordance with the English LP Law;[9] or
- if a limited partner takes part 'in the management[10] of the partnership business[11],' either directly or indirectly.

On its face, the English LP Law circumscribes the extent of a limited partner's loss of limited liability as a result of its participation in the management of partnership business to the debts and obligations of the firm incurred *during the period in which the limited partner so took part*.[12] As such, a strict construction of the relevant provisions would suggest that a limited partner will not have unlimited liability in respect of any debt or obligation incurred after its limited liability status has been re-established, even where the debt or obligation has been incurred because of the subsequent implementation by the general partner of a prior management 'decision' of the limited partner. Of course, it is possible that a court could nevertheless construe such provisions in such a way that the limited partner would retain unlimited liability for debts and obligations incurred in such circumstances.

As with the Delaware RULPA, the key question raised by this aspect of the English LP Law is how to define 'management of the partnership business', which is expressly defined neither in the English LP Law nor apparently in any relevant case law.[13] Leading legal commentators[14] suggest that any decision that constitutes 'an ordinary matter connected with the partnership business'[15] will constitute such management, whereas any decision 'relating to the terms or structure of the partnership (for example, the nature of the business carried on, the admission of new partners, or the profit sharing ratios) will not'.[16] Obviously there is still substantial uncertainty among leading authorities regarding those limited partner actions that would constitute management and those that would not.

Over time, legal practitioners have attempted to narrow the parameters,[17] and market practice (while not tested in the courts) has to some extent reduced the grey area surrounding the question of what constitutes 'management of the partnership business ...'. In that context, we believe that the following actions would generally be regarded as likely to breach the restriction:

- taking part in the general partner's decision-making process with regard to the making of investments;
- being involved in the hiring or firing of general partner employees or investment executives (though this should be distinguished from the ability of limited partners to replace the general partner itself);
- approving or rejecting the suitability of general partner employee or investment executive expenses or otherwise being involved in the making of decisions regarding their terms of employment or engagement;
- being involved in decisions as to the operational procedures of the general partner, whether generally or with regard to specific day-to-day general partner administrative activities;
- involvement in the negotiation of the terms of any investment (or of the terms of engagement of any third party adviser, to be retained in connection with the evaluation, analysis, negotiation or closing of such investment);
- any attempt to influence the general partner with regard to any of the activities set out above (depending on the circumstances, relationship between the parties and so on); or
- any entitlement (by virtue of voting control, committee position or otherwise) with regard to the activities set out above (depending on the circumstances, relationship between the parties and so on).

The following activities, on the other hand, would generally be regarded as not likely to breach such limits:

- taking part in any decision or decision-making process that relates to the relationship between the various partners, as opposed to the business of the partnership (for example, profit allocations, rules for (and the process governing) the admission of new members or the transfer of existing interests, the increasing of commitments, liquidation or termination of the partnership, etc.);
- being involved in any general partner replacement or sanction/disciplinary process, or otherwise, in the negotiation or agreement as to the general partner's role, duties and financial entitlement; and
- involvement in the nature of the business to be carried on by the partnership. This could extend to involvement in the making of a strategic investment decision that the fund should focus on a specific industry or industry sector, depending on the circumstances (such involvement would be more likely to fall foul of the management restriction if it could be shown to relate to the performance of a specific target or targets, as opposed to the industry or industry sector trend).

From this standpoint, therefore, the English LP Law presents a significant contrast to the Delaware RULPA. Where the Delaware RULPA has not only provided extensive detail as to what involvement is permitted by limited partners but also erected high standards for challenging their limited liability protection, the English LP Law remains silent as to what involvement, if any, is specifically permitted. As described above, this presents interpretive challenges to any limited partner seeking clear guidance regarding what actions he or she may be permitted to take with respect to an English limited partnership.

## Cayman Islands

The applicable rule governing Cayman Islands limited partnerships, the Exempted Limited Partnership Law (2003 Revision) (the 'Cayman LP Law'), presents an apparent compromise between the extensive detail of the Delaware RULPA and the more generally stated principles of the English LP Law. Section 7(1) of the Cayman LP Law sets forth a general rule consistent with that of the other common fund formation jurisdictions, stating that '*[a] limited partner shall not take part in the business of an exempted limited partnership*, and all letters, contracts, deeds, instruments or documents whatsoever shall be entered into by the general partner on behalf of the exempted limited partnership' [emphasis added].

Failure to observe the general rule can result in a loss of limited liability for the limited partner:

> If a limited partner takes part in the conduct of the business of[18] an exempted limited partnership in its dealings with persons who are not partners, that limited partner shall be liable, in the event of the insolvency of the exempted limited partnership, for all debts and obligations of that exempted limited partnership incurred during the period that he so participates in the conduct of the business as though he were, for such period, a general partner....[19]

As with other limited partnership statutes reviewed in this chapter, the Cayman LP Law provides additional protections to the limited partner, namely by imposing a *scienter* requirement on behalf of the potential claimant and also providing multiple safe harbours for activities in which a limited partner may engage without risking increased liability.

First, the Section 7(2) loss of limited liability occurs only to the extent a person who transacts business with the partnership during such period has *actual knowledge* of the limited partner's participation (that is, in the conduct of the business) and *who then reasonably believes such limited partner to be a general partner*. As with the Delaware RULPA requirement of a 'reasonable belief' that the limited partner was a general partner, this standard is likely to be difficult to meet.

Secondly, Section 7(3) provides an extensive list of safe harbours for actions a limited partner may take without being deemed to be taking part in the conduct of the business,[20] including:

- being a contractor for or an agent or employee of the exempted limited partnership or of a general partner or acting as a director, officer or shareholder of a corporate general partner;
- consulting with and advising a general partner with respect to the business[21] of the exempted limited partnership;
- investigating, reviewing, approving or being advised as to the accounts or business[22] affairs of the exempted limited partnership or exercising any right conferred by this Law;
- acting as surety or guarantor for the exempted limited partnership either generally or in respect of specific obligations;
- approving or disapproving an amendment to the partnership agreement; or
- voting[23] as a limited partner on:
  - the dissolution and winding up of the exempted limited partnership;
  - the purchase, sale, exchange, lease, mortgage, pledge or other acquisition or transfer of any asset or assets by or of the exempted limited partnership;
  - the incurrence or renewal of indebtedness[24] by the exempted limited partnership;
  - a change in the nature of the business[25] of the exempted limited partnership;
  - the admission, removal or withdrawal of a general or limited partner and the continuation of business of[26] the exempted limited partnership thereafter; or
  - transactions in which one or more of the general partners have an actual or potential conflict of interest with one or more of the limited partners.

In addition, a limited partner may bring an action on behalf of the partnership to the extent that a general partner with authority to do so has, without good cause, refused to do so.

The Cayman LP Law, while not as protective of limited partners as the Delaware RULPA, provides at least a clear list of safe harbours for limited partners. It is worth noting, however, that the Delaware RULPA provides a safe harbour to limited partners for several activities that are not included in the Cayman LP Law, including:

- the right to terminate any third party law suit in right of the limited partner; and
- serving on the board of directors or a committee thereof, to consult with or advise, to be an officer, director, stockholder, partner, member, manager, trustee, agent or employee of, or to be a fiduciary or contractor for, any person in which the limited partnership has an interest or any person providing management, consulting, advisory, custody or other services or

products for, to or on behalf of, or otherwise having a business or other relationship with, the limited partnership or a general partner of the limited partnership.

While Cayman Islands law is clearly influenced by the Delaware standard, there are certain differences with the Delaware RULPA, which cause the Cayman LP Law to be less protective of limited partners.

Limited partners can be certain of protecting their limited liability status by restricting their activities to the safe harbour activities enumerated in Section 7(3) of the Cayman LP Law. For example, a limited partner will not be deemed to be taking part in the conduct of the business of an Exempted Limited Partnership by voting on 'the incurrence ... of indebtedness by the exempted limited partnership' in accordance with Section 7(3)(f)(iii). Certain such enumerated activities, however, are inherently ambiguous, and, hence, do not by themselves make clear the safe limits of limited partner involvement – that is, 'consulting with and advising a general partner with respect to the business of the exempted limited partnership' consistent with Section 7(3)(b). Just what manner of and how much advice can be rendered before the limited partner is actually conducting the business is not obvious on the face of the statute.

In order to achieve optimal protection for the limited partner in a partnership agreement, therefore, the applicable provisions of the Cayman LP Law should be considered as a whole. Section 7(2), in particular, should be referred to when interpreting any of the more ambiguous Section 7(3) provisions. Given that Section 7(2)'s provisos regarding the knowledge of the third party are a question of fact (and, hence, would likely proceed to a trier of fact in any enforcement scenario), a limited partner should seek to ensure the benefit of Section 7(2)'s protections via avoiding third party contact if possible with respect to fund activities. In connection with a limited partner who will be, for example, a member of an investment or advisory committee, therefore, the investment or advisory committee provisions in the partnership agreement should contain a clause providing that, to the extent that a member of the investment or advisory committee is a limited partner, it shall not, in acting as a member of such committee, communicate with any third party who is not a limited partner or a general partner. Although, as a practical matter, it is unlikely that a third party will have notice of such (or any) provision in the partnership agreement, such a provision would at least serve as a proscriptive reminder to a limited partner of safe parameters to the extent that a limited partner does have contact with a third party.[27]

## Channel Islands: Jersey and Guernsey

### Jersey

Under Article 18 of the Limited Partnerships (Jersey) Law 1994 (the 'Jersey LP Law'), a limited partner is liable to the limited partnership only for the difference, if any, between the value of money or other property contributed by the limited partner to the limited partnership and the value of money or other property specified in the records kept by the general partner to be contributed by the limited partner to the limited partnership. Under Article 19 of the Jersey LP Law, a limited partner is not liable for the debts or obligations of the limited partnership unless otherwise provided under the Jersey LP Law. The Jersey LP Law provides for a loss of limited liability under two circumstances. The first is if the surname or corporate name of a limited partner appears in the name of the limited partnership. In such a case (other than in certain limited circumstances set out in Articles 7(2) and (3) of the Jersey LP Law), the limited partner is liable as a general partner to any creditor of the limited partnership who has extended credit without actual knowledge that the limited partner is not a general partner.[28]

The other circumstance under which a limited partner can become liable for the debts and obligations of the limited partnership is if a limited partner participates in the 'management' of the limited partnership with persons who are not partners. This management prohibition, set forth in Articles 19(2) and 19(3) of the Jersey LP Law, only applies in the event of insolvency of the limited partnership. In such case, the limited partner will be liable as a general partner for all debts and obligations of the limited partnership incurred during the period that he or she participated in the management of the limited partnership. The limited partner, however, is only liable to persons who transacted with the limited partnership with actual knowledge of the participation of the limited partner in the management of the limited partnership and who reasonably believed the limited partner to be a general partner.

As with the Delaware RULPA, the Jersey LP Law provides several safe harbours for actions that limited partners can take that do not constitute 'management' of the limited partnership. These are:

- being a contractor for or an agent or employee of the limited partnership or of a general partner or acting as a director, officer or shareholder of a corporate general partner;
- consulting with and advising a general partner with respect to the activities of the limited partnership;
- investigating, reviewing, approving or being advised as to the accounts or affairs of the limited partnership or exercising any right conferred by the Jersey LP Law;
- acting as surety or guarantor for the limited partnership either generally or in respect of specific obligations;
- approving or disapproving an amendment to the partnership agreement;
- voting on, or otherwise signifying approval or disapproval of, one or more of the following:
  - the dissolution and winding up of the limited partnership;
  - the purchase, sale, exchange, lease, pledge, hypothecation, creation of a security interest, or other dealing in any asset by or of the limited partnership;
  - the creation or renewal of an obligation by the limited partnership;
  - a change in the nature of the activities of the limited partnership;
  - the admission, removal or withdrawal of a general or a limited partner and the continuation of the limited partnership thereafter; or
  - transactions in which one or more of the general partners have an actual or potential conflict of interest with one or more of the limited partners; or
- bringing an action on behalf of the limited partnership pursuant to Article 28(3) of the Jersey LP Law.[29]

As with the Delaware RULPA, Article 19(6) of the Jersey LP Law provides that the list of safe harbours is not exclusive and shall not imply that 'the possession or exercise of any other power by a limited partner will *necessarily* constitute the participation by such limited partner in the management of the limited partnership' [emphasis added].

Consequently, while the Delaware RULPA provisions are more protective of limited partners, the protection of limited partners under the Jersey LP Law is still quite broad. There has been relatively little litigation with respect to the Jersey LP Law, as the terms of most limited partnership agreements, and in particular the usual control rights requested by limited partners such as certain approval rights or participation on an advisory board, fit squarely within the permitted safe harbours.

## Guernsey

Unlike those of the states of Delaware, Jersey or the Cayman Islands, the Guernsey laws with respect to limited partners, set out in Article 12 of the Limited Partnerships (Guernsey) Law 1995, as amended (the 'Guernsey LP Law'), are on their face more restrictive regarding the kinds of actions limited partners are permitted to undertake. Article 12(1) states:

> A limited partner:
>
> (a) shall not participate in the *conduct or management of* the business of the lim ited partnership;
>
> (b) shall not *transact the business of*, sign or execute documents for or otherwise bind the limited partnership [emphasis added].

This standard appears on its face to be broader and hence more limiting of the kinds of activities in which a limited partner can engage than the Delaware RULPA or the Jersey LP Law. The Guernsey LP Law elsewhere, moreover, expressly allows a limited partner only certain very limited rights, including, under Article 12(2):

> (a) to inspect the books of the limited partnership;
>
> (b) with such assistance as may reasonably be required of the general partners, examine and inquire into the state and prospects of the partnership business; and
>
> (c) advise the partners thereon.

Article 12(5) similarly permits a limited partner the same rights as a general partner '(a) to: inspect, make copies and take extracts from the partnership books at all times; (b) to be given, on demand, true and full information of all things affecting the partnership; and (c) to be given a full and formal account of partnership whenever circumstances render it just and reasonable' and a limited partner has the same rights as a general partner to have the partnership dissolved by order of the Royal Court.

Article 12(3), moreover, sets forth what appears on its face to be a fairly strict standard for failure of a limited partner to live within such limits, stating that:

> A limited partner who *in whatever capacity acts or purports to act in contravention* of subsection (1) shall be liable as if he were a general partner in respect of all debts of the limited partnership incurred while he so acts or purports to act [emphasis added].

Article 12(3) of the Guernsey LP Law is apparently less protective of limited partners' limited liability status than any of the laws of the states of Delaware, the Cayman Islands or Jersey. Nonetheless, the Guernsey LP Law does provide a list of safe harbours for limited partners in Article 12(4), including:

- being a contractor, agent or employee of the limited partnership or of a general partner;
- acting as a director, officer or shareholder of a corporate general partner;
- acting as a partner in a partnership which is itself a general partner;
- consulting with and advising a general partner as to the business of the limited partnership;
- investigating, reviewing, approving or being advised as to the accounts or affairs of the limited partnership;
- exercising any right or power conferred on limited partners by the Guernsey LP Law;
- acting as surety or guarantor or providing any other form of security for the limited partnership, generally or in respect of specific debts;
- approving or disapproving an amendment to the partnership agreement;
- filing a declaration under Section 8(2)(d) [of the Guernsey LP Law][30]; or
- applying to the Royal Court under section 16(2) for the appointment or removal of an auditor; or
- voting as a limited partner on any of the following matters:
  - the dissolution and winding up of the limited partnership;
  - the acquisition, sale, transfer, exchange, lease or charging of or other dealing with any property or assets by or of the limited partnership;
  - the incurrence, renewal, repayment or discharge of any debt by the limited partnership;
  - any change in the nature of the business, objectives or policies of the limited partnership;
  - the admission, removal, retirement or resignation of a general or limited partner and the continuation of the limited partnership thereafter; or
  - any transaction in which a general partner has an actual or potential conflict of interest with a limited partner.[31]

As in the Delaware RULPA and the Jersey LP Law, the Guernsey LP Law also contains a provision clarifying that the list of safe harbour actions does not comprise an exclusive list of actions that may be undertaken by a limited partner without losing limited liability. Article 12(6) states that it should not be assumed that 'if a limited partner exercises any other right, power or function, he has necessarily, by reason of that fact alone, participated in the conduct or management of the business of the limited partnership within the meaning of this section'. That said, however, the Guernsey LP Law does not provide a clear definition of what 'management of the business' means. As a result, while the list of safe harbours is virtually identical (in scope of topics, if not language) to that in Jersey, it seems less protective of a limited partner's limited liability, certainly than the Delaware RULPA and potentially than the Jersey LP Law, as well.

## Conclusion

Perhaps not surprisingly given the commercial context of fund sponsors and their investors, the issue of when a limited partner has exceeded its authority to the extent of losing its limited liability status has not been the subject of detailed legislation and appears rarely to have been litigated. Hence, even in the key fund formation jurisdictions examined here, relevant case law and other interpretive guidance regarding how to avoid such a pitfall is thin at best. It is clear from the face of the relevant statutes, however, that, in theory at least, the extent of participation by a limited partner in the 'conduct' or 'management' of a partnership's business that is required in order to compromise a limited partner's limited liability status varies, sometimes significantly, among even commonly used jurisdictions for private equity limited partnerships.

Such differences may become relevant in the formation of a limited partnership for several reasons. First, the statutory provisions provide a prescriptive benchmark for the participation of limited partners in the business of the fund and this may affect the negotiation of the working relationship between the limited partners and the general partners. Such differences should be considered in the choice of formation jurisdiction. Secondly, given the specificity of the relevant safe harbour provisions, the differences suggest that there should be a different approach to any given fund agreement's provisions, at least to the extent dealing with the powers and duties of limited partners. Finally, presuming that sooner or later such provisions will be litigated, probably in a loss scenario, optimising a limited partner's certainty in respect of his or her limited liability status cannot be taken for granted, but should reflect applicable law.

---

[1] Although the opinions expressed in this chapter are the sole responsibility of the authors, they would like to extend their appreciation to each of Ben Robins and Brian Scholfield of Mourant du Feu & Jeune, Iain McMurdo, David Whittome and Sarah Priaulx of Walkers, and Tai Hsia, Jonathan Jacobs and Derek Vander Heide of Kirkland & Ellis International LLP for their generous assistance in the preparation hereof.

[2] 6 Del. Code Ann. §17-303(a).

[3] For a complete list, see 6 Del. Code Ann. §17-303(b).

[4] See 6 Del. Code Ann. §17-303(b)(8)(n).

[5] See 6 Del. Code Ann. §17-303(c).

[6] See 6 Del. Code Ann. §17-303(a).

[7] The little further legislation there has been since the adoption of the English LP Law has tended to focus on the alleviation of certain original requirements more suitable to the commercial context of its adoption. With the passage of time, such requirements have been found to be unduly restrictive – for example, note the removal in 2002 of the 20 partner limit.

[8] See Section 4(2) of the Limited Partnerships Act 1907.

[9] See Section 5 of the Limited Partnerships Act 1907. On formation, a form LP5 is required to be filed with Companies House, setting out, among other things, the name of the partnership, the names of the partners and the details of their capital contributions (see Section 8(1) of the Limited Partnerships Act 1907). Section 5 states that a limited partnership must be registered in accordance with the English Law in order for limited partners to have limited liability status – that is, if the initial registration is not properly made, all partners will be treated as general partners. A question therefore arises as to the effect of breaching the obligation to register further changes in the partnership (for example, transfers by one limited partner to a new limited partner, etc.) under Section 9(1) of the Limited Partnerships Act 1907. There is an argument that a failure to register such changes will mean the firm is no longer 'registered in accordance with the [English LP Law]' (again, see Section 5 of the Limited Partnerships Act 1907) and that *all* limited partners will lose their limited liability status. However, and bearing in mind: (a) the existence of an explicit sanction for breach of Section 9(1) of the Limited Partnership Act 1907 (that is, the payment of a daily default fine under Section 9(2) of the Limited Partnerships Act 1907); and (b) the inability of any limited partner to ensure that the details of any change are properly registered (only the general partner can validly file the relevant forms), our view is that the risk, while genuine, is remote.

[10] Note how this formulation differs from that of the Delaware RULPA, namely 'participates in the control of ...' (6 Del. Code Ann §17-303(a)). Although there is little available guidance, and one could read the English formulation with the addition of '... either directly or indirectly ...' as materially synonymous with the Delaware formulation, the difference raises a potential question regarding whether the Delaware RULPA captures forms of limited partner control *other than management of* the partnership business, but which are not captured by the English LP Law.

11 See Section 6(1) of the Limited Partnerships Act 1907.

12 See ibid.

13 In the Canadian case of *Hutchinson v. Bowes, McDonnell and Cotton* (1857) 15 UCR 156, the purportedly limited partner became chairman of what described itself as an advising committee. It was held that: 'They did more than advise, they directed and acted, and while they did that they could not escape the consequences of interfering in the transaction of the business by calling themselves an advising committee.' While not binding in English law, the case is at least persuasive owing to the similarities between the English LP Law and the Limited Partnerships Act of Upper Canada 1849, and the fact that Canada's highest judicial authority remains the House of Lords in England (owing to the fact of Canada's membership in the British Commonwealth).

14 See generally, R. C. I'Anson Banks (*Ed.*) *Lindley & Banks on Partnership* (18th edition), (London: Sweet & Maxwell, 2002).

15 The phrase is derived from Section 24(8) of the Partnership Act 1890, which applies to partnerships generally, and Section 6(5)(a) of the English LP Law.

16 Op Cit., *Lindley & Banks on Partnership,* p. 872, ft. 14.

17 This is at least partly due to the fact that the law firm acting for the proposed general partner or management team, in relation to a fund formation, is now expected as a matter of market practice to deliver an opinion to the proposed limited partners to the effect that, on 'closing' of the fund, they will enjoy limited liability status. In order to be able to give that opinion, but at the same time ensure that it is not so restrictive as to be prohibitive to a limited partner's desire to invest, lawyers in this field have attempted to develop a common approach to the management restriction.

18 Note that Article 19(3) of the Limited Partnerships (Jersey) Law 1994 (the 'Jersey LP Law') contains a potentially narrower formulation, which would be more favourable to limited partners: 'participates in the *management* of ...' [emphasis added]. The Jersey LP Law also compares favourably from a limited partner's perspective to the Limited Partnerships (Guernsey) Law 1995, as amended (the 'Guernsey LP Law'), which, among other things, states in Section 12(1)(a) that the limited partner 'shall not participate in the *conduct or* management of the business of the limited partnership' [emphasis added].

19 Section 7(2) of the Exempted Limited Partnerships Law (2003 revisions).

20 The analogous provision of the Jersey LP Law refers to 'management ...' (Article 19(5), Jersey LP Law). Again, the Guernsey LP Law is more strict on this point, stating not that any of the subsequently enumerated activities is in itself a safe harbour, but rather only that '[a] limited partner shall not be deemed to have participated in the conduct or management of the business of a limited partnership within the meaning of this section *by reason only of* any one or more such circumstances ...' [emphasis added]. In other words, engaging in one of the enumerated activities *may* risk a limited partner's limited liability status in combination with other activities. This implies a greater burden for the limited partner seeking to avail itself of the Guernsey LP Law safe harbours.

21 Under Article 19(5)(b) of the Jersey LP Law, the broader term 'activities' is used instead of 'business'.

22 The word 'business' is not included in the analogous Jersey LP Law provision.

23 Under the Jersey LP Law, this is expanded to include 'or otherwise signifying approval or disapproval of ...'.

24 Under the Jersey LP Law, this is expanded to 'an obligation ...'.

25 See endnote 18: the Jersey LP Law uses 'activities' instead.

26 '[O]f business of' is not included in the analogous Jersey LP Law provision.

27 It should be noted that a number of revisions to the Cayman LP law are currently under review which if enacted would expand the safe harbours and protection to limited partners.

28 It is worth noting that the Delaware RULPA includes a contrary provision explicitly stating that 'a limited partner does not participate in the control of the business within the meaning of subsection (a) of this section by virtue of the fact that all or any part of the name of such limited partner is included in the name of the limited partnership'.

29 Article 19(5) of the Jersey LP law.

30 Such section relates to the filing by a general partner of the declaration (containing details relating to the limited partnership) which must be filed with the Guernsey Greffier upon the registration of the limited partnership.

31 Section 12(4) of the Limited Partnerships (Guernsey) Law 1995.

Exhibit 4.1

**Limited partner safe harbours in key jurisdictions**[i]

| | **Delaware*** | **Cayman Islands**** | **Jersey***** | **Guernsey****** |
|---|---|---|---|---|
| **General rule** | A limited partner is not liable for the obligations of a limited partnership unless he or she is also a general partner or, in addition to the exercise of the rights and powers of a limited partner, he or she participates in the control of the business. (DC 2004 §17-303(a)) | A limited partner shall not take part in the conduct of the business of an exempted limited partnership, and all letters, contracts, deeds, instruments or documents whatsoever shall be entered into by the general partner on behalf of the exempted limited partnership. (ELPR 2003 §7(1)) | Except as provided in this Law, a limited partner is not liable for the debts or obligations of the limited partnership. (LPJL 1994 Art. 19(1)).<br><br>A limited partner is not liable as a general partner unless he participates in the management of the limited partnership. (LPJL 1994 Art. 19(2)) | A limited partner:- shall not participate in the conduct or management of the business of the limited partnership; (LPGL 1995 §12(1)(a))<br><br>shall not transact the business of, sign or execute documents for or otherwise bind the limited partnership. (LPGL 1995 §12(1)(b)) |
| **Consequence of violation** | | If a limited partner takes part in the conduct of the business of an exempted limited partnership in its dealings with persons who are not partners, that limited partner shall be liable, in the event of the insolvency of the exempted limited partnership, for all debts and obligations of that exempted limited partnership | If a limited partner participates in the management of the limited partnership in its dealings with persons who are not partners, that limited partner shall be liable in the event of the insolvency of the limited partnership for all debts and obligations of the limited partnership incurred during the | A limited partner who in whatever capacity acts or purports to act in contravention of subsection (1) shall be liable as if he were a general partner in respect of all debts of the limited partnership incurred while he so acts or purports to act. (LPGL 1995 §12(3)) |

*(Continued)*

Exhibit 4.1 *(Continued)*

| | **Delaware*** | **Cayman Islands**** | **Jersey***** | **Guernsey****** |
|---|---|---|---|---|
| | | incurred during the period that he so participates in the conduct of the business as though he were, for such period, a general partner …. (ELPR 2003 §7(2)) | period that he participated in the management of the limited partnership as though he were for that period a general partner. (LPJL 1994 Art. 19(3)) | |
| **Knowledge required** | However, if the limited partner does participate in the control of the business, he or she is liable only to persons who transact business with the limited partnership reasonably believing, based upon the limited partner's conduct, that the limited partner is a general partner. (DC 2004 §17-303(a)) | [P]rovided always that he shall be rendered liable pursuant to the foregoing provision only to a person who transacts business with the exempted limited partnership during such period with actual knowledge of such participation and who then reasonably believed such limited partner to be a general partner. (ELPR 2003 §7(2)) | A limited partner shall be liable under paragraph (3) only to a person who transacts with the limited partnership with actual knowledge of the participation of the limited partner in the management of the limited partnership and who then reasonably believed the limited partner to be a general partner. (LPJL 1994 Art. 19(4)) | |
| **Safe harbour** | A limited partner does not participate in the control of the business within the meaning of subsection (a) of this section by virtue of possessing or, regardless of whether or not the limited partner has the rights or powers, exercising or attempting to exercise one or more of the following | A limited partner does not take part in the conduct of the business of an exempted limited partnership within the meaning of this section by: (ELPR 2003 §7(3)) | A limited partner does not participate in the management of a limited partnership within the meaning of this Article by doing one or more of the following: (LPJL 1994 Art. 19(5)) | A limited partner shall not be deemed to have participated in the conduct or management of the business of a limited partnership within the meaning of this section by reason only of any one or more of the following circumstances: (LPGL 1995 §12(4)) |

| | Delaware* | Cayman Islands** | Jersey*** | Guernsey**** |
|---|---|---|---|---|
| | rights or powers or having or, regardless of whether or not the limited partner has the rights or powers, acting or attempting to act in one or more of the following capacities: (DC 2004 §17-303(b)) | | | |
| **Specific safe harbours** | | | | |
| **Contractor, agent or employee; Director, officer or shareholder of corporate general partner, or partner of partnership general partner** | To be an independent contractor for or to transact business with, including being a contractor for, or to be an agent or employee of, the limited partnership or a general partner, or to be an officer, director or stockholder of a corporate general partner, or to be a partner of a partnership that is a general partner of the limited partnership, or to be a trustee, administrator, executor, custodian or other fiduciary or beneficiary of an estate or trust which is a general partner, or to be a trustee, officer, adviser, stockholder or a beneficiary of a business trust | being a contractor for or an agent or employee of the exempted limited partnership or of a general partner or acting as a director, officer or shareholder of a corporate general partner; (ELPR 2003 §7(3)(a)) | being a contractor for or an agent or employee of the limited partnership or of a general partner or acting as a director, officer or shareholder of a corporate general partner; (LPJL 1994 Art. 19(5)(a)) | he is a contractor, agent or employee of the limited partnership or of a general partner; (LPGL 1995 §12 (4)(a))<br><br>he acts as a director, officer or shareholder of a corporate general partner; (LPGL 1995 §12(4)(b)).<br><br>he acts as a partner in a partnership which itself is a general partner; (LPGL 1995 §12(4)(c)) |

*(Continued)*

Exhibit 4.1 *(Continued)*

| | **Delaware*** | **Cayman Islands**** | **Jersey***** | **Guernsey****** |
|---|---|---|---|---|
| | or statutory trust which is a general partner or to be a member, manager, agent or employee of a limited liability company which is a general partner; (DC 2004 §17-303(b)(1)) | | | |
| **Consulting and advising** | To consult with or advise a general partner or any other person with respect to any matter, including the business of the limited partnership, or to act or cause a general partner or any other person to take or refrain from taking any action, including by proposing, approving, consenting or disapproving, by voting or otherwise, with respect to any matter, including the business of the limited partnership; (DC 2004 §17-303 (b)(2)) | consulting with and advising a general partner with respect to the business of the exempted limited partnership; (ELPR 2003 §7(3)(b)) | consulting with and advising a general partner with respect to the activities of the limited partnership; (LPJL 1994 Art. 19(5)(b)) | he consults with and advises a general partner as to the business of the limited partnership; (LPGL 1995 §12(4)(d)) |

| | Delaware* | Cayman Islands** | Jersey*** | Guernsey**** |
|---|---|---|---|---|
| **Investigating, reviewing, approving accounts and business affairs** | | investigating, reviewing, approving or being advised as to the accounts or business affairs of the exempted limited partnership or exercising any right conferred by this Law; (ELPR 2003 §7(3)(c)) | investigating, reviewing, approving or being advised as to the accounts or affairs of the limited partnership...; (LPJL 1994 Art. 19(5)(c)) | he investigates, reviews, approves or is advised as to the accounts or affairs of the limited partnership; (LPGL 1995 §12(4)(e)) |
| **Surety or guarantor** | To act as surety, guarantor or endorsor for the limited partnership or a general partner, to guaranty or assume one or more obligations of the limited partnership or a general partner, to borrow money from the limited partnership or a general partner, to lend money to the limited partnership or a general partner, or to provide collateral for the limited partnership or a general partner; (DC 2004 §17-303(b)(3)) | acting as surety or guarantor for the exempted limited partnership either generally or in respect of specific obligations; (ELPR 2003 §7(3)(d)) | acting as surety or guarantor for the limited partnership either generally or in respect of specific obligations; (LPJL 1994 Art. 19(5)(d)) | he acts as surety or guarantor or provides any other form of security for the limited partnership, generally or in respect of specific debts; (LPGL 1995 §12(4)(g)) |

*(Continued)*

Exhibit 4.1 *(Continued)*

| | Delaware* | Cayman Islands** | Jersey*** | Guernsey**** |
|---|---|---|---|---|
| **Filing details of limited partnership** | | | | he files a declaration under Section 8(2)(d)[ii]; (LPGL 1995 §12(4)(i)) |
| **Call meetings** | To call, request, or attend or participate at a meeting of the partners or the limited partners; (DC 2004 §17-303(b)(4)) | | | |
| **Winding up** | To wind up a limited partnership pursuant to §17-803 of this title; (DC 2004 §17-303(b)(5)) | | | |
| **Bring derivative actions** | To take any action required or permitted by law to bring, pursue or settle or otherwise terminate a derivative action in the right of the limited partnership; (DC 2004 §17-303(b)(6)) | | bringing an action on behalf of the limited partnership pursuant to paragraph (3) of Article 28. (LPJL 1994 Art. 19(5)(g)) | |
| **Committees** | To serve on a committee of the limited partnership or the limited partners or partners or to appoint, elect or otherwise participate in the choice of a representative or another person to serve on any such committee, and to act as a | | | |

| | Delaware* | Cayman Islands** | Jersey*** | Guernsey**** |
|---|---|---|---|---|
| | member of any such committee directly or by or through any such representative or other person; (DC 2004 §17-303 (b)(7)) | | | |
| **Voting** | | | | |
| **Prologue** | To act or cause the taking or refraining from the taking of any action, including by proposing, approving, consenting or disapproving, by voting or otherwise, with respect to one or more of the following matters: (DC 2004 §17-303 (b)(8)) | voting as a limited partner on: (ELPR 2003 §7(3)(f)) | voting on, or otherwise signifying approval or disapproval of, one or more of the following: (LPJL 1994 Art. 19(5)(f)) | he votes as a limited partner on any of the following matters: (LPGL 1995 §12(4)(k)) |
| **Dissolution** | the dissolution and winding up of the limited partnership or an election to continue the limited partnership or an election to continue the business of the limited partnership; (DC 2004 §17-303 (b)(8)(a)) | the dissolution and winding up of the exempted limited partnership; (ELPR 2003 §7(3)(f)(i)) | the dissolution and winding up of the limited partnership; (LPJL 1994 Art. 19(5)(f))(i)) | the dissolution of the limited partnership; (LPGL 1995 §12 (4)(k)(i)) |
| **Sale of assets** | the sale, exchange, lease, mortgage, assignment, pledge or other transfer of, or granting of a security interest in, any asset or assets of the limited partnership; (DC 2004 §17-303 (b)(8)(b)) | the purchase, sale, exchange, lease, mortgage, pledge or other acquisition or transfer of any asset or assets by or of the exempted limited partnership; (ELPR 2003 §7 (3)(f)(ii)) | the purchase, sale, exchange, lease, pledge, hypothecation, creation of a security interest, or other dealing in any asset by or of the limited partnership, (LPJL 1994 Art. 19(5)(f))(ii)) | the acquisition, sale, transfer, exchange, lease or charging of or other dealing with any property or assets by or of the limited partnership; (LPGL 1995 §12 (4)(k)(ii)) |

*(Continued)*

Exhibit 4.1 *(Continued)*

| | **Delaware*** | **Cayman Islands**** | **Jersey***** | **Guernsey****** |
|---|---|---|---|---|
| **Incurrence of debt** | the incurrence, renewal, refinancing or payment or other discharge of indebtedness by the limited partnership; (DC 2004 §17-303 (b)(8)(c)) | the incurrence or renewal of indebtedness by the exempted limited partnership; (ELPR 2003 §7(3)(f)(iiii)) | the creation or renewal of an obligation by the limited partnership, (LPJL 1994 Art. 19(5)(f))(iii)) | the incurrence, renewal, repayment or discharge of any debt by the limited partnership; (LPGL 1995 §12 (4)(k)(iii)) |
| **Change in business** | a change in the nature of the business; (DC 2004 §17-303 (b)(8)(d)) | a change in the nature of the business of the exempted limited partnership; (ELPR 2003 §7(3)(f)(iv)) | a change in the nature of the activities of the limited partnership, (LPJL 1994 Art. 19(5)(f))(iv)) | any change in the nature of the business, objectives or policies of the limited partnership; (LPGL 1995 §12 (4)(k)(iv)) |
| **Admission or removal of partners** | the admission, removal or retention of a general partner; (DC 2004 §17-303 (b)(8)(e))<br><br>the admission, removal or retention of a limited partner; (DC 2004 §17-303 (b)(8)(f)) | the admission, removal or withdrawal of a general or limited partner and the continuation of business of the exempted limited partnership thereafter; or (ELPR 2003 §7 (3)(f)(v)) | the admission, removal or withdrawal of a general or a limited partner and the continuation of the limited partnership thereafter, or (LPJL 1994 Art. 19(5)(f))(v)) | the admission, removal, retirement or resignation of a general or limited partner and the continuation of the limited partnership thereafter; or (LPGL 1995 §12(4)(k)(v)) |
| **Conflicts of interest** | a transaction or other matter involving an actual or potential conflict of interest; (DC 2004 §17-303 (b)(8)(g)) | transactions in which one or more of the general partners have an actual or potential conflict of interest with one or more of the limited partners. (ELPR 2003 §7(3)(f)(vi)) | transactions in which one or more of the general partners have an actual or potential conflict of interest with one or more of the limited partners; (LPJL 1994 Art. 19(5)(f))(vi)) | any transaction in which a general partner has an actual or potential conflict of interest with a limited partner. (LPGL 1995 §12(4)(k)(vi)) |
| **Amendment** | an amendment to the partnership agreement or certificate of limited | approving or disapproving an amendment to the partnership agreement; or (ELPR 2003 | approving or disapproving an amendment to the partnership agreement; (LPJL 1994 | he approves or disapproves an amendment to the partnership agreement; (LPGL 1995 |

| | Delaware* | Cayman Islands** | Jersey*** | Guernsey**** |
|---|---|---|---|---|
| | partnership; (DC 2004 §17-303 (b)(8)(h)) | §7(3)(e)) | Art. 19(5)(e)) | §12(4)(h)) |
| **Merger** | the merger or consolidation of a limited partnership; (DC 2004 §17-303 (b)(8)(i)) | | | |
| **Appointment or removal of auditor** | | | | he applies to the Royal Court under Section 16(2) for the appointment or removal of an auditor; or (LPGL 1995 §12(4)(j)) |
| **Matters requiring approval by law** | in respect of a limited partnership which is registered as an investment company under the Investment Company Act of 1940, as amended [15 U.S.C. §80a-1 *et seq.*], any matter required by the Investment Company Act of 1940, as amended, or the rules and regulations of the Securities and Exchange Commission thereunder, to be approved by the holders of beneficial interests in an investment company, including the electing of directors or trustees of the investment company, the approving or terminating of investment | | | |

*(Continued)*

Exhibit 4.1 *(Continued)*

| | Delaware* | Cayman Islands** | Jersey*** | Guernsey**** |
|---|---|---|---|---|
| | advisory or underwriting contracts and the approving of auditors; (DC 2004 §17-303 (b)(8)(j)) | | | |
| **Indemnification** | the indemnification of any partner or other person; (DC 2004 §17-303 (b)(8)(k)) | | | |
| **Determinations regarding contributions** | the making of, or calling for, or the making of other determinations in connection with, contributions; (DC 2004 §17-303(b)(8)(l)) | | | |
| **Determinations regarding investments** | the making of, or the making of other determinations in connection with or concerning, investments, including investments in property, whether real, personal or mixed, either directly or indirectly, by the limited partnership; or (DC 2004 §17-303 (b)(8)(m)) | | | |
| **Management of entities in which** | to serve on the board of directors or a committee of, to consult with or advise, to | | | |

| | Delaware* | Cayman Islands** | Jersey*** | Guernsey**** |
|---|---|---|---|---|
| **partnership has an interest** | be an officer, director, stockholder, partner, member, manager, trustee, agent or employee of, or to be a fiduciary or contractor for, any person in which the limited partnership has an interest or any person providing management, consulting, advisory, custody or other services or products for, to or on behalf of, or otherwise having a business or other relationship with, the limited partnership or a general partner of the limited partnership; or (DC 2004 §17-303(b)(9)) | | | |
| **Rights at law** | any right or power granted or permitted to limited partners under this chapter and not specifically enumerated in this subsection. (DC 2004 §17-303(b)(10)) | | | he exercises any right or power conferred on limited partners by this law; (LPGL 1995 §12(4)(f)) |
| **Other acts not excluded** | The enumeration in subsection (b) of this section does not mean that the possession or exercise of any other powers or having or acting in other capacities by a limited partner | Subsection (3) shall not import any implication that the possession or exercise of any other power by a limited partner will necessarily constitute the taking part by such limited | Paragraph (5) shall not import any implication that the possession or exercise of any other power by a limited partner will necessarily constitute the participation by such limited | the provisions of subsection (4) shall not be taken as implying that, if a limited partner exercises any other right, power or function, he has necessarily, by reason of that |

*(Continued)*

Exhibit 4.1 *(Continued)*

| | **Delaware*** | **Cayman Islands**** | **Jersey***** | **Guernsey****** |
|---|---|---|---|---|
| | constitutes participation by him or her in the control of the business of the limited partnership. (DC 2004 §17-303(c)) | partner in the business of the exempted limited partnership. (ELPR 2003 §7(4)) | partner in the management of the limited partnership. (LPJL 1994 Art. 19(6)) | fact alone, participated in the conduct or management of the business of the limited partnership within the meaning of this section. (LPGL 1995 §12(6)) |
| **Name included in the name of the limited partnership** | A limited partner does not participate in the control of the business within the meaning of subsection (a) of this section by virtue of the fact that all or any part of the name of such limited partner is included in the name of the limited partnership. (DC 2004 §17-303(d)) | | | |
| **Rights and powers not excluded** | This section does not create rights or powers of limited partners. Such rights and powers may be created only by a certificate of limited partnership, a partnership agreement or any other agreement or in writing, or other sections of this chapter. (DC 2004 §17-303(e)) | | | |

| | Delaware* | Cayman Islands** | Jersey*** | Guernsey**** |
|---|---|---|---|---|
| **Extent of safe harbour** | A limited partner does not participate in the control of the business within the meaning of subsection (a) of this section regardless of the nature, extent, scope, number or frequency of the limited partner's possessing or, regardless of whether or not the limited partner has the rights or powers, exercising or attempting to exercise one or more of the rights or powers or having or, regardless of whether or not the limited partner has the rights or powers, acting or attempting to act in one or more of the capacities which are permitted under this section. (DC 2004 §17-303(f)) | | | |

[i] We have not included England here because of the lack of explicit statutory safe harbours applicable to English law capable of easy comparison.
[ii] Such section relates to the filing by a general partner of the declaration (containing details relating to the limited partnership), which must be filed with the Guernsey Greffier upon the registration of the limited partnership.
*Delaware Code §17-303 (2004), hereinafter referred to in the table as '(DC 2004: §17-303)'.
**Exempted Limited Partnership Law (2003) Revision, hereinafter referred to as '(ELPR 2003)'.
***Limited Partnerships (Jersey) Law (1994) as Amended, Article 19, hereinafter referred to as '(LPJL 1994 Art.19)'.
****Limited Partnerships (Guernsey) Law 1995 as Amended, hereinafter referred to as '(LPGL 1995)'.

Chapter 5

# The governance of private equity owned firms

Carsten Bienz
*Financial Markets Group – London School of Economics and Centre for Financial Studies – JW Goethe Universitat Frankfurt*

Jeremy Grant and Thomas Kirchmaier
*Financial Markets Group – London School of Economics*

## Introduction

In 1989, Michael Jensen argued in an article entitled 'The Eclipse of the Public Corporation'[1] that privately held companies provided a superior alternative to publicly owned firms with widely dispersed shareholders, because they eliminated the principal–agent problem between shareholders and management over free cash flow. Therefore, it followed that assets in privately held companies should be used in the most productive way and their ownership structure would be economically superior to alternatives. Free cash flow would be paid out to the owners, instead of wasted on low or negative net present value capital expenditure projects, and empire building acquisitions with low expected future returns. However, at the time, corporate governance, as a term used to describe mechanisms to mitigate the principal–agent problem, had nothing like the prominence in the vocabulary of the senior managers of public corporations as in today's post-Enron world.

Since 1989 we have come a long way. Corporate governance of the public corporation has improved considerably, not least because corporate boards are taking their role as the guardians of shareholders' interests more seriously.[2] In parallel, private equity – later stage buyouts and venture capital – has filled a void by positioning itself half way between the private and public company with new and innovative ownership and governance structures. Private equity firms are, by their nature, activist investors, and avoid the typical private control benefits where dominant owners try to extract rent from their minority shareholders.[3] Put simply, in leveraged buyouts widely dispersed ownership is replaced by a single owner that governs the firms through two mechanisms.

- An extensive array of legal control and information rights that are assigned to the board members who are general partners of the private equity firm. These often extend far beyond those to which shareholders in a publicly listed enterprise are entitled.
- Highly incentivised senior management, usually through an increased ownership stake in the enterprise.

Venture capital investing, at the other end of the spectrum, essentially relies on similar structures with strict legal control and information rights codified in the initial shareholders' subscription agreement and the articles of association. Early-stage ventures are often managed by their founders, who retain a sizeable stake in the firm, thus directly aligning their interests with the general partners. Unlike leveraged buyouts, early-stage investing will see an increase in a firm's shareholder base.

In this chapter we will examine the particularities of governance structures for private equity financed firms, concentrating first on the role of the board of directors and, secondly, on the elaborate series of contractual rights demanded by private equity investors, which extend far beyond those available to investors in public firms.

## Corporate governance in public companies

To begin with, what does corporate governance in public companies amount to, and what kind of conclusions can be drawn for the private equity sphere?

In public companies, the principle aims of corporate governance are two-fold. Primarily, it aims to protect the suppliers of equity capital. In public companies, shareholders have limited contractual rights covering the repayment of their funds. Corporate governance therefore provides a number of mechanisms ensuring that the lack of contractual rights is compensated for in other ways. In the private equity world, this is not a major concern as there is a more extensive framework of private contracts in place that govern the relationship between owners and managers. We will discuss this relationship in detail later on in the chapter.

Secondly, and often overlooked, corporate governance aims to put in place management and governance structures that ensure the firm is organised and run in the most productive way, thereby guaranteeing the health of the company and maximising the long-term cash flow and shareholder wealth. Private equity relies heavily on executive compensation contracts, offering the managers income possibilities, often unparalleled in public markets, in case of success. The argument goes that the strong incentive contracts solve the principal–agent conflict by aligning the interests of the investors and managers. While there is some evidence that this approach delivers the desired effect, there is also increasing evidence that oversimplistic use of high-incentive contracts is not without danger in public markets. Michael Jensen, historically one of the strongest advocates of incentive contracts, recently introduced 'enlightened shareholder theory', and, while still acknowledging the importance of incentive contracts, outlined the dangers of over-incentivising managers.[4] The risks he outlined are that managers might be encouraged to engage in transactions, in particular M&A transactions, that are extremely value destructive in the long run but make the accounts look favourable in the short run.

## Governance in private equity financed firms

Corporate governance in private equity transactions centres around an investor holding most of the firm's equity, with the remainder going to management. Normally there are no minority shareholders (in the case of buyouts) or a small number of outside owners (in the case of venture deals).

The involvement of investors is only temporary and transitory. There are several reasons for this. First, and foremost, the particular skills private equity investors employ can only offer comparative advantages for a relatively short period of time. During this period, the private equity investor helps to facilitate the transition to a higher level of firm performance. This is normally done by optimising the financial structure of the firm and/or finding a new owner who has a better fit with and use of the assets than the previous owner. In addition, the investors themselves are time constrained as they receive their capital for a limited amount of time only. Both factors ensure that receiving private equity finance is only a transitory phase in a firm's lifecycle.

## Board of directors

As discussed above, the existence of a functioning board in private equity owned companies is something of an oddity, as the investors normally hold monitoring rights well in excess of those that a normal board member will be assigned in a public company. For example, tight contractual rights secure the investor the supply of monthly or even weekly updates on the firm's performance. These include pro-forma balance sheets, profit and loss statements and cash flow projections.

It is important to point out that, at least theoretically, the relationship between the private equity house and their portfolio firms could be structured in a way that would allow investors to do without a board.[5] However, this is uncommon, as well-run boards can offer strategic advice (and, to a certain degree, even control) more effectively and cheaply than almost any other mechanism. Boards define clear roles for all parties involved and allow for a relatively easy inclusion of outsiders. As the advice function is of particular importance for private equity owned firms, the appointment of the right non-executive directors, and the functioning and structure of the board, become central to the firm's success; so, when the decision is taken to construct a board, extra effort should be put into assembling a group of individuals who together are fully capable of discharging the advisory function. This means that, while there is sufficient diversity in terms of functional background, there is also enough social cohesion and mutual respect among the board members so that the board can also function from a social perspective. Here, a more structured approach to board building might be advisable for private equity houses; one that goes beyond reliance on personal contacts. The Digitas case study examines how a well-structured board functioned at a private equity owned firm in Boston.

### Case study

### Digitas:[6] How to structure a board of directors

In 1999, the US private equity fund, Hellman & Friedman (H&F), invested US$100m in Digitas, a Boston-based direct marketing firm. As part of the deal, Digitas's board was restructured to comprise two management representatives, two independent directors and two general partners from H&F, who had significant experience from prior investments in the marketing and advertising industries, including an investment in Young & Rubicam. Despite the fact that H&F had purchased a majority of Digitas's equity (67 per cent), they did not gain control of the board. This was due to the fact that firm wanted to retain the services of

*(Continued)*

Digitas's founder, Michael Bronner, and knew from previous experience that marketing was a 'people business' where a significant part of the value of the firm was in its human capital, which required a consensual approach to governance.

### Board structure

Therefore, it was agreed that there should be two independent directors appointed to the board, with strategic experience in the industry, who could mediate in case of a difference of opinion between the management and investors. One was a founding director of Yahoo, while the other was the chairman of the strategic consultancy Bain & Company.

Initially, H&F, with management, set the business plan objectives for Digitas going forward, focusing on capital budgeting, corporate and financial strategy and managerial remuneration. Subsequently, each group of directors focused primarily on monitoring different aspects of the business plan. Management focused on the revenues, H&F's general partners focused on the costs, while the independent directors monitored strategy and implementation.

### Board meetings

In 1999, the board met six times. Five of these meetings lasted a day, while the sixth meeting was held over two days. These sessions were built around board books prepared by the management. These contained extensive financial data, including client statistics, investment targets and minutes of previous board and committee meetings. Due to the human capital intensive nature of the business, the board also required an extensive human resources report, which detailed new hires, promotions, attrition rates, current employee issues and compensation.

Thanks to its effective structure, which reflected both diversity and cohesion, and recognised the value of employees to the firm, the board was able to lead Digitas to a successful IPO in March 2000.

Beyond the basic structure of the board, private equity firms often maintain an impressive array of control and veto rights,[7] which force management to obtain the permission of investors for all major strategic decisions including capital structure changes, deviations from the firm's business plan, head-count increases and even for permission to pursue lawsuits. These arrangements ensure that the formal monitoring rights that come along with board membership are normally not essential for an investor.

In summary, boards are important for the structured interaction they provide between all parties involved in the firm, as in the Digitas case. In this sense it is an arrangement that is used to minimise frictions between parties and gives guidance on key aspects of the firm's success, while, at the same time, the typical control function is widely replaced through contractual rights. It is these contractual rights that we will examine in the next section.

## Contractual governance

Private equity firms use different types of securities, both debt and equity, and contractual clauses contained in the subscription agreements, articles of association/by-laws and even managerial

Exhibit 5.1

**Typical contracts and generic categories of covenants for private equity investments**

**Contracts**

Securities issued
By-laws
Shareholder agreements
Employment contracts

**Information rights**

Net turnover (monthly)
Balance sheet (quarterly/annually)
P&L (quarterly/annually)
Cash flow projections (quarterly/annually)

**Control / veto rights**

Capital structure changes
Capital distribution
Firm dissolution or asset sales
Acquisitions or major investments
Deviations from business plan
Employment of key personnel

**Other rights**

Right to replace management
Anti-dilution protection
Right to force an exit after a specified time period

*Source*: Authors' own.

labour contracts, to protect their rights and maximise shareholder returns. The appendix to this chapter includes a selection of these terms and conditions in a model heads-of-terms agreement.

Securities issued offer differing mixes of property rights (claims on the portfolio company's assets, and ultimately cash flows) and control rights (which directly influence the behaviour of management). On one side of the spectrum, debt offers strong property rights but weak control rights, while straight equity offers the opposite. Hybrid securities offer differing quantities of property rights and control provisions, allowing investors and managers/entrepreneurs to find an optimal mix.

## Equity securities

### Ordinary shares/common stock

These denote a direct ownership interest in the company with associated rights including the right to elect directors to the board and vote on major strategic issues (including acquisitions, divestitures and changes in capital structure). These securities also carry information rights to financial data. Holders of common stock are the residual recipients of cash flows and in cases of bankruptcy they are the last to be paid after creditors, debenture holders and owners of preference shares. Dual classes of common stock can also be issued with differential voting rights. For example, a widely used structure authorises the issuance of two classes of common stock, which differ only in the number of directors each class is entitled to elect. This arrangement can be deployed to ensure an investor a seat on a company's board of directors while, at the same time, ensuring that control of the board will remain with management.

**Preferred stock**
This allows the holder a preferential right over the holders of common stock – for example, preference in payment of a dividend and on liquidation of the company. Often this dividend will be fixed. Overall, the holders of preferred stock have a greater claim over the company's assets than those of common stock.

**Convertible preferred stock**
This allows investors to convert into common stock based on a predetermined formula. The preferred status gives the holder preference in the case of an acquisition or liquidation. Convertible preferred stock is often deployed by venture capitalists in early-stage ventures as they allow the investor to receive back his initial investment, plus a certain guaranteed rate of return before proceeds of a sale are distributed to holders of common stock. Convertible preferred stock will usually have dilution protection against future share issuances at a price below which the convertible stock was purchased. Because these securities give the payout preference to the investor and guarantee a certain return, the willingness of an entrepreneur to sign up to their terms is often used as a signalling mechanism to identify those with the strongest execution skills. Also, convertible preferred stock allows for more favourable tax treatment in the United States for managers and employees who are heavily incentivised by stock grants.

**Redeemable preferred stock**
This class of securities can require the company to redeem preferred stock after a predetermined period for an amount that guarantees the holder a pre-set return. Some types allow the company to force a redemption or conversion to common stock after a set period of time.

## Debt securities

If convertible preferred stock dominates early-stage financing, debt securities become more important in later-stage financings where there are fewer information asymmetries between investors and managers, and monitoring is more straightforward. Debt contracts tend to be characterised by strong underlying property claims and weaker intermediate control rights, as the costs of financial distress will tend to be borne disproportionately by senior managers/entrepreneurs who tend to have both significant equity stakes in private equity backed firms, which will be wiped out in bankruptcy, and large human capital investments, which will be similarly degraded along with their reputations.

**Loans, bonds and notes**
These are forms of straight debt, which have seniority in terms of payout on liquidation, both in relation to subordinated debt and, subsequently, the equity capital of the firm.

**Convertible debt**

This allows the lender to convert debt securities into equity under certain predefined scenarios and at a pre-set ratio. This security allows the holder to receive the downside protection of debt and the upside bonus of equity. From the firm's perspective, convertible issuance lowers the cost of debt (that is, current and future interest payments) in return for a lower value of current outstanding equity due to future dilution on conversion.

**Subordinated convertible debentures**

These represent a special form of convertible debt where the principal and interest payments are convertible into stock at a pre-agreed ratio. Subordinated convertible debentures are sometimes used in lieu of convertible preferred stock to fund a portion (or all) of a company's funding needs. These convertible debentures are usually less attractive to growing companies because they accrue interest and require scheduled repayments unless and until they are converted.

Beyond the control mechanisms related to the securities listed above, private equity firms have an array of other control rights embedded in the articles of association, by-laws and subscription agreements.

## Control rights

**Board rights**

As discussed above, private equity firms will require significant board representation. Best practice dictates that the majority of directors be independent of management, and that the board's sub-committees, including the audit and compensation committees, be composed entirely of independent directors. Board members should have rights to certain information – for example, monthly consolidated net turnover, unaudited quarterly financial statements reviewed by management and audited year-end financial statements.

**Voting rights**

These usually force the company to gain investors' permission before undertaking any major strategic decisions including mergers and acquisitions, new equity issuance, new debt issuance, changes in management compensation, issuance of employee stock options and amendments to the articles of association. Convertible preferred stock is normally voted as common stock on these issues.

**Veto rights**

Equally, private equity investors can have veto rights over all major strategic decisions, even if they do not control a majority of the outstanding equity.

**Access and information rights**

With reasonable time and notification, investors should have full access to the books, records and management of the company.

**Right to replace senior management**

This contractual right often requires board approval, and is usually accompanied by the right to repurchase the manager's shares at book value. Such rights are less common in Europe than in the United States, and it is more often the case that private equity firms in Europe will have to use the next round of funding negotiations to restructure management.

**Other rights**

Other control rights stem from management contracts with senior executives of the portfolio firm and include the following.

- *Non-compete clauses*. As part of their employment agreement, senior managers are required to give the company their full-time attention, protect its trade secrets and undertake not to enter into a competing business venture for a set period after they leave its employment.
- *Keyman insurance*. Where the success of a company is dependent on a small number of key managers, the private equity firm will often require the company to take out life insurance policies on these individuals. The investors will be the beneficial owners of these policies to enable them to protect their investment in the company.

Future financing provisions structure the terms and conditions for the raising of further financing. Subscription rights state the conditions under which a capital increase will be approved by shareholders; for example, the need for the support of a majority of shareholders at a general meeting. Typically, current shareholders will have pre-emption rights to subscribe on a pro-rata basis to new equity. If they do not take up this right, the shares must be offered to other current shareholders before being offered to external parties.

Anti-dilution provisions give investors the right to acquire additional equity when the share capital of a company is increased. This anti-dilution measure can be costless for the investors concerned, and so can have a very significant impact on other investors – often management and employees.

Exit provisions are a way to guarantee investors a return on their money by giving them an option to force, if necessary, a liquidity event such as an initial public offering (IPO), strategic sale or a secondary transaction. They include the following.

- *Demand rights*. These allow investors to force a public offering by registering their shares for sale to the public.
- *Automatic conversion rights*. These convert preferred stock into ordinary stock in the run up to a liquidity event. Such conversions usually take place on a majority (or supermajority) vote of the convertible preferred stockholders, and can also be conditional on a particular valuation of the company and whether the IPO is fully underwritten. Upon conversion, special rights attached to the convertible preferred stock, such as special information rights and veto rights, cease to exist.
- *Drag-along/tag-along rights*. Drag-along rights allow the private equity firm to force other shareholders to sell their stock to a buyer in a strategic sale. However, this right may not be enforced if the buyer wants the management to stay on. To exit completely, management needs a tag-along right.

While the reasons for the use of these contractual mechanisms seem clear, there exists more than one possible explanation for their existence. The normal explanation centres around the moral hazard problems of investment, requiring the investor to assign more control. However, there are at least two other lines of reasoning. The first line emphasises the fact that the entrepreneur is cash-constrained and is in need of outside support. To ensure that the investor at least earns his required rate of return, the entrepreneur usually needs to give up a large share of the firm's equity. By trading off control against equity, the entrepreneur may retain more cash flow rights but gives the investor more say in the governance of the firm, ensuring a higher return for the investor in 'bad states of nature'.[8] This means that the investor can restrict asset sales, ensuring that in bad states of nature no asset stripping occurs or he is given the right to replace management in case of incompetence.

The second line of reasoning emphasises the fact that, by granting the investor a dominant position in the governance of the firm, the entrepreneur signals his confidence in the prospects of the firm and his own management qualities. The idea behind this explanation is that only confident entrepreneurs will be willing to offer contractual terms that allow for their replacement or restrict their behaviour as managers. Alternatively, instead of entrepreneurs offering terms, rather investors may use contractual elements to screen between good and bad investment opportunities.[9]

The last open question with respect to the use of explicit contractual mechanisms is the question of the actual use of these rights. Investors often emphasise the need for good working relations with the entrepreneurs/managers. This is in stark contrast to the impressive array of rights given to them. It is therefore not quite clear whether the presence of these rights is sufficient for good corporate governance or whether these rights have to be actually exercised.

## Differences compared with public firms

This structure is remarkably different to public firms, where monitoring is performed both by the market and by shareholders via the board.[10] The last fact requires that shareholdings exceed a minimum threshold that makes monitoring worthwhile. This is, of course, the case for private equity firms, but not necessarily for public firms. Also, shareholders do not hold rights in addition to those spelt out in the regulations for public firms and have to rely on the board's right to information and its ability to sanction the management's behaviour if appropriate. This is emphasised by the fact that there exist various codes of conduct for public firms, ensuring a minimum level of monitoring performed by the board and facilitating market monitoring.[11]

The question that arises is why there is a need for differences in the governance structure of public and private equity financed firms. The answer is that, most often, private equity is either used for very young, innovative firms or for relatively stable, mature firms. In both cases, a more restrictive form of corporate governance is desired. For early-stage private equity (venture capital), general riskiness and both issues of moral hazard and adverse selection force investors to use more intensive monitoring. First, there is a priori uncertainty about the quality of new management. Secondly, management might not work as hard as desired or may funnel funds into unproductive uses.

For older firms a change in the firm's leverage will increase its returns, turning it into a much more risky enterprise that calls for closer monitoring. This more intensive form of monitoring does not come without costs – in particular, employing a team of specialised private equity managers is expensive. Beyond this fact several issues arise. First, investors may abuse their position, especially when dealing with founder-managers in young firms. While this is a real concern, several measures are used to overcome it, the most important being that venture capital investors are repeat players in the market with reputations to gain or lose. Any too overt abuse of power may lead to punishment by the market.

Secondly, there may be over-monitoring of management. This aspect will most likely arise in older, more mature firms that have stable and experienced management. In these cases, intensive monitoring may either deter the hiring of good management or may stifle investment in new ideas.

## Advice

The investors' role should not be limited to monitoring, but should also include advice to management. Private equity can be implicitly defined by the need of a firm for both tight monitoring and advice. Most firms that receive such funds are in need of such advice primarily because their management is inexperienced and due to the complexity of the business environment. Both reasons apply to venture firms, while the latter is more applicable to buy-out firms.

Also, in many cases there exists a positive externality between monitoring and advising management. Well-informed monitors also make better advisers, reaping performance benefits for the firm. This externality is best seen when one considers the type of advice given by investors. Often advising is not restricted to business strategy, but also covers professionalising management.[12] This may include the search for additional members for the management team through to the replacement of the entrepreneur as CEO, or any of the other roles assigned to the CEO. Naturally, the question whether size limits exist for such types of arrangements remains. However, given the size of new commitments to funds, this question will only be tested in future, as private equity firms leverage their business model applying it to even larger firms.

It is clear that the need to run boards as described requires the recruitment of people familiar with the types of problems encountered in private equity. For venture capital investments the problem is often solved by means of syndication, grouping together investors with expertise in different fields or countries. This allows management to draw advice from an experienced group of professionals.

## Conclusion

This chapter has reviewed the structure of corporate governance in private equity financed firms. Corporate governance relies on a two-tier system, the first layer being a nexus of contracts that define the roles of all parties involved, and the second being a board that focuses on the support of the private equity firm rather than actual control. Reasons for the use of these mechanisms include lowering risk, the need to retain enough equity for the entrepreneur and the fact that management wants to signal confidence in the firm.

# Annex

## Model heads of terms agreement between private equity firm and founders of Company X

**1. Subscription of B Shares**

1.1 The Investment shall comprise the subscription by Investor X of a new class of ordinary shares to be designated as 'B shares', which shall be identical in all respects with the existing ordinary shares of the Company (to be known as 'A shares') in respect of rights as to income, return of capital and voting. On an IPO (as defined below), all classes of shares shall be redesignated (on a one for one basis) as ordinary shares. The B shares shall benefit from certain additional rights in relation to issues of new shares and transfers of shares as described below.

1.2 The Investment by PE firm X shall comprise a total subscription for B shares of US$xm at a pre-money valuation of the Company of US$xxxm (the 'First Round Financing').

1.3 The proceeds of the First Round Financing shall be applied by the Company in:

(a) marketing the business of the Company and its subsidiaries (the 'Business');
(b) developing the technology used in the Business;
(c) making further acquisitions to develop the Business; and
(d) other general corporate purposes.

1.4 The Investor acknowledges that:

(a) The Company proposes to adopt a Share Option Scheme (the 'ESOP') whereby it may grant options to employees to subscribe for ordinary shares representing up to 10 per cent of the diluted (pre IPO) equity share capital and to date has made commitments in respect of xxx per cent.

**Further Financing and IPO**

It is the Company's present intention that a public offering and listing of the Company's shares ('IPO') on an internationally recognised exchange/trading facility will take place within 18 months of the closing of the First Round Financing and that, prior to the IPO, further equity financing (a 'Further Financing') may be required by the Company by way of one or more private placements. In this connection:

1.5 Holders of all existing B shares shall have proportional pre-emptive rights in relation to any such private placement whereby they will be entitled to subscribe to the new shares proposed to be issued (the 'New Shares') in proportion to their holding of B shares as at closing of the First Round Financing. To the extent that any holder of B shares does not exercise its primary pre-emptive right, wholly or in part, the remaining holders of B shares will have secondary proportional pre-emptive rights in respect of the remaining New Shares. For the avoidance of doubt, such pre-emptive rights shall not apply to:

(a) issues of shares otherwise than for cash;
(b) the issue of options or the exercise thereof pursuant to the ESOP; and

1.6 The Investor will be entitled to a discount of 10 per cent on the subscription price required to be paid by other investors in relation to any Further Financing insofar as the Investor subscribes for shares at a cost of up to US$xm (after such discount).
1.7 Provided that the Investor exercises in full its pre-emptive right in relation to any Further Financing, to the extent that the subscription price per share (that is, pre new money) in relation to the New Shares (the 'New Subscription Price') is less than the Subscription Price per share for the B shares in the First Round Financing (or its equivalent), then each holder of B shares shall be entitled to subscribe such number of additional shares at par as shall result in the average subscription price for such holder across his entire holding of B shares being equal to the New Subscription Price after having taken account of the discount referred to above.
1.8 A majority of the holders of the B shares shall have the power to veto any Further Financing which values the Company at less than US$xxxm.
1.9 Any Further Financing shall be made in the form of a further class of shares.

**2. IPO**

2.1 Should no IPO have been undertaken within 18 months of Closing, management will, within a further 12 months, propose and implement alternative financing and/or exit mechanisms to the Company's shareholders. If all proposed alternatives prove unsuccessful within such further 12 month period and the Company requires additional financing, holders of a majority of the B shares shall be entitled to require an IPO within a further period of 6 months.
2.2 If, within such further period of 6 months ('the Resolution Period'), no IPO has been implemented, then the holders of a majority of the B shares shall be able to require a trade sale of the Company by exercising drag along rights.

**Transfer of Shares**

2.3 No transfers of A shares may be effected prior to the earlier of (a) IPO and (b) 30 months from Closing ('the Lock Up Period') save that any holder of A shares may transfer up to 5 per cent of his or her holding of A shares at the date of the Closing at any time.
2.4 No transfer of B shares may be effected prior to the earlier of (a) IPO and (b) 30 months from Closing save that 'intra group' transfers shall be permitted where Private Equity Firm X remains the [manager] of the investment.
2.5 If, following expiry of the Lock Up Period, a holder of B shares wishes to transfer all or some of its shares to a third party, it will inform the holders of the A shares who will then have a period of 30 days during which to offer to acquire such B shares. If the holders of the B shares do not accept such offer within 14 days of receipt of the offer, they shall only be entitled to sell their B shares to a third party at a price which exceeds that offered by the holders of the A shares and within a further period of 90 days.
2.6 Upon an IPO, holders of A shares and B shares will be required to enter into new lock up agreements with the underwriter of the IPO. The holders of A shares acknowledge that the period applicable to their shares is likely to exceed that applicable to the B shares.
2.7 If following the Resolution Period the Company is unable to raise finance in order to meet the commitments incorporated in its then latest budget and holders of any class of shares receive an offer for all such shares ('the Subject Shares') from a third party which offer

(a) is in cash payable on closing and (b) contains no unusual terms and conditions, e.g. reps, indemnities etc., then such holders shall be entitled to require the holders of all other classes of shares to transfer their shares to such third party at the same time as selling their entire holding of shares, provided that such third party extends its offer to all of such other classes of shares on identical terms as those applying to the Subject Shares.

2.8 If, following the Lock Up Period, a holder of A shares wishes to transfer all or some of his or her shares as a result of which transfer a person or persons acting in concert (who do not then have control of the Company) acquire control of the Company, he or she must, prior to such transfer, ensure that the proposed purchaser extends an offer in identical terms to the holders of all other shares in the Company offering to acquire all such shares. For this purpose, 'control' means the ability to direct the overall policy of the Company and its subsidiaries.

**3. Board Representation and Vetos**

3.1 Private Equity Firm X shall be entitled to appoint and maintain one person approved by Founders as a director of the Company ('B Director') provided that its shareholding constitutes at least 1 per cent of the issued equity share capital of the Company.

3.2 Holders of a majority of the B shares shall have power to veto any of the following:

(a) any transaction involving any affiliate of the Founders;
(b) any significant transaction (including acquisitions), which shall be defined as any transaction outside the normal course of business not provided for in the then current budget, involving the Company or its subsidiaries (together 'the Group') for a consideration in excess of US$15m (such figure to be renegotiated at the time of any Further Financing);
(c) the incurring of bank indebtedness which has no equity features by the Group in excess of US$7.5m (such figure to be renegotiated at the time of any Further Financing);
(d) the granting of security by a member of the Group or the guaranteeing by a member of the Group of a third party's obligations other than in the ordinary course of business and save for specified exceptions;
(e) an IPO where the market capitalisation envisaged is less than US$xxxm;
(f) any variation of the rights of the B shares contained in the Company's Articles of Association; and
(g) any change to the Company's current dividend policy (which presently does not envisage the payment of any dividend).

3.3 In the event that (a) EBITDA of the Group achieved in 20xx is less than 50 per cent of that included in the budget or (b) first half revenues for 20xx (tested during August in relation to the previous 6 months) are less than 50 per cent of those included in the budget, then no budget for 20xx will be adopted by the Board without the consent of the holders of a majority of the B shares. The same mechanism shall apply for subsequent years.

**4. Reporting and budget**

4.1 A representative of the holders of the B shares shall be entitled to inspect the books and records, and operations, of the Group at times reasonably convenient to the Group but not more than once in any period of six months.

4.2 Each holder of B shares shall be entitled to receive the following financial information prior to IPO:

(a) monthly consolidated net turnover;

(b) unaudited quarterly financial statements which have been reviewed by management; and

(c) audited year end financial statements.

**5. Founders lock up and non compete**

5.1 Term – the Founders will commit to serve the Group for 3½ years or, if less, 2 years post IPO provided that, if the Company is sold after 3 years from Closing but prior to such 3½ year period, the term shall continue for 6 months following the closing of such sale.

5.2 Non compete – the Founders shall not (subject to specified exceptions to be agreed) be involved in any xxxx business for a period of 18 months following their ceasing to work for the Company.

**6. Miscellaneous**

6.1 The parties shall bear their own costs and expenses in relation to the negotiation and implementation of the Investment. It is understood that the Investor shall in principle lead negotiations and due diligence on behalf of all Investors taking part in the First Round Financing.

6.2 The parties shall endeavour to achieve Closing no later than 20xx.

6.3 It is expressly agreed that notwithstanding any other provision of these Heads of Terms, the Founders shall retain both board and shareholder control of the Company prior to the IPO or, if earlier, the date falling 18 months from Closing.

---

[1] *Harvard Business Review*, September/October 1989.

[2] Owen, G. and T. Kirchmaier, 'The Changing Role of the Chairman of the Board: The Impact of Corporate Governance Reform in the UK, 1995-2005' (London: Chairmen's Forum, 2006).

[3] Grant, J. and T. Kirchmaier, 'Financial Tunnelling and the Revenge of the Insider System' (*FMG Discussion Paper DP536*, 2005).

[4] Jensen, M. C., 'Agency Costs of Overvalued Equity', *Financial Management*, 34(1), 5–19 (2005).

[5] In Germany, with its two-tier board system, about 50 per cent of all VC firms have no supervisory board.

[6] Based on Jay Lorsch, *Digitas (A)* (Boston: Harvard Business School, 2004).

[7] Kaplan, S. and Stromberg P., 'Contracting Theory Meets the Real World', *Review of Economic Studies* (2003) and Bienz, C. and Hirsch, 'The Dynamics of Venture Capital Contracts'(*FMG Working Paper No 552*, 2005)

[8] Aghion P., Bolton P., "An 'Incomplete Contracts' Approach to Financial Contracting", *Review of Economic Studies*, 59, pp.473–494, (2002).

[9] Dessein, W., 'Information and Control in Ventures and Alliances', *Journal of Finance* (2005).

[10] Demsetz, H. and K. Lehn, 'The Structure of Corporate Ownership: Causes and Consequences', *Journal of Political Economy*, 93(6), 1155–1177 (1985).

[11] Arcot and Bruno, 'In Letter but Not in Spirit: An Analysis of Corporate Governance in the UK', *Working Paper* (London: London School of Economics, 2005).

[12] Hellmann, T. and M. Puri, 'Venture Capital and the Professionalization of Start-up Firms: Empirical Evidence', *The Journal of Finance*, Vol. 57, No. 1, pp. 169–197 (2002).

# Part III

# Investment strategies and performance

Chapter 6

# Private equity funds of funds

Joe Sovran
*Capvent AG*

## Introduction

A private equity fund of funds may be broadly defined as a portfolio of several investments in funds organised and run by private equity fund managers (referred to in this chapter as 'general partners' or 'GPs', and their funds as 'GP funds'), who themselves invest that capital in a variety of securities – usually in unlisted/private companies. This definition includes:

- pooled funds of funds established and managed by independent specialists groups who collect, pool together and invest capital from third parties;
- proprietary funds of funds, or segregated accounts, managed by discretionary or non-discretionary managers/advisers; and
- captive groups within banks and asset management organisations.

This chapter is directed particularly towards private and institutional investors – also known as limited partners (LPs) – who invest in or are potentially interested in investing capital in the private equity asset class, and for whom a fund of funds is one possible option.

## Why funds of funds exist

Private equity is an asset class that offers investors the opportunity to make attractive long-term returns that exceed the publicly quoted markets. However, these returns do not come without effort. Private equity is specialised and heterogeneous. The differences among private equity firms span a number of parameters: geographic focus, investment style, size of fund, types of portfolio companies, industry sectors and types of security invested in. There are thousands of private equity groups worldwide, encompassing a tremendous variety of strategies. Since the private equity groups are themselves rarely publicly listed entities, there is little publicly available information about their performance.

The variation in performance among the best and poorest performing private equity managers is high. According to Venture Economics, the top quartile net internal rate of return (IRR) for all private equity funds in Europe between 1980 and the beginning of 2005 was 23.4 per cent and the median net IRR was 14.7 per cent. This difference of over 8 per cent per year compounded over 24 years is considerable. Since the dispersion in terms of performance is much higher in private equity than in listed equity or fixed income, it is imperative to deploy one's capital with the better-performing private equity GP funds.

These GP fund managers invest in private companies in which they play a central role in facilitating the creation of value while managing varying degrees of risk. The investments are by nature illiquid until the GP completes an exit, which typically takes between two and eight years. Therefore, a single investment in a GP fund bears much more risk for the investor than an investment in a diversified fund of funds. An empirical study[1] demonstrates two points.

- The probability of receiving a negative return on invested capital is over 20 per cent for a single GP fund investment. This falls to between 0.1 per cent and 1.7 per cent for a fund of funds portfolio of 20 GP funds.
- The risk as the standard deviation of IRRs is much smaller for funds of funds than for individual GP funds. For example, the standard deviation for individual venture capital funds in Europe is 27.47 compared to 5.53 for a portfolio of 20 venture capital GP funds. The difference in standard deviation is similar for buyout funds.

Because of the variety and private nature of the asset class, a specialised set of skills is needed to evaluate the risk and return potential of GP fund investments. However, many investors have the problem that private equity represents only a small proportion of their overall allocation of financial assets – usually less than 3 per cent and not often more than 5 per cent. These investors therefore cannot justify the cost of having a dedicated, in-house team focused on it. Therefore, funds of funds can play the role of agent for investors who cannot, or choose not to, invest themselves in the resources necessary to determine who the future outperformers will be (and to avoid the future underperformers).

In addition, for many entities the amount of capital available to invest in private equity is small from the standpoint of GP fund managers. The reason for this is that the process by which GPs raise capital from investors can be long and tedious. GPs therefore have strong incentives to establish long-term relationships with investors who are able to invest significant amounts of capital in the GP's current fund and potentially in successive funds. Since GP funds vary in size significantly, from approximately US$50m at the small end to US$10bn plus at the large end, what they consider to be 'significant' can vary. A rough estimate may be taken from the minimum investment suggested by most private placement memoranda (PPMs, effectively the GP's main marketing document when raising a new fund); this usually ranges from US$2m to US$20m, with the majority being in the area of US$5m. A well-diversified private equity portfolio of 15 investments would therefore require approximately US$75m to be invested, and should ideally be invested over several vintage years. If the objective were to reach a 3 per cent overall allocation in the LP's portfolio, this means that only investors with at least US$2.5bn of capital under management are able to build their own programme. However, even making these 15 investments may be more difficult than it would appear. For the reason indicated above, many GPs may not wish to have a one-time investor in their fund who may not have additional capital to invest in their subsequent funds. This may limit the LP's choice of GPs in which to invest, and undermine its ability to deploy the desired capital optimally.

Funds of funds address all of the above issues. As dedicated participants in the private equity market, they also collect a tremendous amount of information on macroeconomic and sector trends, and on the broad variety of GPs' approaches to opportunities in the market. A good fund-of-funds manager can use this information to triangulate data originating from differing sources and perspectives to separate real opportunities from good salesmanship on the part of GPs. Virtually every GP claims that their fund is top quartile, and is able to give a reasonable justification for this. Funds of funds also have relationships with GPs that have been built over time, or by reputation. These are often important in providing access to GPs whose funds have performed so well in the past that they can effectively select their investors, and are always over-subscribed. A proactive fund-of-funds manager is also on the lookout for new teams that show exceptional promise on the basis of their experience, motivation and differentiated strategy – and only by continuously meeting many teams is it possible to distinguish which teams are truly 'exceptional' in this regard.

Funds of funds may also be useful for investors to obtain specific exposure to niches of the private equity market that do not form a core part of the investor's programme, are relatively difficult for an investor to access, or are particularly specialised. Examples of such riches are as follows.

- Different geographies: for example an Asian fund of funds for investors whose current portfolios have little exposure to Asia.
- Different types of private equity funds: such as a venture capital fund of funds for investors who wish to have some exposure to venture capital, but would find it difficult to establish a diversified portfolio of investments without going the fund-of-funds route.
- Variations on the above two, such as a fund of funds focused on mid-market buyouts in Europe for US investors. A number of these investors have some exposure to large pan-European buyout funds but little or no allocation in the vibrant lower end of the European mid-market because of geographic remoteness and higher language and cultural barriers when accessing funds operating in more local markets.

In this way, a tailored fund-of-funds investment can complement an existing portfolio of GP funds and/or direct or co-investments.

## Investing in a fund of funds versus in GP funds

A familiar commercial analogy to contrast the ways in which one can invest in private equity is the 'make or buy' decision.

### 'Buy'

Choosing to invest in a fund of funds is comparable to outsourcing the manufacturing of a product, or the full provision of a service, to an arm's-length third party. The third party supplier may provide a product or service from its existing suite of offerings (a pooled fund of funds), or may customise an offering to suit the client's needs (a proprietary fund of funds, or segregated account). There are a number of advantages to this approach.

- A fund of funds will have an existing, experienced team that is already fully mobilised, is benchmarking active funds in the market against each other and is making investments. Also,

funds of funds are more able than many investors to attract and compensate specialised, high-quality private equity investment professionals. A fund of funds can offer a career path from junior to senior roles at competitive remuneration, plus the future prospect of sharing the profits of the business (carried interest). Many investors are not able to match this.
- It is easier to achieve diversification in two ways: first, by outsourcing the selection process to a private equity investment specialist who has economies of scope; and, secondly, by piggy-backing on the fund-of-funds manager's scale, a small amount of capital can command the same diversification as larger commitments of capital.
- It distils the investor's approval process down to one decision, instead of having to make multiple decisions at the GP level.
- A quality fund of funds will have a good reputation and established relationships with well-regarded GPs, making it an attractive investor to the GPs. This is a particular advantage when trying to obtain access to funds that have a strong past track record, can often be oversubscribed and can therefore be selective in admitting new investors.
- It reduces the overall administrative burden for the investor, because negotiating the terms of each investment, maintaining communications with the GPs, monitoring the progress of investments and dealing with issues that arise are all undertaken by the fund-of-funds manager.

There are, however, a few disadvantages to this outsourcing approach.

- The main one is the additional layer of fees that must be paid for the above services. For a pooled fund of funds, these would typically consist of an annual fixed fee of 50 to 150 basis points on the amount of capital committed, plus usually a share of the profits (carried interest) of 5 per cent to 10 per cent after return of the investor's original capital and costs, often linked to a preferred return of between 5 per cent and 8 per cent.
- Choosing a mediocre fund of funds is likely to result in the investor achieving no better than average private equity returns, which are at best comparable to public market returns.
- Compared to making GP fund investments, the investor is not as directly involved with the investing activity, and therefore has less opportunity to build its own base of direct knowledge that would improve its future ability to invest in the asset class.

## 'Make (with partners)'

Choosing to invest directly in GP funds is akin to deciding to undertake manufacturing in-house, or having an in-house department provide a service, but where outside suppliers (the GPs) provide components or service elements to support the effort. This of course requires that the investor has appropriate in-house resources in order to execute the strategy. The advantages for the investor are as follows.

- It acquires its own proprietary expertise in private equity investing.
- It is able to fully control the investment strategy at the GP level, and to choose exactly which GP funds to invest in, in accordance with the investor's particular needs.
- GP funds report directly to the investor, who can establish and build long-term relationships in the private equity market.

- A successful strategy may, over time, allow the investor to establish its own fund-of-funds business offering fund-of-funds investment opportunities to other investors.

However, undertaking this task in-house is an initiative that requires management time and effort, and a serious long-term commitment of resources. It carries disadvantages.

- The need to build sufficient scale to make the initiative worthwhile. Building an in-house team can be very expensive, and therefore it is necessary to establish that the long-term programme of private equity investment warrants the effort and expense.
- The difficulty of identifying, attracting and incentivising top private equity investment professionals to join a captive, in-house team versus working for an independent specialist.
- If the commitment to private equity weakens at some point, the portfolio may never achieve a healthy level of diversification, leaving a half-baked effort that exposes the investor to excessive risk.
- It takes time to build the relationships and credibility that gives one organisation preferential treatment over another. GPs have seen varying degrees of commitment by investors to private equity, and have a preference for steady, long-term investors.

### 'Pure make'

Choosing to make direct investments in companies, through either a direct strategy or a co-investment strategy, is like having the whole manufacturing process or service function kept in-house. This in fact is the most flexible way to invest in the sector and attracts no fees from intermediary players. However, the fixed costs of this option are very high, and worldwide only a small number of typically large, highly sophisticated investors make significant numbers of direct investments.

Many investors are put off by the extra layer of fees charged by funds of funds, which are on top of the fees that will have been charged by the GP funds in the underlying portfolio. If the fund-of-fund's performance is no better than the average performance across the private equity market, then this concern is wholly justified. However, since the top GP funds significantly outperform the market average, the overall value that a high-quality fund-of-funds manager brings to its investors in terms of returns and the associated services that come with them easily exceeds the cost of the extra layer of fees. For this reason, it is so important that an investor conducts a thorough review before choosing a manager. There follows an outline of the main fund-of-funds structures and useful tips in selecting a fund-of-funds manager.

## Different types of funds of funds

There are two main structures for funds of funds – pooled and proprietary.

### Pooled funds of funds

This is a structure established by an organisation that is specialised in investing in private equity funds. It typically consists of a standard limited partnership into which investors pool their capital. All investors in this limited partnership structure invest in the same set of GP interests from this pool of capital, in proportion to their commitments.

**Advantages**

- There is a broad selection of funds of funds available for investors to choose from at any one time. It includes funds of funds that provide broad exposure across private equity, and specialised sector, style, stage, or geographically focused funds of funds.
- An investor can acquire exposure to private equity with only a very small commitment (for example, a few million dollars) to start.

**Disadvantages**

- The strategy cannot usually be changed during the investment period, because it was the basis upon which the fund of funds convinced investors to commit capital. The investment strategy can therefore be inflexible, and unable to adapt to changes in the investment environment.
- Once the choice to invest in a specific fund of funds has been made, all investors in the LP structure invest in the same assets, and small to mid-sized investors have limited influence over how the fund of funds directs its investment strategy, as in the following examples.
  - A fund of funds that deploys capital too quickly risks being overexposed to a specific vintage year. Private equity returns can vary significantly by vintage year.
  - A fund of funds that invests in too many GP funds risks diluting its overall return. A good fund of funds should not make average private equity returns – which are no better than the returns from the public market – but rather exceptional returns from investment in a selection of only the best prospective performers.

## Proprietary funds of funds / segregated accounts

This structure is established jointly by the fund-of-funds manager and the investor to meet the latter's legal, tax, strategic and other specific needs.

**Advantages**

- The investor can have significant influence over the investment strategy and execution.
- The strategy can be adjusted during the investment period. Such adjustments may be needed in response to changes in the investment environment, such as macroeconomic shocks or increasing competition in the original areas of focus. In addition, adjustments may be useful to address changing investor needs, such as the shifting of focus in the remainder of the asset mix, or to refine cash deployment.
- Depending on the investor's needs and interests, the structure can involve a deep transfer of knowledge on private equity investing to the investor.

**Disadvantages**

- It requires some additional effort on the part of the investor to identify the fund-of-funds manager to work with and to determine the optimal investment structure.
- The investor needs to make a minimum commitment (in the order of US$30m to US$50m

over several years – varying by fund-of-funds manager) so that establishing and managing a customised offering is worthwhile both for the investor and for the fund-of-funds manager.

## How to choose a fund-of-funds manager

Fund-of-funds managers enjoy a significant asymmetrical information advantage over most investors, particularly over new investors to the asset class. This can make it difficult for an investor to differentiate between them, to understand the relative significance of the benefits each offers, and to choose the ideal fund-of-funds manager or adviser. This section aims to help redress this imbalance. It discusses factors that are important to consider, and provides some practical advice as to how to effectively make evaluations. Although the first few factors – team, track record and investment strategy – are often cited and are indeed important, there are a few additional points less often mentioned that should help potential investors to take their evaluations a level deeper.

### Team/organisation/motivation

Clearly the overall quality of the firm's management and investment team is critical. Relevant and extensive past investment experience is a must. Aside from this, there is a range of past expertise and experience that can add value to the team, so there is no set formula to evaluating it. It is important to assess the range and depth of the intellectual rigour that the team is able to bring to bear to its decision-making. It is equally important to get a sense for how well oriented and motivated all of the individuals in the organisation are to generating the best results for clients/investors. Here are a few questions to ask.

- Are the same professionals who were responsible for the firm's successful track record still as engaged and motivated to repeat that success going forward?
- How are rewards shared across the team; does everyone have a good incentive to perform?
- What mistakes has the fund of funds made in the past, and how have the managers learned from them? Regardless of whether they consider them 'mistakes' or not, ask them to discuss their poorest performing GP investments to date, and particularly any recent ones. Despite the poor results in these cases, had the fund of funds conducted rigorous due diligence, followed their own disciplined internal process and executed on their purported investment strategy?
- Who are the owners of the firm, and what are their aims in building their business going forward? Does their answer indicate that they are truly aligned with their investors, or are they more interested in just building a larger business (remember, more capital under management equals more fees)?
- How hands-on are the most experienced members of the team in investment analysis and investment decisions?
- If the firm has had considerable past success and its principals are already well-off, how hungry are they to maintain their success, and how oriented are they to the ongoing needs of their clients/investors (rather than 'coasting' on past success)? For example, do they commit a significant amount of their own capital to their funds?

## Track record / performance

As a result of the number of years it takes private equity firms to make and then exit investments, much more time is needed to clearly demonstrate performance in this asset class than in most others. A prospective investor should review the most recent performance reports of a fund of funds, covering all its past investments, and ask the following.

- How has the track record been calculated? Does it include all relevant investments the firm has made, and if not what has been excluded?
- What does the current unrealised part of the investment portfolio look like? Remember, the great majority of the 'proven part' of the track record of a fund of funds is already at least three or four years old, because capital is typically deployed over a four-year investment period and then requires time for exits to generate returns. Therefore, the 'proven track record' is usually already old news.

## Investment strategy

Because the variance between the best and poorest performing GPs is so great, choosing the GPs that will *in the future* outperform their peers is a central objective of a fund-of-funds manager. Therefore, it is important to understand how the fund-of-funds manager intends to achieve this. Is the firm a thought leader or a follower? As with any other investment, past performance is not necessarily a good indicator of future performance. The private equity market is just that – a market, or more precisely a set of niche markets, driven by the same supply and demand dynamics as any other market. The danger of being a follower in any market is chasing momentum. This was illustrated on a grand scale during the dot-com boom: many early investments did well, but almost everyone else who followed behind suffered after excess supply of capital drove prices to unsustainable heights. While this is a somewhat extreme example, capital mobility into and out of niches in the private equity market has a strong effect on GPs' abilities to outperform. As a result, a potential investor should ask a fund of funds manager the following questions.

- What is their investment philosophy and how does it lead to exceptional performance? How rigorous are they in their thinking? What kind of research do they undertake to support their investment theses?
- How proactive is the firm, and what work does it do to stay ahead of the curve?
- Where in the private equity market do they see the best risk-adjusted returns coming from in the next one to two years? Does their response demonstrate a proactive approach to finding opportunities, or a complacent backward-looking approach?
- It is all well and good to spend time analysing the well-known funds, but how does the firm identify emerging managers – the 'hidden jewels' – from the several thousand GPs operating worldwide? How have the emerging GPs they have invested in performed to date? If they do not invest in them, it is necessary to make a judgement as to whether the firm's investment strategy is more forward-looking or backward-looking.
- Ask the firm to give examples of where it took a lead in committing to a GP, and then call the GP to ask about the fund-of-funds manager's investment approach.

A potential investor could also call one or more placement agents (whose role is to help GPs raise capital from institutional and other investors) to ask which fund of funds they consider to be the most rigorous, proactive and forward-looking.

## Investment execution

A sound private equity investment strategy needs to be backed up by solid processes that impose a consistent level of intellectual rigour, discipline and effort – from the early research and identification stages through to investment. An investor should ask the firm to demonstrate:

- how many GPs with whom it is in contact, and how it tracks them;
- what analysis it undertakes at various stages of assessment;
- the scope and depth of its due diligence processes;
- the number and types of references it takes before making an investment; and
- the involvement of the most experienced members of the firm in the details of the investment process.

## Fees

The fact that a fund of funds will add a layer of fees on top of the GP funds' fees is certainly an issue with many investors considering funds of funds. In principle, the advantages of a fund of funds should justify its fees. However, it is also useful to consider how fees are broken down between the annual management fee, which typically ranges between 50 and 150 basis points, and the performance fee, which is typically a percentage of profit (called 'carried interest') earned after whatever preferred return is first provided to the investor. Does the revenue stream that the fund-of-funds manager earns from the fees from all of the funds it manages just cover the firm's reasonable operating costs, or does this fee stream already provide rich compensation for its partners? This again is an indication of where lie the motivations of the firm's principals.

## Loyalty to investors versus GPs

The focus of fund-of-funds managers on 'access to top-quartile GPs' as their key selling point to investors has merit, but there is a risk that this emphasis shifts the fund-of-funds manager's loyalties from investors to GPs. If obtaining a good allocation from perceived top-ranking GP fund 'X' is overly important to a fund of funds, then necessarily it needs to maintain a good, long-term relationship with X in order to preserve that access. This is not itself a bad thing. However, when it comes time to negotiate terms for the next fund, to review valuation policy for the investment portfolio or to provide feedback to the GP on an issue, there is more incentive for the fund-of-funds manager to acquiesce on these issues with the GP, since playing too strong a hand in the investors' interests may strain the relationship. Because these are the very GP funds that tend to be oversubscribed, and the process of allocating the investment capital of the GP's next fund to existing and new investors is totally within the GP's own discretion, why not then give larger allocations to the investors that have been most cooperative? Investors should ask a fund-of-funds manager about their policy on 're-ups' (investing in a GP's subsequent fund to the one the fund of funds had previously invested in). Also, the firm should be asked to provide a complete record of past decisions to re-up or not, and the justification for the decision made in each case.

## Resolving allocation conflicts

A fund of funds that operates only one fund for all of its clients is likely to have a simple task in allocating investment in proportion to the respective commitments of these clients. However, where the firm operates several funds and/or separate accounts for clients, there may be instances where the firm must divide a limited allocation to a GP among them. It is therefore useful to understand what exposure the investor will obtain to the kinds of GP funds that are of interest, within the context of the vehicle being proposed and the entirety of the fund-of-funds firm's obligations.

## Client service

As with any service, big or important investors/clients may be given more attention and higher priority than smaller clients. Therefore, an investor should ask up-front for the firm's list of clients/investors, and get clear answers on what standard and ad hoc services will be provided. For example, it is commonly thought that a fund of funds is a good first step for new investors in the asset class to learn about how private equity works, before thinking about establishing their own private equity investment programme. Some investors have then been disappointed when they find that the chosen fund of funds does little to actually transfer knowledge, and that after several years of investment the investor knows little more about the asset class than it did before. The specific data, knowledge and time commitment being provided by the fund-of-funds manager needs to be clarified, and also needs to be credible when considering the resources the firm has available for all of its investors/clients. Prospective investors should ask the firm for a complete list of clients/investors, and should take references with a variety of these to verify the level of service and attention the firm provides to its clients.

## Monitoring

A GP fund will typically provide quarterly and annual reports to its investors. These are the basic source of information regarding the progress of a private equity investment. However, a proactive fund of funds will maintain an ongoing dialogue with its GPs. Sophisticated investors can provide helpful feedback regarding strategy, capital flows and competition in the market to GPs, because following the market is a central activity of a specialist investor in private equity. Furthermore, in informal discussions GPs often provide best-guess indications of future likely capital calls and drawdowns, which assist in planning future cash flow management. Overall, a fund of funds that has a strong ongoing dialogue with its GPs reinforces its commitment to the success of the GP's fund and therefore its relationship with the GP – putting the fund of funds in a better position to take up a favourable allocation in the GP's next fund, if it so chooses.

Finally, GPs will almost always organise advisory committees for each of their funds, which consist of a handful of selected investors in that fund. While it is not possible to have a place on the advisory committee for every GP fund invested in, this is another opportunity for a fund of funds to influence its GPs and further develop the relationship. Since GPs like to have well-informed, sophisticated investors on their advisory committee (although in many cases the de facto rule is that it consists of the largest investors in that fund), whether a fund of funds sits on any advisory committees is indicative of the esteem in which they are held in the GP community.

A prospective investor should ask a fund of funds how proactive it is in communicating with its GPs, and what its policy is in terms of sitting on advisory committees.

### Reporting

Just as GPs report to their investors, funds of funds should equally provide clear, detailed, relevant and timely reports to their investors. A prospective investor should ask a fund of funds to provide examples of the types of reports that it currently provides to its investors.

## Future directions for funds of funds

The fund-of-funds industry experienced its major growth phase during the 1990s, riding on the coat-tails of the great expansion of the private equity market itself. In the United States, there were 20 fund-of-funds managers in 1991 and 65 by 2001. In Europe, there were 11 managers in 1995 and 47 by 2001. As at the beginning of 2005, 131 funds manage US$161bn of discretionary assets. Around 48 per cent of these funds are independent specialists, 34 per cent are assets managers and 18 per cent are banks. The majority of funds – 61 per cent – are headquartered in the United States and 36 per cent are headquartered in Europe.[2]

The funds of funds that established themselves early and maintained respectable track records are now the large brand names in the industry. Over time, they have tended to raise increasingly larger funds, and multiple funds focused on different geographies or parts of the market. The large general funds of funds have also started to offer more options to allow investors to choose how they wish to deploy capital in specific sub-strategies. The other, smaller funds of funds include niche players with specific strategies as their core offering to investors. With the main barrier to entry to this market being the challenge of raising capital to invest, small players will continue to enter.

However, as noted earlier, it takes many years for the feedback loop of returns on investments to close. There are undoubtedly funds of funds with mediocre track records that continue to operate, but which will eventually struggle to raise further capital as their returns slowly come to light. This could even include long-standing players that have established strong brand names for themselves. Because of their momentum, most of these large players can be expected to continue to be seen as the safe option for private equity investing, much like how, for several decades, a computer systems manager 'would not be fired for buying an IBM computer'. However, this perception outlasted the actual superiority of IBM's products and services. While small funds may struggle to establish a credible track record with investors, some of the large, successful and profitable funds of funds may struggle to maintain their hunger, motivation and discipline over time. With comfortable fixed fee revenues it could take a number of years before investors become aware that these players are no longer in fact top performers on a risk/return basis. Just like at the GP level, some of the future top-performing funds of funds will come from the ranks of current lesser-known players.

In the meantime the dedicated, professional approach that funds of funds take to investing has had broad positive impacts on the private equity market as a whole. GP funds are generally conscientious about providing information during due diligence, establishing reasonable terms for investors and reporting on the progress of their investment portfolios. However, having relatively more sophisticated investors tends to raise the bar in these areas. Funds of funds review large numbers of GP funds every year and demand high-quality information and corporate governance from them throughout the investment cycle. They can be expected to monitor performance closely, and to be active and informed participants in issues that arise, such as conflicts of interests or appropriate valuations for portfolio assets. For first-time GPs or small or regional GPs in particular, funds of funds can assist in imparting industry best practices, and in this way can help to professionalise the industry. Because funds of funds need to be very selective, in the broadest sense they also play a positive role in allocating capital to strong GPs who do perform well, and not to weak ones, which in turn positively reinforces the entire private equity industry.

## Conclusions

Private equity funds of funds are an excellent option for investors who want to obtain or increase exposure to the asset class but can only allocate small amounts of capital to it, or do not wish to build dedicated, in-house resources to achieve this. It is an equally viable means for investors to gain exposure to niche areas of private equity without having to deploy large amounts of capital. A fund-of-funds manager who performs satisfactorily easily justifies the extra layer of fees that an investor incurs, by the added value of specialised selection and due diligence, and by greatly diversifying the investor's risk.

---

[1] T. Wiedig, A. Kemmerer and B. Born, 'The Risk Profile of Private Equity Funds of Funds', *Journal of Alternative Investments*, Spring 2005.

[2] Almeida Capital, *A Review of private equity funds of funds 2005*, April 2005.

Chapter 7

# Where next for the secondaries market?

Christophe Nicolas
*Greenpark Capital*

## Introduction

The private equity secondaries market has evolved beyond recognition since its cottage industry beginnings in the early 1990s. Originally a private equity secondaries transaction involved the sale of a limited partner position in a private equity fund, usually by an institutional investor who did not wish, or was not able, to stay for the duration of the life of the fund. Since then, the secondaries industry has developed into an advanced facility regularly used by sophisticated private equity investors and international corporations to optimise the management of their balance sheet by releasing cash from illiquid investments that, over time, have become non-strategic to their requirements and reusing such cash proceeds in investment opportunities offering higher return prospects.

This chapter will address the following topics.

- The drivers behind the consistent growth in the secondaries market.
- The increasing diversity of assets traded in the private equity secondaries market.
- The types of secondaries transactions, and their increasing sophistication.
- The hurdles to be overcome in a successful secondaries transaction.
- Growth expectations for the secondaries market.

## Drivers of growth in the secondaries market

### Increased awareness

Up until 2000 for many investors and/or limited partners with commitments to private equity funds, exiting before the maturity of the fund (typically after a duration of 10 years plus one or two extension years if necessary) was either:

- unthinkable, due to perceived potential reputation issues for themselves and/or the general partner;
- unfeasible, because of the limited universe of buyers and a reluctance to get involved in a secondaries sale process for the first time; or
- simply unattractive, due to the price often representing a serious discount to the book value.

Secondaries transactions, however, are now commonplace in the United States and Europe, and are increasingly a feature of the Asian private equity landscape. Potential reputation issues for the selling investor and for the general partner have largely disappeared as it is now commonly

Exhibit 7.1
**Value range of base global secondaries transactions, 2002–05**

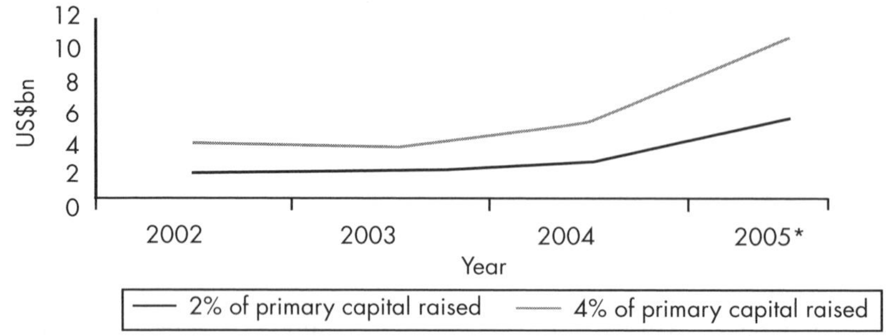


*2005 figures estimated.
*Source*: Greenpark Capital.

accepted that, on average, 2–4 per cent of the total commitments made by investors to private equity funds change hands each year (see Exhibit 7.1). In addition, increasing competition between buyers and the emergence of intermediaries focusing on private equity secondaries transactions contribute to giving the selling party comfort that an appropriate and attractive exit price and relatively straightforward process are achievable.

## Changes within institutional sellers

Internal developments at some limited partner organisations also drive the market in a substantial way, and traditionally many secondaries transactions have been prompted by such developments. These changes include major public bid or merger activity, or the appointment of new decision-makers at senior investment/trustee level. A new senior team member often instigates a critical review of the existing portfolio with a view to undertaking some housekeeping, including partial divestments via a secondaries sale.

## Volume of primary capital committed to private equity

The secondaries market is highly dependent on the total pool of private equity capital committed globally, because secondaries transactions are purely a consequence of investors wanting to exit from primary investments they made some time ago. The huge growth of the pool of primary private equity capital since 2003 (see Exhibit 7.2) has resulted in a major increase in the number and value of private equity positions for sale. This in turn has generated serious interest at investor level in capitalising secondaries funds that specialise in the purchase of secondaries positions. Overall, the significant increase in primary funds raised is proving to be a significant driver behind the secondaries market.

Exhibit 7.2
**Private equity funds raised globally, 1999–2005**

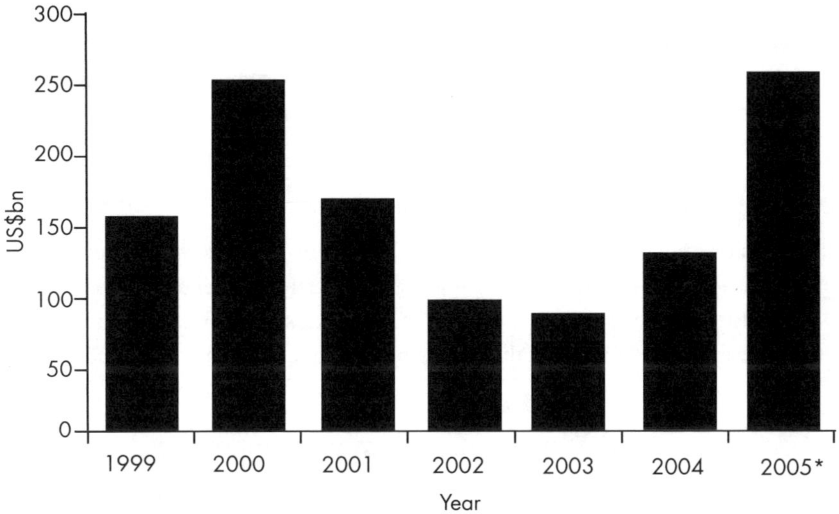


*2005 figures estimated.
*Sources*: Private Equity Analysis; EVCA; PriceWaterhouseCoopers; Thomson Financial Venture Economical; AVCJ.

## Regulatory developments

The regulatory environment in Europe and the United States has played a significant role as a driver for secondaries transactions. Between 2001–2004, Basel II regulation has triggered an unprecedented quantity of secondaries transactions as most major banks were forced to realise that the core capital allocated to private equity investments was not complying with the new financial adequacy ratios required by their regulator. Currently, International Financial Reporting Standards (IFRS) are forcing large institutions to look at the valuation of private equity assets on their balance sheets. In many instances, those institutions, which used to account for their private equity investments at the lower of cost or fair market value, already have or will have to report valuations marked-to-market. A number of institutions who invested in private equity for its lack of short-term volatility and attractive long-term prospects are now reconsidering their investment policy to meet the new IFRS accounting standard requirements.

## The worldwide economic situation

An analysis of the trend in secondaries deal volume and value since 1990 shows that an economic downturn period, such as the post-internet bubble, caused a peak of activity in the secondaries market. However, it is believed that such a peak mainly represents additional volume above a base volume of continuous growth in secondaries deal flow caused by the drivers indicated in this section. When the economic climate is favourable, some potential sellers are reluctant to approach the secondaries market, even though they would otherwise be so inclined, for a variety of internal reasons. The most quoted rationale for the postponement of a sale is that distributions are coming through at an attractive rate. However, this does not mitigate the attraction of a secondaries sale; on the contrary, the seller could achieve a better overall price while there are companies with good exit potential still in the portfolio. Once all the investee companies with exit potential have been sold it will be very difficult to achieve a sale of the remainder. Also, such an argument for postponement fails to address the opportunity cost of reinvesting the proceeds of a sale into a potentially more attractive investment, private equity-related or not.

## Developments within general partner organisations

Limited partners remain sensitive to key executive changes at the general partner level, particularly in relation to long-expected succession issues, or because a general partner's performance is not satisfactory. In these situations we often note that some limited partners prefer to sell their position because of concern for the future performance of their investment.

## Use of the secondaries market as a portfolio management tool

Finally, the main driver behind the growth of the private equity secondaries market since 2004 has been the increasing use of secondaries as a portfolio management tool. As outlined above, historically the secondaries market represented a mechanism for investors with cash constraints or requirements to create liquidity out of long-term illiquid holdings. Only in that situation would an investor be prepared to go through a sale process with which he would typically be unfamiliar. Nowadays, the secondaries market is being used for a whole range of portfolio management actions. Sales of private equity positions enable investors to:

- optimise investors' portfolios in line with their most current investment strategy by type of funds (buyout, VC, mezzanine, etc.) or geography;
- rebalance future currency exposure;
- increase positions with preferred general partners;
- undertake long overdue housekeeping;
- take advantage of arbitrage opportunities in private equity or other alternative assets;
- optimise long-term returns; and
- address particular balance sheet requirements.

Since 2005 transaction examples have included the following.

- A large pension fund with hundreds of private equity fund investments decided to sell a large portion of its private equity portfolio in order to refocus its private equity allocation on to the top 50 key general partner relationships.
- A large corporation decided to sell part of its direct investment portfolio with a view to reinvesting the proceeds into more strategic organic R&D/industrial investments.
- Private equity investors decided to sell part of their portfolios of US mid-market buyout or European VC programmes to reallocate their resources to other types of alternative assets such as hedge funds or real estate investments.

The shortening of the fund-raising cycle has become an important additional factor in the use of the secondaries market as a portfolio management tool. The increased fund-raising frequency at the primary level coupled with the increasing size of these funds impose major constraints on the ability of private equity investors to meet the requirements of successful general partners. We can now see more and more situations where larger buyout funds are requesting several hundred millions of US dollars/euros from each of their larger investors every two to thee years, resulting in certain of these investors recycling some older private equity holdings to free up capital for reinvestment. In addition, the amounts of capital required often mean that smaller investors decide to sell the older funds of these general partners when the relationship becomes too diluted. This enables these smaller investors to reallocate their capital to teams (established or emerging) that better suit their investment policy and capacity.

## Increasing diversity of assets traded in the secondaries market

Traditionally, secondaries transactions would have involved one or several limited partner positions in mature private equity funds (often at least 70 per cent drawn and in year five to seven of the fund's life). Many of these traditional secondaries would have comprised positions in the buyout and growth capital areas of investment.

In 2005, the range of alternative assets traded in the secondaries market is growing to include the following.

1. Limited partnership positions in:
   - less mature funds – that is, funds that are around 20–40 per cent drawn down; these secondaries are usually referred to as 'early secondaries' or 'manager secondaries' because the role and track record of the general partner is still highly important in the analysis of the secondaries transaction, given the lower visibility on the underlying assets;
   - technology and life science venture capital funds;
   - private finance initiative (PFI) funds where the ultimate objective is to consolidate several public project investments or funds into a vehicle with a more efficient capital structure;
   - real estate funds;
   - energy funds;
   - mezzanine funds; and
   - funds that are near, and sometimes past, the standard 10-year maturity; these 'tail-ends' usually involve a small number of underlying investments from older generations of funds that do not justify, from a time and economic return perspective, the continuing effort of the general partner when compared with more current investments.
2. Portfolios of direct private equity investments. These portfolios involve investments in all types of private companies from relatively recent start-ups to mature/buyout types of companies. These portfolios are generally divested in the following circumstances.
   - They are owned by financial institutions that initially sought to put capital to work in private equity directly or to cement a client/service provider relationship; after a number of years of holding the underlying investments the strategy changed and the portfolio has been put up for sale.

- Portfolios of direct investments can also be owned by large industrial corporations, particularly (but not exclusively) in the telecoms, media and technology (TMT) and life science industries, which over time have outsourced some of their research and development by investing in third party companies. After a number of years such corporations divest all or part of these underlying investee companies if, for example, their strategy changes; if some companies are no longer useful; or if conflicts arise with their core business.

## Types of secondaries transactions and their increasing sophistication

As the range of assets traded on the secondaries market has significantly widened since 2003, as described above, the complexity and sophistication of transaction structures has evolved at a faster pace. Reasons behind this phenomenon are the increasingly competitive nature of the private equity secondaries market and the overall maturing of this sub-segment within the private equity industry. These two factors in themselves are a direct consequence of increasing awareness among investors of the secondaries sale option as a portfolio management tool, matched by the even faster surge in the pool of capital available in the private equity secondaries market.

The increasing level of competition in the secondaries market is pushing prices up for all parties, thereby prompting buyers and sellers to look for alternatives to a simple one-off payment/straight sale. Ultimately, both buyers and sellers need to reach their return expectations for any transaction to be consummated, and new types of secondaries transactions are emerging to help both parties achieve their respective return objectives. The following illustrate the increasing level of sophistication and diversity of secondaries transaction structures.

- *'Stapled' secondaries cum primary transaction.* These transactions involve the spin-off/spin-out of a captive or semi-captive private equity investment team from its parent company, typically a large financial institution. The background situation might be that such a team seeks to raise a larger fund once it has established a successful private equity portfolio. The parent, however, may not be able – or strategically inclined – to allow this development. A synthetic transaction of this kind will consist of one or several private equity secondaries funds providing liquidity to the parent for part or all of the existing portfolio in parallel with the establishment of an independent general partner staffed by the existing team on an independent basis. The team sometimes raises a new fund capitalised by the same investors plus new investors.
- *The increasing use of leverage on a deal-by-deal basis in secondaries transactions.* The debt lenders to primary buyout transactions have entered the secondaries market since 2004. These lenders are either banks or, increasingly, hedge funds attracted by the comparatively low level of risk of secondaries transactions where future cash flows are spread over multiple (tens and sometimes hundreds) underlying private equity-backed companies in the portfolios.
- *Securitisation.* A number of leveraged private equity vehicles (collateralised fund obligations, or CFOs) have been successfully launched and invested. These vehicles sell the debt component at the start of the vehicle's life to various types of debt investors. The number of such vehicles so far has been limited due to their high set-up cost, relative inflexibility and the reluctance of traditional limited partners to provide the equity component.

- *Challenged fund situations*. This refers to troubled private equity funds where either the limited partners, out of concern for the future of their investment, or the general partner, faced with a situation his carried interest might be worthless and potentially more money is required by the portfolio, have decided to act before the end of the life of the fund. Generally, a secondaries firm offers LPs an exit and/or a rollover option into a new fund backed by the private equity secondaries firm. A high level of selectivity is needed on the part of the secondaries player in these situations.
- *Fund extensions*. Some secondaries transactions have also taken place through the extension of an existing private equity fund where some of the current investors are seeking an exit and new capital is required by the general partner to fund existing portfolio commitments or new investments.
- *Publicly quoted portfolios of direct private equity investments*. This refers to the complete or partial disposal of assets held by quoted investment/holding companies lacking the financial resources and scale to remain attractive quoted investment vehicles. Those companies can be too small to be followed by the financial analyst community and usually display low levels of trading in their shares. Hence they are a very illiquid investment for their shareholders. Private equity secondaries firms have offered attractive exit solutions for those shareholders faced with an illiquid publicly quoted investment, while being able to provide the necessary capital to the management to finance the portfolio going forward.
- *Tail end of funds*. These secondaries transactions involve the buyout by a private equity secondaries fund of the assets left in earlier generation funds that are reaching or have already reached the end of their 10-year life. Generally, the general partner's attention has moved to its more recent funds and limited partners would like to see a complete exit from the assets in the older fund(s) in order to recycle the capital into new opportunities.
- *Structured secondaries transactions*. These transactions involve the transfer of a portfolio of limited partner positions or direct private equity investments into a newly created special purpose vehicle capitalised by a private equity secondaries firm and the seller. Capitalisation of this form of joint venture structure is unique to the transaction requirements and often includes various levels of equity, debt provided by the lender and quasi-equity layers shared according to the needs of the parties involved. These transactions are more complex to execute and therefore usually require both an experienced buyer and a greater time commitment from all parties involved than a straight sale.

## The hurdles to overcome in a successful secondaries transaction

The first hurdle is the proactive decision to create liquidity in a portfolio of private equity holdings rather than wait for their natural maturation. That decision is usually followed by apprehension regarding what process to follow for those investors with no prior experience. Once the decision to take a more proactive approach in the management of the portfolio has been made, the next hurdle becomes how to organise the process and what should be the price expectation range.

Decisions as to whether or not to use an adviser and whether one or more buyers should be approached will determine the level and type of involvement that the individual responsible for the process will have in the transaction. It is a fact that no two secondaries transactions are the same and, therefore, processes involving negotiations on the customisation of an offer to satisfy a particular requirement of a seller are more frequent than an easy and quick transaction. The best way to optimise the chance of a successful process is to involve from the outset experienced purchasers with a reputable track record. Whichever way the process is going to be handled, it is vital that one or more (as required) appropriate potential purchasers are approached – that is, those with an investment strategy that matches the profile of the investments for sale. Typically, the more complicated the transaction, from a structuring and portfolio composition standpoint, the fewer and more qualified the parties one should involve to maintain a timely transaction pace and workable process.

As regards what would amount to an appropriate price (see Exhibit 7.3), this is usually not an obvious figure. Sellers in many cases only have the most recent book value or net asset value as reported by the underlying fund, which may or may not reflect the value one can achieve in a secondaries transaction. The price most often depends on which transaction structure is being developed, with deferred payments and upside sharing arrangements just two of the alternatives available to a one-off payment. The underlying analysis that most buyers would undertake involves predicting the likely exit value range and timing for each underlying company, adjusted for fund costs such as management fees and carried interest, a component of the net asset value often overlooked when determining fund valuations. Most transactions can be customised in some way, including the pricing aspects if more flexible payment schedules are allowed for. However, the lower-quality funds (for instance, underperforming funds with relatively high unfunded commitments) may not be attractive at any price!

Exhibit 7.3
**The pricing process**

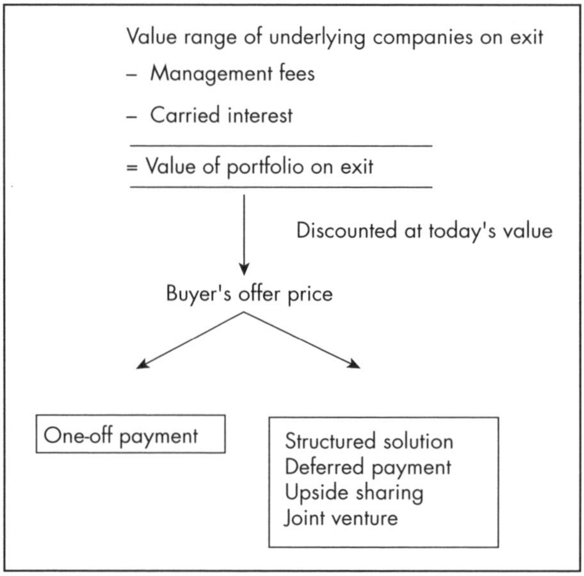


*Source*: Author's own.

The next hurdle is working through the due diligence and legal process. Sellers need to be aware that this is not only a transaction between them and a buyer, but the general partner or the manager of the fund in which they are selling a position also has a say, and typically needs to give consent to the transfer. They also have information on the portfolio companies that in many cases the buyer needs to receive to complete the due diligence on the fund or the portfolio.

Finally, it is worth noting that, while most transactions close successfully, the ones that do not complete usually fail because of a lack of preparation or commitment on the part of the seller.

## Growth expectations for secondaries

As indicated above, the private equity secondaries market has evolved enormously since its infancy in the early 1990s but never has its pace of change been as fast as it is in 2006. New transaction types and large secondaries transactions hit the headlines of the private equity press on a regular basis. This reflects private equity investors increasingly using the secondaries market as a tool to optimise the performance of their portfolios over time, and large corporations and financial institutions becoming more proactive, either voluntarily or as a result of shareholder pressure, in managing their long-term holdings or non-core activities in a more aggressive way.

Here is a summary of how we see the future of the private equity secondaries industry.

- *The secondaries market has become a well-established part of the wider private equity industry; it is here to stay and will develop further.* This is fuelled by the substantial growth of investor interest in alternative assets versus quoted assets and by the use of secondaries as a portfolio management tool. While this will result in a healthy growth of base secondaries deal flow, the much talked about over-leveraging of some large and medium buyout transactions is likely to negatively affect some funds and result in additional secondaries deal flow a few years down the road, as some recent investors get 'spooked' by highly visible investment failures.
- *The barriers to entry are becoming higher due to the increasing complexity of transactions.* Since 2000 the analysis and valuation of secondaries transactions, sometimes with hundreds of underlying companies, require enormous skill and expertise, particularly if a transaction has a tight timetable. The increasing sophistication of the market also requires extensive transaction structuring on a bespoke basis to suit the specific, ever-changing needs of vendors of private equity positions.
- *There is clear trend towards investment strategy differentiation.* The evolving secondaries market is giving rise to strategy differentiation and specialisation between the funds investing in this area. This includes geographical focus: some funds will focus more on US transactions, while others have a particular interest in European assets. It also includes type of assets: some secondaries players prefer to invest the majority of their funds in old economy assets rather than venture secondaries. Size is also a distinguishing factor: larger funds of, say, well over €1bn, more or less by necessity need some sizeable transactions to fill up their investment capacity, whereas smaller funds can afford to be more flexible in terms of the transactions that they choose to complete. On the one hand this strategic differentiation and specialisation within the secondaries arena is taking place and the emergence of 'stapled' transactions and 'early secondaries' deals is in some instances blurring the frontiers between primary private

equity and secondaries firms. On the other hand, a number of secondaries transactions involving portfolios of direct investments, requiring hands-on operational input to create value, look closer to the direct investment model than the primary private equity model.

- *Expect to see the emergence of funds dedicated to portfolios of direct investments.* More firms are likely to start their own 'managing-out' operations. Currently there are relatively few of these, with the most established teams located in the United States, the United Kingdom and Germany, where they are looking for portfolios they can buy and manage-out using special purpose vehicles capitalised by secondaries funds. These vehicles have adjusted terms and conditions, reflecting the amount of work still required in relation to the acquired portfolio. This relatively new activity is most helpful to secondaries funds whose investment teams are typically focused exclusively on purchasing secondaries investments. Over time, we would expect these firms to start raising their own funds as one US managing-out company has already. Beyond this, expect traditional secondaries funds building their own managing-out capabilities to fill the gap!
- *Secondaries market developing in areas where currently the primary market is growing; for example, in Asia and South America.* A prerequisite for this will be a sufficiently mature primary market for potential sellers to actually have anything to sell and for potential buyers to see enough to want to buy!

Secondaries in alternative assets are simply a prerequisite for the growth of this increasingly popular asset class to be able to continue. Although, due to the nature of alternative assets, it will not be feasible to have an open market for these products, transparency and ease of transaction will improve somewhat as alternative assets become an increasingly important part of institutional portfolios. In the United States and Europe, where secondaries of private equity investments are more established, we may well see other secondaries products developing. A fund focused on secondaries of hedge fund positions comes to mind, as liquidity periods for hedge funds with 'longer' strategies and/or a private equity focus are lengthening.

Chapter 8

# Beyond financial engineering: Value-added investing

Oliver Markl
*Monitor Clipper Partners*

The year 2005 was the strongest ever for buyouts. Global fund-raising amounted to US$106bn and totalled nearly twice as much as the previous year. Completed buyouts reached a volume of US$260bn and eclipsed 2004's record of US$151bn. While these numbers indicate that the buyout industry is enjoying great success, the attractiveness of the traditional business model of buyout firms is being reduced by a number of adverse trends.

Funds today have seen the increased supply of capital and an environment of easy credit drive up purchase price multiples. At the same time, previous advantages, such as access to sophisticated financial engineering and proprietary deal flow, have eroded in the onslaught of competition. Today's funds must develop new means of increasing the value of their portfolio companies.

Top private equity firms now seek to add value through hands-on involvement in the operations of their portfolio companies. Successful buyout funds bring a variety of best practices to their buyouts, which helps improve their operational performance, thereby increasing investment value.

This chapter begins with a brief overview of how the industry has changed in recent years and then examines what techniques buyout funds are using to help their portfolio companies succeed operationally. Next we look at how the structure and focus of the buyout fund itself can create advantages leading towards better performance of portfolio companies. Finally, we examine how strategic alliances can create a competitive advantage for buyout funds.

## Threats to the traditional LBO fund business model

Since the late 1990s, the competitive environment for traditional buyout funds has deteriorated as a number of adverse factors have gained strength. These factors include the growing supply of capital – both equity and debt – which force buyout firms to pay higher prices, as well as the declining ability of buyout funds to differentiate themselves from the competition.

### Growing supply of capital

The European Private Equity and Venture Capital Association (EVCA) quarterly activity indicator shows that total funds raised for European buyouts in the first three quarters of 2005 reached €50.9bn (US$69.2bn), which compares to €17.3bn (US$19.5bn) for 2003 and

€17.3bn (US$21.5bn) for 2004. On a global basis,[1] leveraged buyout (LBO) funds raised US$106bn in 2005 compared to US$56bn in 2004, and surpassed the previous record of US$78bn set in 2000.

This pace is expected to continue in 2006, and increasing demand is expected from European institutional investors in particular; these investors have been slower than their US counterparts in opening up and raising their fund allocations to alternative investments. According to the Russell survey of alternative investing, European institutions' allocation to private equity was at 1.9 per cent in 1996 and grew to 4.5 per cent by 2005: in contrast, North American institutional investors had 7 per cent of their assets allocated to private equity in 2005. As return expectations in the public equity and bond markets remain low, and top private equity continues to generate stellar returns, the pressure on European investors to invest more in private equity will grow.

## Higher leverage multiples

As the amount of equity capital available has grown substantially, so has liquidity in the credit markets: 2004 and 2005 have seen the highest levels of leverage since the late 1990s. Debt multiples reached 4.8× EBITDA (earnings before interest, taxes, depreciation and amortisation)[2] in the second quarter of 2005, compared to 3.6× in 2001.

A factor contributing to this increase in leverage is the increasing acceptance of 'staple financings', where the investment bank running an auction offers an aggressive financing package (which is 'stapled' to the selling memorandum) to all participants in the auction. In fact, the supply of credit is currently so loose that it is not uncommon for private equity firms to take on less debt in a transaction than is actually offered to them by their financing sources.

## Higher purchase prices

Between 2001 and the second quarter of 2005, purchase price multiples grew from 6.1× to 7.3× EBITDA, which corresponds exactly to the increase in debt multiples over the same period. Therefore 100 per cent of the incremental leverage provided to buyout firms during this period was passed on to the benefit of sellers in the form of increased purchase prices. While buyout firms still put the same amount of equity to work on the average transaction, the increase in debt implies that these firms are willing to take on increased risk and lesser returns than four years ago.

The large increase in the amount of capital chasing after the same transactions in recent years has led buyout firms to continuously reduce their return expectations. At the same time, a benign credit environment and surplus liquidity in the debt markets have led to higher debt multiples in LBO transactions. These two factors have resulted in a continual increase in LBO purchase price multiples since 2001.

## Complex financial engineering now a commodity

The 1982 acquisition of the US company Gibson Greeting by Wesray Capital was a seminal moment for the private equity industry. Wesray Capital, which was founded by former Secretary of the Treasury William Simon, acquired Gibson Greeting from RCA for US$81m, of which only US$1m was equity-funded. The company went public one year later for US$290m and William Simon turned a personal investment of US$330,000 into US$66m.

While private equity has been around since the 1970s – and indeed KKR was founded in 1976 – the Wesray transaction helped fuel a buyout boom that lasted for the rest of the 1980s. The key value driver of LBOs during this period was sophisticated financial engineering, the secrets of which were closely guarded by the top players in the industry. These secrets have now become commodities as all participants in the buyout sector, as well as the investment banks advising them, have mastered issues of structuring and financial engineering. This evolution is best illustrated by the rise of the staple financing, as previously described: from the perspective of the bank handling the auction, it in effect can take financial engineering skills entirely out of equation.

### Proprietary deal flow diminished

Another key differentiating factor of the first buyout boom was access to proprietary deal flow. Helped by the relative scarcity of the private equity landscape up to the mid-1990s, well-connected principals were able to routinely secure transactions with minimal competition and on attractive conditions. Today, buyout firms still make claims as to the strength of their proprietary deal flow, whereas in reality truly proprietary deals are few and far between, and the scope for 'arbitraging' – that is, buying companies below their fair price – is very low. The substantial increase in the number of players in the buyout field, the increased sophistication of sellers, and investment banks' increased efficiency in running sell-side auctions have all contributed to making the auction process the standard transaction mechanism in the buyout field, leading to more efficient – and higher – pricing of companies put up for sale.

### Expectation for declining returns

The trends illustrated above result in an increase in the competitive pressure on buyout firms and in an erosion of their traditional areas of differentiation, all pointing towards a deterioration of the competitive environment. In addition, the industry is exposed to the threats of tightening credits possibly combined with a downturn in the economy, and can no longer rely on multiple expansion driven by rising stock markets. As a result, private equity firms are expected to show diminishing returns in the future, on both an absolute basis and compared with public equity markets. The 2005 Russell survey on alternative investing confirms that the expected median three-year return for the European asset class has dropped to 10.5 per cent, compared to a 12.4 per cent annual performance of the Cambridge Associates Private Equity Index for the period 1995–2004.

## LBO key value drivers

After discussing the various reasons contributing to an expected decline in returns in the buyout industry, we now turn to examining what avenues of value creation are left, and how these can best be utilised to achieve above-average returns in such a competitive environment. The key sources of value creation in an LBO are leverage, multiple expansion

Exhibit 8.1

**Typical LBO IRRs under different scenarios**

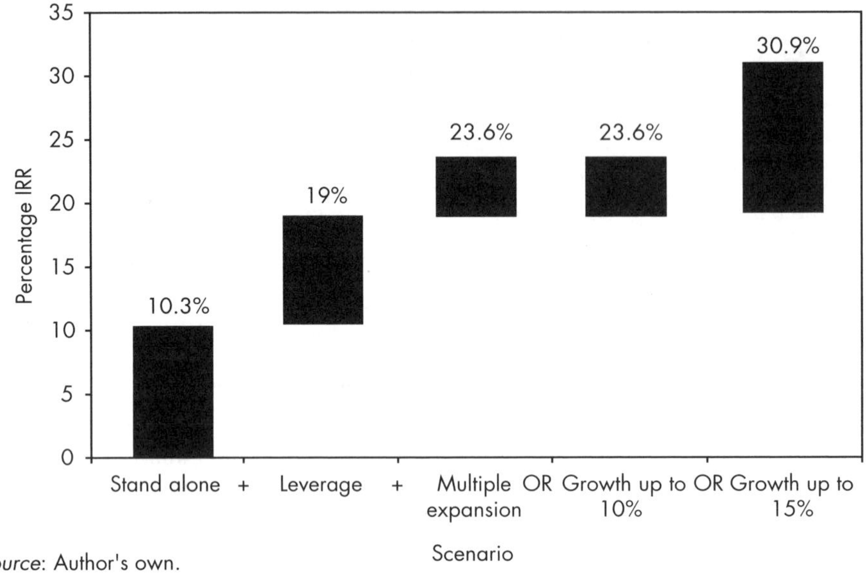


*Source*: Author's own.

and operating performance. The following example illustrates the relative importance of these drivers.

If we acquire a business which is growing EBITDA at 7 per cent per annum without using leverage at the average market multiple of 7.8×, hold it for five years and sell it again at the same multiple, our IRR will be 10.3 per cent – of which 7 per cent corresponds to the increased EBITDA at exit and 3.3 per cent to the amount of cash generated during the holding period. If we execute the same transaction but leverage the company at the average debt multiple of 4.8×, our IRR will increase to 19 per cent. Assuming this LBO benefits from rising markets and obtains a one-turn increase in the exit multiple to 8.3× the IRR would grow to 23.6 per cent. If we exclude the assumption of a multiple expansion, but instead assume that management is able to increase the company's EBITDA growth rate to 10 per cent, the IRR grows to 23.6 per cent as well; and if management succeeds in driving the growth rate to 15 per cent per annum, the IRR shoots up to 30.9 per cent. (Exhibit 8.1 summarises this analysis.)

In summary, the single biggest driver of value in an LBO is the ability to improve a company's operational performance. While leverage is a commodity available to all buyout firms, and multiple expansion is an externality as it depends mostly on stock market performance and the ability of the bank handling the auction at exit, improving a company's operational performance is very much dependent on the buyout firm's skills. Unsurprisingly, successful buyout firms are better at working this value driver, as shown in the study mentioned in the next sub-section.

## Focus on company outperformance

A 2005 study[3] of 11 leading private equity firms, all with better-than-average track records, showed that the main source of value creation in their portfolio was company outperformance. The other factors that were isolated and tested were overall stock market appreciation, sector appreciation and the effect of financial leverage and arbitrage. Company outperformance was the main source of value in two-thirds of the deals in the sample.[4]

Another study[5] shows that buyout firms have recognised over time the importance of increasing their focus on their portfolio companies' operations. Exhibit 8.2 shows how operational improvements have contributed to an increasing portion of average buyout returns over time.

These factors evidence a fundamental shift in the focus of the buyout industry: in the first wave of the 1980s, competitors focused on removing capital market inefficiencies. While some of those opportunities remain as evidenced by the healthy pace of public-to-private transactions, buyout firms are now shifting their focus to reducing operational inefficiencies in their portfolio companies. How do they do it?

## Utilising best practices

Buyout firms have developed a variety of approaches aimed at giving their portfolio companies an edge. The most widespread components of best practice include a thorough due diligence process – in particular at the commercial and strategic levels – putting in place a

Exhibit 8.2

**Components of average buyout returns[6]**

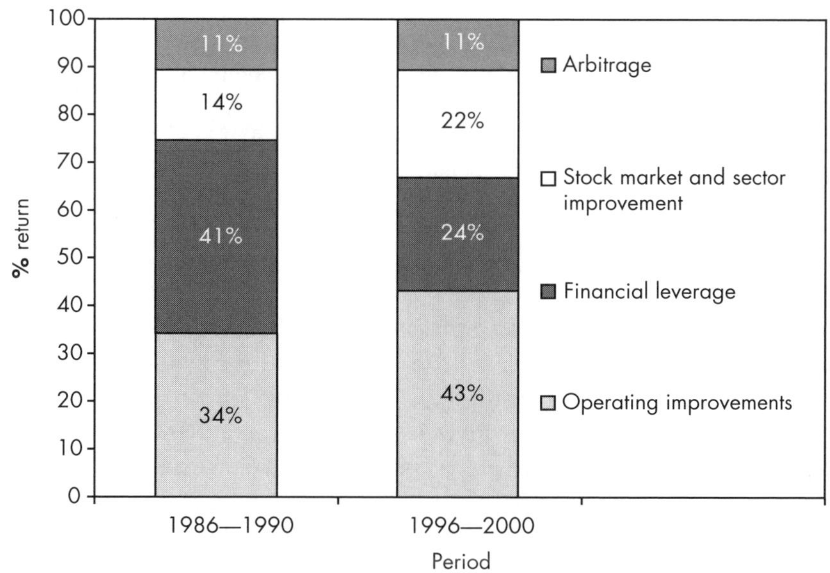


*Source*: *Strategies for Successful Buyout Investing*, Asset Alternatives, 2001.

management compensation system that creates an alignment of interests between management and the buyout firm, and a focus on identifying strong management teams (replacing weaker ones if required). Approaches that are not as consistently employed but which are shown to have a high impact on a portfolio company's performance include the creation of a detailed blueprint for the strategic and operational development of the company over a three to five-year period, and a substantial time commitment by the buyout firms' deal executives in the first year of the investment period.

The following methods are commonly used by buyout funds, although impact varies considerably based on how and to what extent the practices are implemented.

## Due diligence

Commercial and strategic due diligence has evolved a long way from a formality required by lending banks as part of their credit approval process to a key tool for buyout firms to help identify areas of risk and potential upsides in a company's operations or strategic environment. Beyond guiding investment decisions and helping determine a fair price, extensive due diligence allows buyout firms to thoroughly understand their new investment early on, and structure a plan for operational success before the deal has been signed. Proactive firms at this stage utilise their competitive advantages for insights into the industry and begin tackling some of the practices described below, such as creating an action plan and enlisting the support of senior industry experts. By the time the ink has dried on the sale and purchase agreement, these firms are already working hard to add value to their new investment.

## Upgrade management

All private equity firms recognise the importance of having a top quality management team in place, and most pride themselves on their ability to identify top managers. However the key factor[7] that appears to differentiate successful private equity firms is their ability and willingness to change the management team. Successful firms are more likely to replace managers during an investment's life than less successful firms. Even more telling, in 83 per cent of the best deals but only 33 per cent of the worst deals, buyout firms strengthened the management team *before* the closing of the transaction.

## Incentivise management

Most buyout firms systematically put in place a meaningful and focused management compensation package. Such a package can account for more than 10 per cent of fully diluted equity and is generally heavily weighted towards the CEO and a small group of the company's top executives. In addition, this group of executives is strongly encouraged to invest personal money in the deal, or, if relevant, to roll over a large proportion of their personal after-tax proceeds from the original transaction. Solutions need to be tailored to the management team's specific circumstances and should seek to align as much as possible management's incentives with those of the buyout firm – that is, to maximise proceeds at exit.

## Less common best practice differentiators

In addition to the practices listed above – extensive due diligence, new management and correctly aligned management incentives – there are several other steps that add value to the investment through increased operational performance, but which are less systematically applied by buyout firms.

### Creating an action plan

A detailed blueprint created soon after the investment (or, better yet, begun during the due diligence stage), establishes a clear process for how the company's performance will be improved and outlines goals that need to be met. According to the McKinsey study, in 92 per cent of the best performing deals reviewed such an action plan was put in place (versus half as many in the worst deals).[8] Another study[9] found that buyout firms that take an active approach to planning and sequencing initiatives in the first year of their investment outperform others by a two-to-one margin measured on cash return.

### Human capital investment

It is equally critical that buyout firms deploy their human capital to support and push through the action plan. There are two main sources of human capital in a buyout firm.

- *General partners.* Spending more time with portfolio companies allows GPs to cement relationships between company management and buyout executives, to create a consensus on what needs to be done, to allocate responsibilities and to measure performance. GPs' actual time commitment to the investment is a significant source of value. The McKinsey study found that the most successful deals were led by partners who spent more than half their time with the company in the first three months after the investment (versus only 20 per cent of their time in the worst deals) and met almost daily with executives.[10]
- *Senior industry executives.* More recently, buyout firms have started to hire senior industry figures in increasing numbers. Prime examples include Klaus Esser, the former CEO of Mannesmann who is now a partner at the private equity firm General Atlantic Partners; former CEO of GE, Jack Welch, who is now at Clayton, Dubilier, & Rice; and Lou Gerstner, former chairman of IBM, who is now chairman of the Carlyle Group. These 'operating partners' bring their expertise to bear in different roles: as due diligence support, as active board members, as a sounding board for the portfolio company CEO and also as interim executives.

## Organising for success

There are several models that buyout firms have adopted to optimise their ability to follow the best practices described above. Each of these structures creates a competitive advantage, allowing the firm to either develop internal expertise in an area or have privileged access to external expertise. When working with the portfolio company to achieve operational improvements, this expertise provides a clear advantage.

## Industry focus

An increasing number of firms have chosen specialisation, typically by industry sector. Representative buyout firms include Silver Lake Partners (large technology companies), Providence Equity Partners (media and communications), and many others focusing on energy, financial services, retail, etc. Specialisation facilitates a buyout firm's ability to develop deep strategic and operational insights in a sector, to gain an edge in deal sourcing by cultivating potential targets in a focused manner and to develop relationships with a network of potential portfolio company CEOs.

## Product focus

Other types of specialisation are illustrated by turnaround funds and leveraged build-up (LBU) funds. LBUs, pioneered by KKR, are the roll-up of small companies in a similar industry into one loosely organised entity. These companies benefit from the 'parenting advantage' of being part of a larger organisation, similar to the advantages gained by small business units as part of a conglomerate. LBU funds focus on bringing very specific cross-industry technical expertise to bear on their companies – whether via cost-cutting, negotiating with distressed debt holders or utilising their M&A expertise.

## Strategic relationships

Another unique organisational structure involves a strategic relationship between the buyout fund and a consulting firm. Such an affiliation provides a direct link to resources and expertise that are focused solely on operations, providing access to current thinking and tested solutions for increasing operational efficiency. Firms have structured these affiliations in both internal and external ways. Bain Capital and KKR have both set up in-house consulting operations, while firms like Parthenon Capital and Monitor Clipper Partners have established privileged but arms-length relationships with strategy consulting firms Parthenon Group and Monitor Group respectively. To make these models work, much importance is placed on aligning the interests of the buyout firm with those of the consulting arm: typically the latter is rewarded with a material share of the carried interest, or receives a portion of its commercial fees in shares of the portfolio company, or both.

These in-depth relationships with consulting firms provide advantages at every step of the investment process, from qualifying investment opportunities at an early stage by benefiting from the consulting firm's prior experience in the field to identifying strategic buyers. But the biggest gains are made to the actual operational performance of the portfolio company. Often small and mid-market companies do not have access to high-end consulting services on their own – nor would they necessarily be able to take advantage of such resources in an effective manner without the active interface created by the private equity firm. Partnering with a buyout firm with this unusual structure provides a unique opportunity to receive support beyond the traditional scope of smaller companies. The extent of resources that can benefit the portfolio company depends on the expertise of the consulting firm, but would typically include a wide range of cross-industry functional areas such as marketing and branding strategy, pricing strategy, organisational strategy, sales force incentive plans, redesigning manufacturing product flows, identifying new addressable markets and designing market entry strategies.

For instance, in 2002 Monitor Clipper Partners invested in a medium-sized amusement-with-prize machine operator, Codere. On its own, Codere was too small for a high-end consulting engagement, but through Monitor Clipper Partner's relationship with Monitor Group a team was assigned to help with operational improvements. This team would spend 13 man-years setting up and supporting an acquisition methodology, upgrading governance standards, improving the budgeting process and revamping management compensation. As a direct result of these operational improvements, EBITDA increased 58 per cent in under three years. The Monitor team provided support that would have been unattainable without the private equity consulting structure, and the investment performed strongly as a result.

Recently, many buyout funds have chosen to bring on board 'operating principals' as a way to achieve some of the advantages of a consulting relationship in-house. These individuals, who often have a consulting background, are solely focused on improving the performance of portfolio companies rather than splitting their time between evaluating new companies and working with current investments. They bring the advantages of consulting experience without requiring the buyout firm to maintain a formal relationship with a consulting firm.

## Summary

As the private equity industry in Europe and elsewhere has become more competitive in recent years, the traditional model of value creation for buyout funds has lost much of its lustre and it has become necessary for buyout funds to find new ways of creating value.

An influx of capital combined with a benign credit environment and high debt multiples have resulted in inflated purchase prices. Increased competition has diminished buyout funds' ability to access proprietary deal flow, reducing purchases of undervalued companies. Finally, the original lever of value creation for buyouts – financial engineering – is no longer a prized ability but rather a commodity. Private equity funds are therefore under pressure to create greater value, thereby justifying their higher purchase prices, despite being deprived of their traditional means of value creation.

Value-added investing seeks to overcome this issue by creating value through improved operational performance of the portfolio company. Successful funds gain advantage through unique sources of expertise, either internally cultivated or through external partnerships, which they use to guide the purchase and improvement of portfolio companies. They also skilfully use standard (and non-standard) best practices and support their approach with highly skilled human capital resources that buyout funds are uniquely positioned to provide. By utilising these best practices and focusing on improving their portfolio companies' operational performance, top buyout funds can continue to achieve superior returns despite the challenges currently facing the industry.

---

[1] *Private Equity Analyst* (www.privatequityanalyst.com, 23 January 2006).

[2] Standard & Poor's, *Portfolio Management Data*.

[3] Heel, J. and C. Kehoe, 'Why Some Private Equity Firms Do Better Than Others', *McKinsey Quarterly*, Number 1 (2005).

[4] Incidentally, arbitrage was the main source of value in only 5 per cent of transactions, which illustrates the reduced ability of buyout firms to source transactions at a below-market price.

[5] Research Report. 'Strategies for Successful Buyout Investing.' (*Asset Alternatives*, 2001).

[6] As the study was not repeated at a later date, more recent data are not available.

[7] Heel, J. and C. Kehoe, 'Why Some Private Equity Firms Do Better Than Others', *McKinsey Quarterly*, Number 1 (2005).

[8] Ibid.

[9] MacArthur, H. and C. Bierly, 'The New Drill in Private Equity', *Buyouts* (14 November, 2005).

[10] Heel, J. and C. Kehoe, 'Why Some Private Equity Firms Do Better Than Others', *McKinsey Quarterly*, Number 1 (2005).

Chapter 9

# Private equity performance and public equity returns

Didier Guennoc[1]
*EVCA and Origo Management*

## Introduction

Measuring the performance of the private equity asset class is not an easy task. As a consequence, managing the risk relating to a portfolio comprising private equity funds also represents a challenge. This chapter discusses the difficulties encountered comparing private equity returns with public equity returns. Due to a lack of data, but also to challenges inherent to how returns are measured for private equity assets, different routes have to be explored in order to achieve a meaningful comparison. However, it will become apparent that there are currently no definite answers regarding the size of the premium for private equity compared to quoted stocks, or the correlation between private and quoted equities. Therefore, this chapter ends with a brief overview of the consequences of this situation on the risk management of portfolios comprising private equity assets.

The difficulties in performance measurement for this asset class relate to the following factors.

- There is no continuous market providing prices for private equity assets. Although some private equity funds are listed on quoted markets, most of these investment vehicles are unquoted.
- Transactions in fund shares occur only occasionally, and they are not always representative of the value of the funds.
- Because fund managers have significant discretion regarding the timing of cash flows between a fund and its investors, the industry uses performance indicators that are not directly comparable with other measurement tools used for quoted assets.

In other words, the private equity asset class is characterised by a high degree of illiquidity. This illiquidity is at the root of the difficulties encountered in measuring the performance of private equity and managing the risk attached to it. Therefore, and before proceeding further, it is important to clearly define the concept of illiquidity. For an investor, illiquidity means that:

- it will take time to turn private equity assets into cash; and
- the process will be costly – that is, transaction costs will be relatively high.

Investors, practitioners, consultants, academics and other stakeholders have focused their attention on performance measurement for some time. The recurrent question relates to the existence and to the size of the premium that private equity should produce in comparison with quoted securities (shares and bonds). The first section of this chapter presents the difficulties encountered when trying to answer this question.

The second section discusses the main solutions advocated by academics and practitioners in order to conduct a meaningful comparison. The section does not contain a full review of the literature but presents the main solutions applied and also their results.[2] Building a portfolio is not only about the risk/return of each of its components, it is also a matter of correlation between the returns of its different assets. Therefore, this section also looks at the correlation between private equity returns and quoted security returns. While in the 1990s it was commonly accepted that private equity returns were not correlated with those of quoted stocks, this belief has been questioned after the burst of the internet bubble.

Interim valuations made by general partners are at the heart of the problem of performance measurement and correlation. The adoption by the industry of fair value is addressed in the third section of this chapter.

The concluding section deals specifically with risk management. This topic has recently gained in importance due partly to the regulatory pressure coming from banks and insurance companies' regulators (Basel II and the future Solvency Directive). Risk management should be understood at two levels: first, managing the risk within the private equity portfolio; and, secondly, managing the risk of a portfolio consisting of different asset classes where private equity is only one component among others. Here again, the illiquid aspect of the asset class plays a central role.

## Comparing private and public equity returns: A difficult exercise

Stakeholders are generally familiar with the returns of private equity as presented by the European Private Equity and Venture Capital Association (EVCA) and Thomson Financial (see Exhibit 9.1). The most recent data show an internal rate of returns (IRR) of 9.5 per cent per annum between 1980 and 2004. This figure is 12.3 per cent for the buyout segment and 6 per cent for venture capital.

Exhibit 9.1

### Annualised pooled IRR from inception to 31 December 2004

| | No. of | Pooled | Multiples | | | Multiples (as % of TVPI) | | |
|---|---|---|---|---|---|---|---|---|
| Stage | Funds | IRR | DPI | RVPI | TVPI | DPI | RVPI | TVPI |
| Early-stage | 252 | 0.2 | 0.40 | 0.60 | 1.00 | 40.0 | 60.0 | 100.0 |
| Development | 173 | 8.2 | 0.74 | 0.68 | 1.42 | 52.1 | 47.9 | 100.0 |
| Balanced | 146 | 7.9 | 0.66 | 0.59 | 1.25 | 52.8 | 47.2 | 100.0 |
| **All venture** | **571** | **6.0** | **0.60** | **0.62** | **1.22** | **49.2** | **50.8** | **100.0** |
| Buyouts | 307 | 12.3 | 0.70 | 0.67 | 1.37 | 51.1 | 48.9 | 100.0 |
| Generalist | 78 | 8.7 | 0.98 | 0.37 | 1.35 | 72.6 | 27.4 | 100.0 |
| **All private equity** | **956** | **9.5** | **0.72** | **0.60** | **1.32** | **54.5** | **45.5** | **100.0** |

*Sources*: EVCA; Thomson Financial.

As well as IRR, stakeholders receive information on the multiple achieved by the industry in terms of paid-in capital. At the end of 2004, the distributed to paid-in capital (DPI) was at 0.72 for the full industry, the residual value to paid-in (RVPI) was estimated at 0.60 and consequently the total value to paid-in (TVPI = DPI + RVPI) was 1.32. The right-hand column of the exhibit shows also that, out of this value of 1.32, a little less than 55 per cent has already been distributed to investors while 45 per cent is still unrealised and still in the funds.

Observers with experience of quoted stocks always find it difficult to deal with the returns of the private equity industry as presented in Exhibit 9.1. These difficulties relate to:

- the relative scarcity of data on private equity returns;
- the different methodologies used to measure returns for public equity and private equity; and
- the impact of interim valuations.

## Relative scarcity of data on private equity returns

The first difficulty encountered is the relative scarcity of data on private equity returns. This scarcity is explained by three factors.

- This asset class is relatively young. Data on stock markets extend over a century, but data on private equity returns are available only for four decades for the United States and around two decades in Europe, while data series have only recently started to be built for emerging markets. Most funds have been established in the last decade: for example, of the total amount raised by the European industry between 1984 and 2004, 67 per cent was raised between 1999 and 2004.[3]
- Many practitioners think that the private equity industry is and should stay private, and therefore refuse to take part in surveys covering the industry.
- Returns on private equity assets are only intermittently measured. Because there is no market operating continuously, returns are partially based on periodic valuations performed by general partners. As a consequence, returns cannot be measured on a daily basis like stock market indices. In the best case, returns are made available quarterly.

Despite this relative scarcity of data, returns are made available through different channels. In close collaboration with the EVCA, Thomson Financial provides data on European private equity returns. Moreover, gatekeepers like Cambridge Associates release data on fund returns. Limited partners also occasionally disclose to a larger public or to academics the returns of their investment programmes.[4] However, it is true that the scarcity of data increases when one looks at some specific sub-segments of the industry. With French early-stage funds, for example, there is a relatively small sample in comparison with the full population, which of course raises doubts about the representativeness of the sample.[5]

## Different methodologies used to measure returns for public equity and private equity

The measure of private equity funds' performances is an internal rate of return (IRR) while performance of public equities is measured with a time-weighted return (TWR). The time-weighted return formula is $\bar{R} = ((1 + r_1) * (1 + r_2)\ldots(1 + r_T))^{(1/T)} - 1$. $r_t$ is the periodic return. The IRR is the solution of the following equation:

$$\sum_{t=0}^{T} CF_t (1 + IRR)^{-t} = 0$$

where $CF_t$ are the different cash flows between the investors and the fund.

The IRR calculation is based on the reinvestment assumption of the distributions. In other words, when looking at the IRRs of two funds one can compare the performance of the two funds only if their distributions are reinvested at the same rate shown by the respective IRRs. Unfortunately, this is not the case for private equity funds. As a consequence, one can directly compare the performance of private equity funds only by combining their respective IRRs with their respective multiples (that is, the amount returned divided by the amount invested). This explains why both indicators, IRR and multiples, are used. The IRR is used for private equity and not the TWR because private equity houses, at least for the most common structure (the closed-end fund with a fixed lifetime), control the timing of the cash inflows and outflows. On the other hand, managers of open-end evergreen funds do not control these flows.

The missing reinvestment of distributions also means that private equity returns are not directly comparable with returns calculated from stock market indexes. For example, €100 invested in private equity with a distribution to investors of €120 at the end of the second year and a net asset value estimated at €5 at the end of the fifth year produces an IRR of 11 per cent per annum. If an initial amount of €100 and the resulting proceeds are invested over the same period of time in a stock market index with a time-weighted return of 5 per cent per annum, the investment will result in an amount around 1.28 times higher than the initial capital invested. This multiple is above that for the private equity investment, which is 1.25.

This example also includes one of the trickiest aspects of performance measurement for private equity – estimation of net asset value.

## Impact of interim valuations

Price data on quoted securities can be available on a continuous basis. This is not the case for private equity, which is characterised by holding periods of 10 years or more. It is important to differentiate between the value of the fund itself and the value of the underlying portfolio companies. Meyer and Mathonet (2005) show clearly that the aggregation of the net asset value of each portfolio company is an oversimplified way of assessing the value of an investment's stake in a fund, arguing correctly that this approach ignores material factors such as the undrawn commitments still to be paid into the fund and the quality of the fund manager itself. Both underlying unquoted portfolio companies and stakes in unquoted private equity funds are characterised by non-frequent pricing.

Stakes in private equity funds, at least for the most common structure (unquoted closed-end funds with a fixed lifetime), are not exchanged except in the case of a secondary sale. However, prices agreed in secondary events have to be treated carefully as indicators of the value of the fund. The seller might be confronted with a liquidity crisis, resulting in a discounted price. In those cases, applying valuation methodologies will produce a better estimate of the value of the fund than the price of the actual transaction.

Valuation methodologies also have to be applied to portfolio companies if no substantial new investment has taken place in these companies. When it comes to comparison either between private equity funds or between private equity and quoted securities, applying valuation methodologies raises fundamental questions.

Comparing two private equity funds with substantial assets still unrealised, managed by two different private equity houses, requires an in-depth knowledge of their valuation policy. The more aggressive team in terms of valuation might have the higher interim IRRs but might end up with lower returns than the other team when funds are fully realised. The analysis of historical performance of the industry shows that it takes on average more than six years *after* the inception date of a fund before interim IRRs reasonably equate with final IRR that this fund will effectively produce at the end of its lifetime. This is due to the fact that interim IRRs are based on valuation of net asset value. This dimension is of crucial importance when an investor makes its investment decision based on data for funds at the end of their investment phase.

Moreover, when comparing private equity returns with public equity returns, the use of valuation methodologies might result in stale pricing (that is, the evolution in value is not reported when it occurs but only at a later date). As a consequence, the use of valuation methodologies might translate into overestimated returns and also into an artificially low correlation with other asset classes – two quite disturbing aspects when it comes to asset allocation and risk management.

## Comparing private and public equity returns: The quest for solutions

EVCA and Thomson Financial work on increasing the size of the sample of funds covered in their statistics. Moreover, the implementation of valuation guidelines for the industry (discussed later) should impact on interim valuations. This section focuses on solutions to the problems raised by different methodologies used to measure returns for public versus private equity, and solutions to stale pricing.

### 'Public market equivalent'

The first tentative attempt to reconcile private equity returns with quoted stock returns was initiated by several practitioners during the 1990s. The Bannock, Long, Nickles and Coller methodology[6] is based on the duplication of private equity cash flows on a chosen quoted market index. When a private equity drawdown is made, the same amount is invested in a specific index. When a distribution is made, the same amount is exited from the quoted market index. This methodology, called 'public market equivalent' (or also comparators in Europe), results in IRRs in a given period for quoted stocks that can be compared with IRRs of private equity investment. This methodology is adopted by Thomson Financial and EVCA. Exhibit 9.2 shows the results of this approach for each stage of investment (early-stage, development, buyouts and generalist) and on several indexes (Morgan Stanley Euro, HSBC Small Company Equity and JP Morgan Eurobonds). It can be seen that early-stage has underperformed all indexes, while buyouts have outperformed all indexes. However, it is not possible to gauge if the premium observed for buyout compensates adequately for the risk.

Exhibit 9.2

**Public market equivalent for Europe, funds formed 1980–2004 (annualised pooled IRR since inception to 31 December 2004)**

| Stage | European private equity return | Morgan Stanley Euro Index | HSBC Small Company Index | JP Morgan Eurobonds |
|---|---|---|---|---|
| Early-stage | 0.2 | 0.7 | 8.3 | 9.8 |
| Development | 8.2 | 7.0 | 9.2 | 9.5 |
| Balanced | 7.9 | 3.7 | 9.0 | 9.5 |
| **All venture** | 6.0 | 4.2 | 8.5 | 9.6 |
| Buyouts | 12.3 | –2.0 | 7.1 | 9.6 |
| Generalist | 8.7 | 5.8 | 6.5 | 9.4 |
| **All private equity** | 9.5 | 0.7 | 7.8 | 9.6 |

*Sources*: EVCA; Thomson Financial.

This methodology suffers from several drawbacks.

- When distributions from private equity are huge, it can lead to a negative net asset value on the quoted market index[7] at the end of the studied period.
- The schedule of private equity cash flows is used to determine the investment and the divestment strategy on the quoted market index, which can be seen as an oversimplistic approach. General partners, and not investors, are in control of cash flow timing. They determine the dates of the drawdowns and can, at least to a certain degree, influence the timing of distributions. Moreover, such an approach implies that investors would not use the highest degree of liquidity of quoted securities. However, one should not conclude too hastily that this feature increases artificially the premium of private equity. Exhibit 9.2 shows that the JP Morgan Eurobonds Index has outperformed private equity (an annual IRR of 9.6 per cent compared to 9.5 per cent). This puzzling result raises questions about the attractiveness of the asset class as a whole. However, this can be explained by the underlying methodology. As mentioned earlier, the bulk of the money invested in the asset class had started to flow at the end of the 1990s. According to the public market equivalent methodology that duplicates the private equity cash flows on the quoted index, the bulk of investments in the bond index took place post the end of the 1990s, which is a period characterised by a decrease in interest rates, which impacted positively on the performance of bonds while private equity assets were still not producing distributions. The bursting of the internet bubble and the writing off of a significant part of venture capital portfolios in Europe are legitimate elements that negatively impacted the performance of the asset class in comparison with other assets. However, it is also true that the J-curve phenomenon, which describes the fact that private equity managers must wait several years before any distribution can be made, impacts artificially on this comparison. During this phase of non-distribution, the

results of the comparison will depend significantly on the degree of conservatism involved in interim valuations made by general partners.
- The quoted market index chosen to conduct the comparison should match the risk of the private equity asset in order to conclude that a higher IRR for private equity actually corresponds to an outperformance and not to normal compensation for a higher risk.

Despite its drawbacks, this methodology has inspired several researchers. For example, Kaplan and Schoar[8] studied 746 funds (although not specified, most were probably US entities) in comparison with the S&P 500 over the period 1980–2001. They found that the pubic market equivalent, net of fees and carried interest and expressed in their document as a multiple, was 1.21 for VC funds (outperformance vis-à-vis the S&P 500) and 0.93 for buyout funds (underperformance vis-à-vis the S&P 500). Kaserer and Diller[9] used a similar approach (modified because they calculated time-weighted returns for private equity and compared them with quoted markets time-weighted returns; this was done by reinvesting private equity distributions in quoted market indexes). Their analysis covered several samples (the biggest represented 263 European funds). Funds with vintage years starting from 1989 and which could be considered at the end of their lifecycle outperformed the JPM European Government Index and the MSCI Europe. However, underperformance was observed when including funds raised prior to 1989.

## Using quoted indexes to estimate the 'real' VC return

Another route to estimating 'real' private equity returns – that is, a return that does not suffer from stale pricing – is to use econometric models. The underlying assumption is that private equity returns are dependent on the overall economic environment, which can be adequately represented by a stock market index. An econometric model is then constructed in order to estimate the real return with the stock market index being the independent variable. This approach has been followed by Chen, Baierl and Kaplan[10], who used the S&P 500 and data on 148 liquidated VC funds (although not mentioned, probably mostly US funds) over the period 1960–99. Due to a high variance of annual VC returns, they concluded that compounded average annual VC return is underperforming against the quoted US Small-Cap Stocks and comparable to the S&P 500 return.

Artus and Teïletche[11] used a similar approach, determining the 'real' VC return for European funds using the MSCI Europe Index for the period 1994–2003. They deduced from their analysis outperformance of venture capital compared with quoted bonds and equities. Although this result seems to contradict the survey conducted by EVCA and Thomson Financial where VC outperformed only the Morgan Stanley Euro Index but not the HSBC Small Company Index and the JP Morgan Eurobonds (see Exhibit 9.2), the results do not actually conflict. While Artus and Teïletche's study shows arithmetic averages, EVCA and Thomson Financial's results are pooled IRRs, which take into account the relative size of the cash flows. It should be noted that Artus and Teïletche tried with limited success to use their methodology on buyout returns.

## A difficult benchmark to duplicate

As a conclusion of this short examination of the main solutions offered by academics and stakeholders to comparing private equity returns with public equity returns, it appears that there are no easy answers. Moreover, partial results contradict each other. More importantly, comparisons with quoted stock returns do not take into account that it is impossible to buy the private equity index, or at least it is more difficult to duplicate, than reproducing a quoted securities index. Because funds are closed-end vehicles (some of them are only on invitation), an investor might see his or her investment choice limited, leading to serious deviations of the future returns of a private equity programme from the results of the broader index. This constrained choice, plus limited liquidity of the assets, mean that portfolio building is crucial in the management of the risk attached to a private equity programme.

## Impact of valuation methodologies on performance measurement

In March 2005, EVCA together with the British Venture Capital Association (BVCA) and the *Association Française des Investisseurs en Capital* (AFIC) released the *International Private Equity and Venture Capital Valuation Guidelines*.[12] These guidelines are now endorsed by 30 venture capital and private equity associations worldwide who advocate the use of fair value. Fair value is defined as the amount for which an asset could be exchanged between knowledgeable, willing parties in an arm's-length transaction.

If the industry complies fully with these guidelines, it might translate into a reduction of stale pricing, leading to an easier comparison between private and public equity. However, reporting to investors also has a strong commercial aspect attached to it – think no further than overstatement of net asset value. It is also true that conservatism is advocated by players in the industry. These private equity houses prefer to report a value prior to exit that is lower than the effective price they will receive. Moreover, the intellectual challenge of determining the evolution of fair value of early-stage companies should not be underestimated. It is currently too early to undertake an impact analysis of the guidelines on private equity returns and to determine which effect will be the stronger.

## Comparison of the returns of an illiquid versus a liquid asset class: What does it mean in terms of risk management?

Risk management can be divided into two categories:

- the management of risk within the private equity portfolio; and
- the management of risk within a portfolio of assets that includes private equity.

For the second category of risk management, two approaches can be followed by an investor. The first consists of ensuring that other assets will be liquid enough to cover liabilities and potential future losses, and then the investor can devote a small percentage of his or her total assets to private equity. The second approach involves having a significant share of the total assets invested in private equity (such as 15 per cent) and determining the degree of correlation between private equity returns and the returns of other assets. Measuring this degree of correlation first requires being able to compare returns. As mentioned above, the comparison between private and public equity is not easy. Here again academics and practitioners have looked at the issue.

Chen, Baierl and Kaplan[13] determined the correlation between VC returns and the S&P 500 as being 0.04, which is extremely low. Artus and Teïletche[14] found a similar low correlation between European VC returns and the JP Morgan European Government Bond Index, but estimated a higher correlation with quoted equities (MSCI Europe (equity)) at 0.502. Kaserer and Diller[15] confirmed the low correlation of European private equity returns with the JP Morgan European Government Bond Index but found a modest correlation with the MSCI Europe (equity) index estimated at 0.13. Woodward[16] presented a correlation of both US venture capital and buyout returns with the Wilshire 5000 index (equity) superior to 0.5.

Finally Ljungqvist and Richardson[17], basing their study on the capital asset pricing model,[18] calculated the average beta of VC funds at 1.12 and of buyout funds at 1.08, confirming a significant covariation. Woodward[19] estimated the beta to be higher for VC returns, reaching 2.0. These results indicate that the outperformance observed by several studies should be considered as alpha but also as a normal payment of the systematic risk.

Not surprisingly, the results regarding the correlation between private equity and quoted securities do not lead to definite conclusions. Here again it is important to read those data through the filter of the practicalities of a private equity programme.

Ultimately, risk management should secure a reasonable final return. This should be undertaken primarily during the portfolio construction, understood as the proper mix between the different segments that constitute the private equity industry, and also during the due diligence performed on each candidate fund. Information available gives sufficient insight on the differences between the two main segments, venture capital and buyout, to be able to determine the appropriate balance between these two categories. Investors with a lower resistance to risk will overweight the buyout segment. One important feature of the asset class is the relative stability of general partners' performance across time. Due diligence aims at assessing if the current team still has the potential to replicate previous returns.

Moreover, once the commitment is made, monitoring should rapidly detect difficulties with the overriding need being to determine when realisation can be achieved and what would be the cash that can be extracted from an investee fund turning sour – that is, the degree of illiquidity of that specific investment. Another tool is also mobilised by investors: secondary investments. Through secondary positions investors can modify the composition of their portfolio in order to correct their diversification or to modify the cash flow pattern of their investment programme. However, if this tool is an efficient one on the buy side, it can be extremely expensive on the sell side.

## Conclusion

The illiquidity of the private equity asset class, its relative youth and the still conflicting results regarding its risk/return profile and its correlation with other asset classes increase the cost of entry for a potential new investor. Skill is required in order to build an efficient private equity programme.

As time goes by, one can hope that with more data made available to academics a deeper knowledge will be shared with a broader audience. However, even if this improvement occurs, one should keep in mind that future investors will still be confronted with a high diversity of returns among general partners. Selection skills are crucial in order to meet a targeted return while managing the risk attached to a private equity programme.

## References

Artus, P. and J. Teïletche, 'Asset Allocation and European Private Equity: A First Approach Using Aggregated Data' in *Performance Measurement and Asset Allocation for European Private Equity Funds* (EVCA, 2004: http://www.evca.com).

Chen, P., G. T. Baierl and P. D. Kaplan, 'Venture Capital and Its Role in Strategic Asset Allocation', *Journal of Portfolio Management* (Winter 2002).

Emery, K., 'Private Equity Risk and Reward: Assessing the Stale Pricing Problem', *Journal of Private Equity* (Spring 2003).

Grabenwarter, U. and T. Weidig, *Exposed to the J-curve: Understanding and Managing Private Equity Fund Investments* (London: Euromoney Books, 2005).

Jones, C. M. and M. Rhodes-Kropf, 'The Price of Diversifiable Risk in Venture Capital and Private Equity', Columbia University, Working paper (2004).

Kaplan, S. N. and A. Schoar, 'Private Equity Performance: Returns, Persistence and Capital Flows', article submitted to the *Journal of Finance* (2004).

Kaserer, C. and C. Diller, 'European Private Equity Funds: A Cash Flow Based Performance Analysis' in *Performance Measurement and Asset Allocation For European Private Equity Funds* (EVCA, 2004: http://www.evca.com).

Ljungqvist, A. and M. Richardson, *The Cash Flow, Return and Risk Characteristics Of Private Equity* (Social Science Research Network, 2003 downloadable at http://www.ssrn.com).

Mathonet, P-Y. and T. Meyer, *Beyond the J-curve: Managing a Portfolio of Venture Capital and Private Equity Funds* (Chichester: John Wiley and Sons, 2005).

Rouvinez, C., 'Beating the Public Market', 21 *Private Equity International* (December 2003/January 2004).

Swensen, D. F., *Pioneering Portfolio Management: An Unconventional Approach to Institutional Investment* (New York: The Free Press, 2000).

Woodward, S. E., *Measuring Risk and Performance for Private Equity* (Sand Hill Econometrics, draft of 11 August 2004, http://www.sandhillecon.com).

Woodward, S. E. and R. E. Hall, *Benchmarking the Returns to Venture* (Sand Hill Econometrics, 2003, http://www.sandhillecon.com).

---

[1] This paper represents the personal opinion of the author and does not necessarily reflect the views of EVCA or Origo Management.

[2] A review of the literature can be found in Grabenwarter and Weidig, *Exposed to the J-curve: Understanding and Managing Private Equity Fund Investments* (London: Euromoney Books, 2005) and in Woodward S. E., *Measuring Risk and Performance for Private Equity* (Sand Hill Econometrics, draft of 11 August 2004, http://www.sandhillecon.com).

[3] Source: *EVCA Yearbooks*.

[4] While investors might have to disclose data following application of the Freedom of Information Act (FOIA), others, like the European Bank for Reconstruction and Development (EBRD), release data in order to increase the diffusion of market information.

[5] This aspect is often debated between stakeholders. From a pure statistical point of view, one should however keep in mind that the representativeness of a sample is not only related to its size. A small sample structured according to the characteristics of the overall population will provide better quality information than a larger sample with characteristics not corresponding to those of the overall population.

[6] For more explanation on the BLNC methodology, see for example *2004 Investment Benchmark Report: European Private Equity*, Thomson Financial.

[7] In order to solve this difficulty, Rouvinez (2003/2004) suggests a modified methodology that is called a 'public market equivalent plus' where duplicated distributions are adjusted in order to have similar net asset values at the end of the period both in private equity and on the quoted stock market.

[8] Kaplan, S. N. and A. Schoar, 'Private Equity Performance: Returns, Persistence and Capital Flows', article submitted to the *Journal of Finance* (2004).

[9] Kaserer, C. and C. Diller, 'European Private Equity Funds: A Cash Flow Based Performance Analysis' in *Performance Measurement and Asset Allocation For European Private Equity Funds* (EVCA, 2004: http://www.evca.com).

[10] Chen, P., G. T. Baierl and P. D. Kaplan, 'Venture Capital and Its Role in Strategic Asset Allocation', *Journal of Portfolio Management* (Winter 2002).

[11] Artus, P. and J. Teïletche, 'Asset Allocation and European Private Equity: A First Approach Using Aggregated Data' in *Performance Measurement and Asset Allocation for European Private Equity Funds* (EVCA, 2004: http://www.evca.com).

[12] See the text at http://www.privateequityvaluation.com, including the latest from the IPEV Valuation Board, which is charged with monitoring application of the guidelines.

[13] Chen, P., G. T. Baierl and P. D. Kaplan, 'Venture Capital and Its Role in Strategic Asset Allocation', *Journal of Portfolio Management* (Winter 2002).

[14] Artus, P. and J. Teïletche, 'Asset Allocation and European Private Equity: A First Approach Using Aggregated Data' in *Performance Measurement and Asset Allocation for European Private Equity Funds* (EVCA, 2004: http://www.evca.com).

[15] Kaserer, C. and C. Diller, 'European Private Equity Funds: A Cash Flow Based Performance Analysis' in *Performance Measurement and Asset Allocation For European Private Equity Funds* (EVCA, 2004: http://www.evca.com).

[16] Woodward, S. E., *Measuring Risk and Performance for Private Equity* (Sand Hill Econometrics, draft of 11 August 2004, http://www.sandhillecon.com).

[17] Ljungqvist, A. and M. Richardson, *The Cash Flow, Return and Risk Characteristics Of Private Equity* (Social Science Research Network, 2003 downloadable at http://www.ssrn.com).

[18] The capital asset pricing model determines the periodic return of an asset (i) ($r_{it}$ is understood as the excess return over the risk-free rate) as equal to the return of the market $r_{mt}$ (here, again, the excess return of the risk-free rate) multiplied by the factor $\beta_i$ that capture the systematic risk – that is, the covariation between the return of the asset (i) and the return of the market, plus an excess return $\alpha_i$ ($r_{it} = \alpha_i + \beta_i r_{mt}$).

[19] Woodward, S. E., *Measuring Risk and Performance for Private Equity* (Sand Hill Econometrics, draft of 11 August 2004, http://www.sandhillecon.com).

Chapter 10

# Measuring private equity fund performance: the limited partner perspective

André Frei and Michael Studer
*Partners Group*

While most private equity practitioners use internal rate of returns (IRRs) to measure performance, global investment performance standards (GIPS) promulgated by the CFA Institute encourage the use of time-weighted returns (TWRs) in certain situations.

In this chapter, both of these performance measures are analysed, pros and cons of each are highlighted and the prerequisites for meaningful statistics are identified. The two measures are also applied to a hypothetical private equity fund and to the actual private equity market. Finally, an alternative way to present performance is proposed, and two different methods to benchmark private equity using public equity market data are discussed.

## Private equity performance measures

The limited partnership structure of most private equity (PE) fund investments gives rise to irregular cash flow streams that are a hallmark of private equity. In such partnerships, limited partners (LPs) make a commitment to invest over time rather than via an upfront investment. The committed capital is drawn as the general partner (GP) that manages the fund identifies interesting investment opportunities. Thus, the LPs provide capital to the fund in numerous tranches, the precise timing of which is not known at the time of the commitment.

As investments are realised over time, proceeds are distributed to investors. The timing and magnitude of these distributions is also a priori. This portfolio building and liquidation process results in a cash flow stream from LPs to the fund and back (drawdowns and distributions), leading to a highly variable and unpredictable investment exposure. Exhibit 10.1 illustrates the cash flows and the remaining net asset value (NAV) of a hypothetical PE fund investment.

To assess the quality of investments, most investors prefer a single performance figure ('the IRR is 13.0 per cent') to cash flow patterns. The two most common measures are the IRR and TWR, both of which will be discussed in more detail below. Because most people are familiar with IRR, the focus will be on the TWR and its applications to PE.

### Internal rate of return

The most commonly used performance measure for private equity is the IRR. Often the IRR is measured from the first date of an investment until the evaluation date and is referred to as the since-inception IRR (SI-IRR). The IRR is defined as the discount rate that equates the net

Exhibit 10.1
**Illustration of the cash flows of an individual (hypothetical) PE fund**

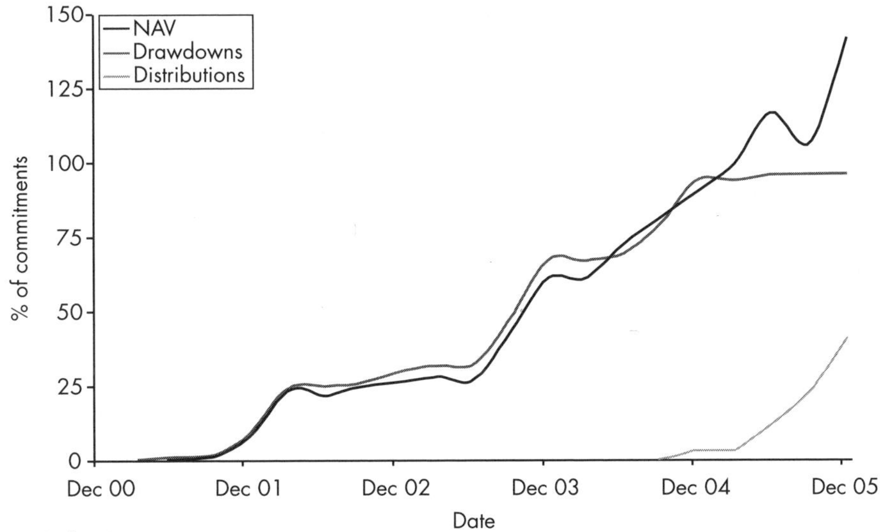


*Source*: Authors' own.

present value (NPV) of the cash outflows, inflows and the final unrealised value[1] of an investment. Practitioners should be aware that IRRs are non-additive (in particular, pooled average IRRs are typically different from capital-weighted IRRs), and that there may be more than one solution to the IRR equation.

Exhibit 10.2 shows the development over quarters of the SI-IRR of the cash flow stream illustrated in Exhibit 10.1. For each date we calculate the IRR of the fund since inception, using the NAV on that date as a final positive cash flow. One observes negative IRRs in the first few years and a significant increase of the IRR thereafter. This IRR development is typical for PE funds and is known as the J-curve.[2] The total multiple or cumulative net cash flows can also be used to illustrate the J-curve over time. Taking an example from Exhibit 10.2, the fund has shown an SI-IRR of 4.7 per cent in December 2004 and 13.3 per cent in June 2005. The dotted line illustrates how the IRR of this fund could develop until liquidation in 2010.

The J-curve phenomenon has a very important implication for performance measurement: early performance comparison of PE investments is difficult and often not indicative for final performance. This statement holds for IRRs and for other performance measures applied to immature PE investments.

## Time-weighted returns

The return, volatility and correlation of traditional portfolios are often measured with the time-weighted return (TWR). Time-weighted returns for investments with interim cash flows can be defined most simply as follows:

$$\sum_{t=0}^{T} CF_t \left(1+IRR\right)^{-t} = 0$$

Exhibit 10.2

**Development of the SI-IRR for the cash flows shown in Exhibit 10.1**

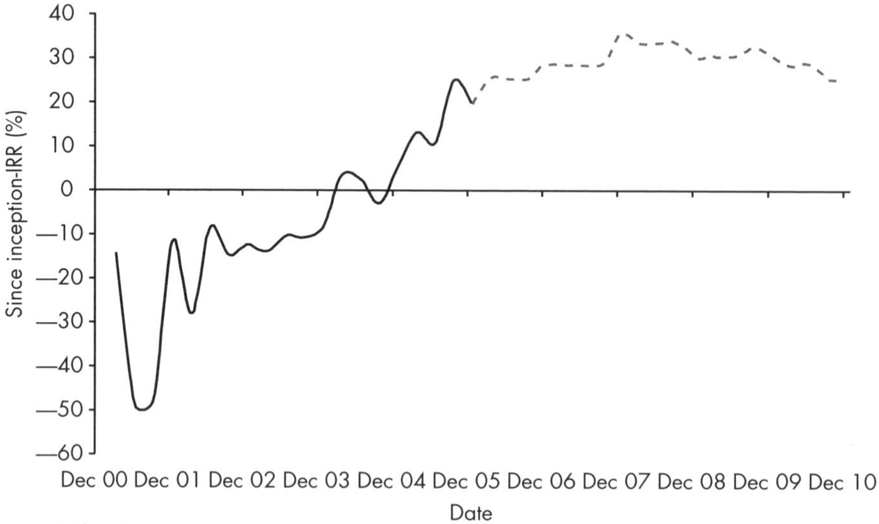


*Source*: Authors' own.

$NAV_t$ is the end residual value, $D_t$ is cumulative distributions over the period, $NAV_{t-1}$ is the residual value at the beginning and $DD_t$ is the paid-in capital over the period. It is important to note that TWRs of individual funds suffer significantly from stale price effects (funds revalue their portfolios infrequently) and that TWRs are highly sensitive to the accounting convention chosen. Although the infrequent valuation of PE investments does not impact on the final IRR of the investment, it may distort TWRs as well as volatility and correlation figures calculated for a PE investment.

As an alternative to the above definition of the TWR, the Original Dietz Method can be applied. The key assumption of this method is that cash flows occur at the mid-point of the period. Therefore, all cash flows are assigned a weight of one-half for the period in which they occur:

$$\text{Original Dietz method: } TWR_t = \frac{NAV_t - NAV_{t-1} - \left(DD_t - D_t\right)}{NAV_{t-1} + \frac{1}{2}\left(DD_t - D_t\right)}$$

Cash flows during the quarter are frequent in private equity, therefore it is also possible to calculate quarterly IRRs. Note that for example Thomson Venture Economics calculates periodic IRRs on a quarterly basis to generate a PE return index.

**GIPS give no clear instruction whether to use TWRs or IRRs**

The investment performance council of the venture capital and PE sub-committee of the global investment performance standards (GIPS)[3] argues that:

> … while the GIPS Private Equity Standards advocate that the IRR is the most accurate measure of performance for an individual private equity manager, it may not be

Exhibit 10.3

**TWRs based on the cash flows in Exhibit 10.1 (above) and comparison of the development of TWR versus SI-IRR (below)**

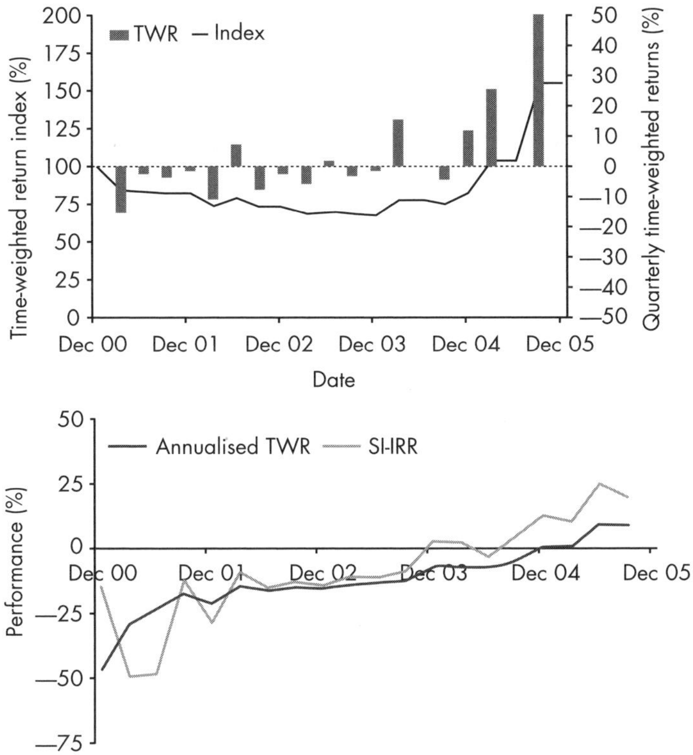


*Source*: Authors' own.

so at higher levels of aggregation. In the case where an investor, for example, a limited partner, is trying to calculate the return at a wider portfolio level, including a number of private equity funds, that investor has no control over the timing of any cash flows. In this situation of a wider portfolio, a TWR is more applicable and will provide a comparability measure at a portfolio level with other private equity portfolios as well as other asset classes.

The GIPS also state that TWRs 'will not offer the best measure for an investor to compare returns between PE funds because the TWR will not capture the critical effects of cash-flow management within the control of the private equity manager'. What are investors to do?

**TWRs do not work for single PE funds**

In particular, TWRs cannot be applied to single funds where the NAV fluctuates significantly over time. Exhibit 10.3 shows the TWRs for the cash flows of the hypothetical fund visualised in Exhibit 10.1. Quarterly returns vary between –15 per cent and +50 per cent. Many

Exhibit 10.4

**Comparison between an investment horizon return and a TWR index as calculated from the cash flows using the Original Dietz Method for US buyout funds with vintage years 1985–2005 over the past 10 years (above) and since inception (below)[i]**

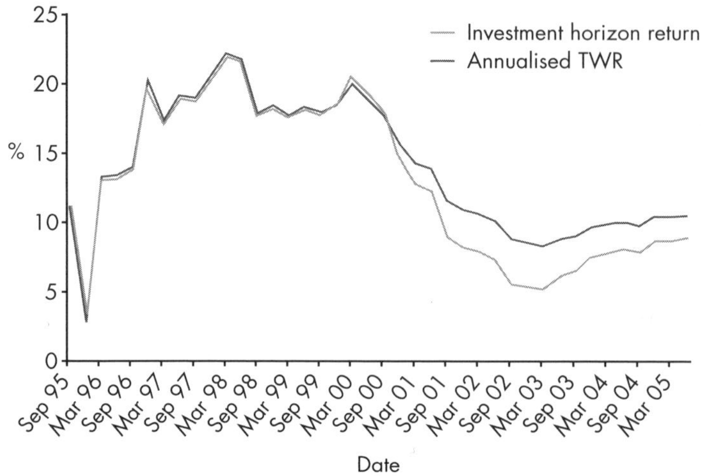


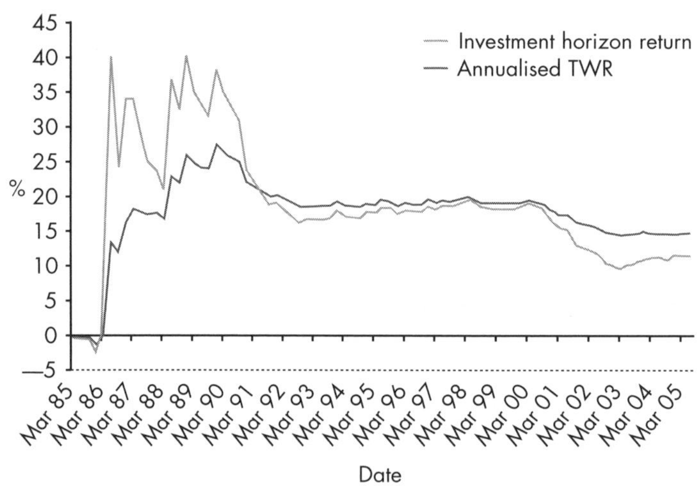


[i]The upper chart shows an example of a diversified portfolio where the use of TWRs is applicable and the lower chart shows a counter-example.

*Source*: Authors' own analysis based on data from Thomsen Venture Economics.

quarters show no big move at all, but big negative returns at inception stem from the impact of management fees on small invested amounts. For example, a negative return of –14.3 per cent is measured for the fourth quarter of 2000. The 1.6 per cent of the commitment that has been invested in this quarter are valued at only 1.4 per cent at the end of the quarter; although this marginal loss (0.2 per cent of the commitment) is not meaningful for the overall final performance the negative TWR of –14.3 per cent will have an impact on the TWR reported for this hypothetical fund. In quarters with revaluations or large exits, TWRs can become substantial (a maximum TWR of 50 per cent would be measured in the second quarter of 2005). Compounding this TWR series yields an annualised performance of 8.9 per cent compared to the SI-IRR of 25.19 per cent. It is interesting to note that compounded TWRs may end higher or lower than the actual multiple – there is 'noise', but no 'bias'.

**TWRs may work for PE portfolios, but must be used cautiously**

In short, TWRs may not be used for single funds. Indeed, it may even be unwise to use the TWR for broadly diversified portfolios. In this sub-section, an example of a diversified portfolio is illustrated, where the use of TWRs is applicable, but also a counter-example. The Original Dietz Method has been applied to the cash flows reported by Thomson Venture Economics for the sample US buyout (vintage years 1985–2005) over the past 10 years and since inception. The results are as follows.

First, an example where the use of TWRs is applicable. The IRR (or more specifically the investment horizon return) over the past 10 years is 8.8 per cent and the annualised TWR is 10.4 per cent. For this time period, the two measures are comparable. These performance figures are, in our opinion, not representative for long-term historic US buyout performance and are simply used to demonstrate the difference between the IRR and the TWR. Note that the IRR and the TWR both suffer from a 'negative bias' due to the following reason. The asset class has grown substantially over the past 10 years and many of the more recent funds are still in the J-curve, during which period the interim IRR is not indicative for final performance. The growth of the asset class is estimated to have a larger impact on the IRR than on the TWR. The upper chart in Exhibit 10.4 shows that the two measures move in parallel for six years until they start to diverge slightly. Note that the maximum net cash flow percentage of the previous end of quarter NAV is 8.1 per cent – that is, the capitalisation moves with relatively small steps.

However, if we change the time horizon for this performance analysis from the past 10 years to the last 82 quarters (that is, since inception) the use of TWRs is no longer applicable. The SI-IRR is at 11.7 per cent and the annualised TWR is 15.1 per cent. For this time period, the lower chart in Exhibit 10.4 shows that the two measures are difficult to compare and it is rather coincidental that the measures move quite close together for some time periods. The IRR is again lower than the TWR, but the TWR series is distorted because the capitalisation over the time period is not stable: in 1986 (second quarter) the TWR is 20.3 per cent for an end-of-quarter NAV equal to US$646m only, and in 2004 (fourth quarter) the TWR is 7.8 per cent for an end-of-quarter NAV equal to US$153bn. Compounding TWRs, both quarters have the same impact on the TWR index, but the first quarter is marginal only for the IRR calculation and will have literally no impact.

In summary, although there are sceptics, it is believed that TWR can be meaningfully applied to fully invested, mature PE portfolios; compounding quarterly TWRs to derive an index typically leads to stable results for portfolios where the capitalisation over the chosen time period is relatively stable (that is, when the quarterly cash flows are small compared to the quarter-end valuation and the capitalisation moves with relatively small steps). Less meaningful results are observed for portfolios that fluctuate significantly in size over the chosen time period, for example with immature portfolios that are being built up over time.

## Measuring GP performance

Performance measurement is thus a difficult issue given the variety of proposed measures and methods. LPs face two challenges: first, they need to analyse the GP performance and track record of individual funds ('Should I commit to the successor of this fund?') and, secondly, they need to assess their overall LP portfolio performance ('Has private equity outperformed other asset classes in my portfolio?'). The first challenge is addressed in this section and the second challenge in the next.

### Separating the wheat from the chaff

PE is an asset class with an extreme dispersion in the returns of underlying funds. Investigating the spread for the 242 US buyout funds tracked in the Thomson Venture Economics database with vintages 1986–97, it can be observed that the best performing fund achieved an IRR of more than 90 per cent, while the worst performing fund returned –42 per cent as of 30 June 2005 (dispersion of more than 130 per cent). A similar analysis for the S&P 500[4] shows a band from –12 per cent to 48 per cent (dispersion of 60 per cent). For the lower and upper quartile, a range of 0 per cent to 19 per cent (inter-quartile range of 19 per cent) can be observed for US buyout and 5 per cent to 15 per cent (inter-quartile range of 10 per cent) for the S&P 500. The spread is even higher for venture capital investments, where the maximum performance for the same vintages exceeds 450 per cent. It is estimated that the dispersion of private equity is at least double the dispersion of S&P 500 companies.

This significant return dispersion of PE funds makes successful fund selection a matter of the utmost importance. The analysis of past performance is one important element of a thorough due diligence process.[5] In order to assess the quality of a GP, the first step is to compare the performance of the GP's past funds with the relevant benchmark figures. For example, a US buyout firm that has raised funds in 1995, 1999 and 2003 should be benchmarked against other US buyout firms that have raised capital in the same years. The status of TWRs as being inapplicable for single funds has already been discussed, and the solution is the IRR.

### The solution is the IRR, but which one?

Data providers such as Thomson Venture Economics report the arithmetic average, the capital-weighted average, the pooled average, and also the median and the top quartile IRR. Which one is the relevant benchmark? The selection of the right performance measure (and the peer group) can be confusing.

- *Arithmetic average.* As the IRR is not an additive performance measure, an arithmetic average performance benchmark is not always meaningful as such a portfolio could not be replicated and outliers can significantly impact the measure.
- *Pooled average.* The pooled average instead gives a number for the performance of the whole sample – that is, it pools all cash flows together to build one large fund and then calculates the performance of this large fund. The pooled average is a representative figure of the performance of the LP portfolio because all actual cash flows are taken into account.

For the benchmark however, the pooled average can be titlted significantly towards the performance of the mega funds. For example, TPG gathered around US$140bn and this will have a weight 140 times larger than some small funds with only US$100m in commitments; however, if one commits to both Warburg Pincus and the small fund, does one commit 80 times more to Warburg Pincus?

- *Unit-valued IRR*. The unit-valued IRR (that is, the performance of a portfolio that gives each fund the same weight irrespective of the fund's size) might on the other hand underweight TPG, as clearly LPs tend to make larger commitments to the mega funds than to small funds. Also, typical venture commitments are lower than buyout commitments because of risk considerations and access issues.
- *Top quartile*. Many investors are tempted to choose the top quartile as a benchmark; however, note that for three out of 10 US venture vintages in the 1990s, the pooled average has actually outperformed the top quartile as of the end of the second quarter of 2005. The top quartile does not denote the pooled average performance of the best 25 per cent of all funds, but the threshold above which a fund belongs to the top 25 per cent performers. Especially for venture funds, spreading the commitments across more funds might even be more successful than trying to pick the right one.

While there is no single figure that is always appropriate, we tend to either choose the pooled average or the top quartile as a benchmark for GP performance. It is believed that the distortion of the average and capital-weighted average are not easily quantifiable and any benchmarking using such figures will suffer from this fact. Using the median should be avoided: given the wide dispersion and the right-skewness of PE returns, it is strongly believed that no LP is in private equity for median returns.

## Measuring LP performance

Just as the GP needs to justify his value-add by proving his ability to generate superior returns, LPs need to prove that they have successfully selected the right funds. Whether you are an adviser, a fund-of-funds manager or a portfolio manager for an endowment fund, somebody will challenge your work. The crucial question is whether you outperformed the benchmark. It is more difficult to measure and benchmark LP performance than to measure GP performance, and there are two ways this can be done: the outperformance over your PE peers can be analysed, or whether a 'public benchmark plus spread' has been beaten. These methods are examined in the next two sub-sections.

### Benchmark against a peer group

How can a PE investor be benchmarked against a peer group? Unfortunately, the PE provisions for the GIPS standards are 'in no way directed towards captive or evergreen funds' in the PE industry and the high-level guidelines that have become effective at the beginning of 2005 can thus not be easily applied. The provisions simply state that open-end funds and evergreen funds (and thus all investors with a long-term private equity allocation, such as pension funds and endowments) 'must follow the main GIPS provisions'. PE is, however, different from public markets and PE evergreen funds are different from public market mutual funds. Therefore, it is believed that a straightforward application of the main GIPS provisions is not satisfactory.[6]

An alternative for evergreen funds is proposed – one that is not in line with the main GIPS provisions (maybe, the following 'cookbook recipe' will contribute to the current discussion on PE performance measurement). One should generally strive to compare apples to apples as much as possible, where the first basket of apples refers to the investments in the actual portfolio and the second basket of apples refers to 'the market', for example, as tracked by Thomson Venture Economics.

Let us assume a global PE mandate is given to invest US$100m in 2000, US$50m in 2001 and US$30m in 2002. Measuring the performance today (at the end of 2005 – that is, only six years after the first investment), the first thing noted would be the average holding period of the investments in the portfolio still being rather young. Although a quantitative assessment is difficult at this stage, most investors require frequent performance updates. How would the performance of that programme be measured and how would benchmarking against the market take place?

- *Neutralise cash flows for currency effects.* In trying to assess fund selection quality, any gains or losses from exchange rates distort the results, so aim to exclude effects from exchange rates wherever possible. In fact, it is typically the client who decides whether or not to hedge the PE portfolio. Because one strives to diversify PE portfolios globally, foreign exchange (FX) impacts may be significant, especially in recent years: many US LPs, for example, have achieved great US dollar IRRs on their post-2001 investments because the US dollar depreciated over the period. In order to neutralise FX impacts, a currency neutralisation would be achieved by simply choosing constant FX rates (such as at the date of the performance comparison).[7] While fluctuating FX rates will change the weighting of the individual funds over time, this impact is typically acceptable and a straightforward currency neutralisation, as proposed, increases the transparency of performance comparisons.
- *Calculate the IRR per segment.* Next, calculate the performance of such currency-neutralised cash flow streams and valuations for each sub-segment and investment year – for example, calculate the SI-IRR (since inception, on a daily basis and pooling all cash flows) for all investments executed in 2000 in the Europe region and the financing stage buyout. In this pool, include all different investment styles (whether primary, secondary or direct investment), because it was a relative value decision as to what particular investments to choose. Note that, if a 1996 vintage is bought as a secondary in 2003, this secondary should be assigned to the investment year 2003, because all distributions prior to purchase belong to the original investor and one will only earn future distributions. For primary and direct investments, the investment year generally equals the vintage year.
- *Benchmark the achieved performance per segment.* Having generated performance figures per investment year, compare the performance of each segment with the benchmark. For example, compare the SI-IRR of all US buyout investments with investment year 2002 in the LP portfolio with the pooled average IRR (as reported by Thomson Venture Economics) for the US buyout funds with vintage year 2002. This detailed analysis is an important tool: it shows whether the LP has learned from mistakes and gives important information about the strengths and weaknesses of the due diligence process.

- *Benchmark the aggregated performance*. More than simply benchmarking the individual segments, benchmark the aggregate portfolio performance also. Because IRRs are not additive, different aggregation methods typically yield different performance results. It is important to measure the manager on the goals that were set at inception: in the above example, it was the client who set the commitment capacity per year and the timing decision is thus with the client (not the assigned investment manager). Therefore, an SI-IRR for the overall PE portfolio may not fairly represent the investment manager's investment success. As a solution, aggregate 'per segment figures' on an investment-level weighted basis: the investment level is calculated as drawdowns divided by commitments (also called the PIC multiple: the ratio of paid-in capital to committed capital). The investment level describes the actual level of the commitment that has already been put to work. Such an aggregation method can reflect the performance achieved by the investment manager and is thus preferable to other methods. This aggregation method is also easy to interpret: it approximates the return assuming a constant commitment schedule for the observed years. Only if the commitment decision is at the full discretion of the investment manager and excess cash can be invested in other asset classes, can an SI-IRR for the entire portfolio fairly represent the investment manager's investment success.

The above proposed method relies on the IRR and the maturity of each investment year. It does not use the TWR and capitalisation is only done partially (within each investment year, but not across investment years). Thus, this method is not in compliance with GIPS.

## Benchmark against public benchmarks

Being asked to ramp up a PE portfolio and outperform an absolute benchmark in the short term is rather like being sent on 'mission impossible' because of the J-curve phenomenon. It is thus of vital importance to pick an appropriate benchmarking methodology. Unfortunately, there is no simple rule that tells us which performance measure to use.

- *TWR*. It was highlighted earlier that TWRs are reasonable only for significantly invested and reasonably diversified portfolios, and that a comparison of private equity TWRs and public market TWRs can make sense for 'market data'.
  *Example*: The TWR methodology works properly for the US buyout funds with vintage years 1985–2005 over the past 10 years, for which sample an annualised TWR of 10.4 per cent was calculated. The total return on the S&P 500 over the same period was actually 9.9 per cent, so US buyout slightly outperformed this benchmark. Note that the large increase in the asset class has a dilutive effect on PE returns (which can be significant) because many funds tranched are still in the J-curve. Over the same time period, European buyout funds achieved a TWR of 16.3 per cent and thus outperformed the S&P 500 by around 6.4 per cent.
- *IRR*. A simple comparison of the achieved IRR with some public market index may not be a meaningful comparison of the two asset classes: simply deducting the public market TWR from the private equity IRR (also called nominal spread) is a 'very direct' method for the calculation of the relative performance and this method does not consider the specific cash flow stream associated with a given PE fund. This independence of the PE fund's cash flow stream eases the performance calculation, but it actually oversimplifies the benchmarking

exercise. Because there is no weighting of returns, all funds incepted at the same time reveal the same benchmark return, irrespective of the timing and amount of draw-downs and distributions. Nevertheless, it is quite common in the PE industry to calculate the relative performance of PE funds versus public markets using this nominal spread.

*Example*: Given the 9.9 per cent return of the S&P 500 over the past 10 years, the IRR of 8.8 per cent measured for US buyout indicates a slight underperformance (again, there is a dilutive effect). Over the same time period, the IRR of European buyout funds was 13 per cent, which results in outperformance of 3.1 per cent.

As alternatives to the nominal spread, the use of the static spread (known from fixed income investments) and 'public market equivalent plus' (PME+) have been proposed recently, and both measures are based on the idea of public market equivalent portfolios (PMEP).[8] Both the static spread and PME+ allow comparing PE portfolios with a benchmark, and neither of the two methods is based on TWRs.

The PMEP is constructed as follows: each time there is a PE drawdown, the same nominal amount is invested in the public market equivalent – for example, the chosen benchmark; each time there is a PE distribution, the same nominal amount is sold from the PMEP; for private equity investments that are not yet liquidated, the unrealised portfolio value is treated as a cash inflow just as actual distributions. A positive (negative) final value of the PMEP implies that the public benchmark would have produced a greater (smaller) return than the PE fund where cash flows were imposed on the benchmark index. The fact that the holdings in the PMEP might become negative, which actually would imply a short selling of the benchmark, is one of the major criticisms of the PMEP approach.

**Static spread**

We propose to use the PMEP in connection with the static spread. In short, the static spread is the spread that must be added to the benchmark returns that will cause the final value of the PMEP to equal zero. If the final value of the PMEP is negative (positive), then we increase (decrease) the return of the benchmark by the static spread and this indicates that PE has outperformed (underperformed) the public market.

For example, a static spread of around 0.6 per cent for US buyout funds is calculated over the past 10 years. In other words, US buyout has outperformed the S&P 500 by 0.6 per cent. Over the same time period, European buyout funds have outperformed the S&P 500 by around 4.8 per cent.

While the GIPS provisions allow public and PE markets to be compared on the basis of TWRs (for 'a wider portfolio, a TWR is more applicable and will provide a comparability measure at a portfolio level with other private equity portfolios as well as other asset classes'), the static spread allows comparing private and public markets on the basis of PE cash flows. The main advantages for the static spread are that (i) it is intuitive, (ii) it takes into account the full cash flow stream of the PE investment, and (iii) it basically overcomes the main criticism of the PME portfolio of short positions in the PME. Moreover, it is well known from fixed-income investments and thus can be easily adopted by PE practitioners.

### PME+

PME+ is an extension of the public market equivalent (PME) and also tries to avoid the shortcomings of short positions in the PMEP. For the PME+ method, the distributions from the private equity portfolios are all scaled such that the final value of the scaled PME portfolio is zero. In case private equity outperformed (underperformed) public markets, we multiply all distributions with a factor less (greater) than one. The scaling can be interpreted as generating a 'similar exposure' in private equity and public markets over time.

At the performance comparison date, the IRRs of both the original PE portfolio as well as the scaled PMEP should be calculated and compared, taking into consideration the remaining value of both portfolios that are now equal. The difference between the two is PME+ and this figure can be readily compared with the nominal spread and the static spread. Note that, while the return of the benchmark portfolio is scaled for the static spread, the private equity distributions are scaled for the PME+.

For example, a PME+ of around 0.9 per cent for US buyout above the S&P 500 is calculated over the past 10 years. This figure is achieved by multiplying each distribution by 0.96. Over the same time period, European buyout funds have outperformed the S&P 500 by around 6.5 per cent.

## Conclusion

It is complex to measure and benchmark private equity performance and there is room for arbitrariness with respect to the applied measure. The use of the internal rate of return and the time-weighted return has been discussed in this chapter, and guidance has been given as to when (and when not) to use which measure. How to benchmark private equity against investors with peer groups and public markets has also been discussed.

It has been argued that the global investment performance standards give good guidance for single private equity funds, but that the application of the standard global investment performance standards for private equity evergreen funds is difficult. Performance appraisal is a delicate task because clients (rather than the investment adviser) often decide on issues such as investment capacity, asset allocation and currency hedging. It is hoped that the example given for a peer group analysis contributes to the discussions on how to benchmark private equity portfolios in a meaningful way.

---

This material has been prepared solely for purposes of illustration and discussion. Under no circumstances should the information contained herein be used or considered as an offer to sell, or solicitation of an offer to buy any security. The information contained herein is confidential and may not be reproduced or circulated in whole or in part. The information is in summary form for convenience of presentation, it is not complete and it should not be relied upon as such. All information, including performance information, has been prepared in good faith; however Partners Group makes no representation or warranty express or implied, as to the accuracy or completeness of the information, and nothing herein shall be relied upon as a promise or representation as to past or future performance. This material may include information that is based, in part or in full, on hypothetical assumptions, models and/or other analysis of Partners Group (which may not necessarily be described herein), no representation or warranty is made as to the reasonableness of any such assumptions, models or analysis. The information set forth herein was gathered from various sources which Partners Group believes, but does not guarantee, to be reliable. Unless stated otherwise, any opinions expressed herein are current as of the date hereof and are subject to change at any time.

---

1 The assumption is that the unrealised value can be sold at the evaluation date at the stated value. Although the issues related to unrealised valuations limit the explanatory power of the IRR (especially for immature funds), it is still the most commonly used measure applied in PE.

2 Most investments are initially valued at cost, and management fees thus significantly impact the overall performance of the fund during the first few years. Funds start to exit their first investments and to write up well-performing companies towards the end of the investment period. The value creation mostly takes place between the fourth and eighth years. Having already written up investments, GPs then need to exit such companies quickly or further grow their valuation in order to keep up with the interim IRR.

3 See http://www.cfainstitute.org/standards/pdf/ipc/sept03/10a.pdf for requirements, recommendations and interpretive guidance for private equity standards and http://www.cfainstitute.org/cfacentre/ips/ for the general standards.

4 This chapter considers all companies that were included in the S&P 500 on 30 June 2005 and that have a 10-year history traceable by Bloomberg – that is, 399 companies are analysed. This approach has been chosen for the sake of simplicity and it is noted that the actual spread (bad performers leave the index whereas good performers, which joined the index recently, are not included in this analysis) is underestimated. On the other hand, TVE does not track the full US buyout universe.

5 Performance analysis of individual funds should of course go beyond the pure comparison of the GP's past funds with the respective benchmark figures. Among other things, it is necessary to make cross-section analyses (for deal captains, industries and exit routes) and to exclude 'homeruns' to find the GP's edge.

6 This is the authors' personal perception: applying the main GIPS provisions to evergreen funds, open-ended products and structured products has turned out to be very difficult!

7 The following describes our methodology to neutralise currency effects from the private equity performance. Let us consider the example of a US dollar investment for a euro investor. In January 2000, one invests US$100; in August 2002 there is a partial realisation of US$20 and, in June 2003, the investment is valued at a NAV of US$110. Given the US dollar cash flow stream, the IRR of this investment is 8.1 per cent. If we consistently apply today's exchange rate rather than the prevailing exchange rates, the currency-neutralised return stream yields an IRR of 8.1 per cent equalling the performance when measured in US dollars. Using the prevailing exchange rates for the above dates – that is, US$/€ = 0.8767, 0.9866 and 1.1511 – the non-neutralised IRR based on the euro cash flow stream is only 0.5 per cent, because the US dollar has depreciated over this time period.

8 See, Frei, A. and Studer, M., 'Practitioner's Guide To Private Equity Benchmarking' *The Journal of Alternative Investments* (Winter 2004) and C. Rouvinez, 'Beating the public market'*Private Equity International* 21 (October 2004).

# Part IV

# New frontiers for private equity

Chapter 11

# The emergence of private equity in eastern Europe

Sylvia Gansser-Potts
*European Bank for Reconstruction and Development*

Dmitry Bosky
*Berkeley Capital Partners*

## Introduction

This chapter traces the emergence of private equity in eastern Europe in the context of major structural and political changes following the collapse of communism throughout the region. It looks at the gradual evolution of private equity opportunities since the early 1990s, as well as examining key factors instrumental for a successful private equity environment. It also highlights the economic clusters within eastern Europe for investment destinations. A Russian country case is included. Although private equity development in Russia lags behind other eastern European countries, it is poised to expand significantly in the coming years given the country's economic and political significance.

The private equity market in eastern Europe, though still small relative to western Europe, has been gaining momentum and recognition since the early 1990s. Driven in part by the favourable macroeconomic environment, structural and political reforms and consistently strong returns, institutional investors' interest in eastern Europe has been steadily increasing. The majority of the largest European investors have either already invested or are actively considering exposure to the region.

## Overview of private equity in eastern Europe

The changes unleashed by the fall of the Berlin Wall and the ensuing collapse of communism created a fertile ground for the emergence of private equity. At the beginning of the 1990s, state-owned enterprises accounted for 70–95 per cent of the region's GDP and in many countries, Russia in particular, the private sector was practically non-existent. The collapse of communism in the region initiated a two-fold transition process – a shift towards capitalism and the consequent privatisation of state-owned enterprises. By the end of the decade, the vast majority of privatisations had been completed and the public sector share of GDP decreased (depending on the country) to 20–35 per cent.

The wave of privatisations and the emergence of a private sector were accompanied by a surge in new business development, including both start-up companies and foreign direct investment. A number of these businesses developed into successful companies, producing a pool of management talent in the region.

The sweeping changes brought about by the privatisations and foreign direct investments created both an entrepreneurial and a commercially driven climate with a much greater degree of acceptance of transfer of asset ownership than in certain western European countries. Resistance to company sale, such as that frequently encountered in the German *'Mittelstand'* where there is a deeply rooted tradition of family ownership, are much less frequent in new and emerging economies.

These developments, coupled with a growing pool of sophisticated entrepreneurs eager to take advantage of the growing economy and favourable market dynamics, created an extensive pool of commercially oriented private equity opportunities.

### Country taxonomy

- *Central and South-eastern Europe (CSEE)*, which is defined as the eight new EU countries (the Czech Republic, Estonia, Hungary, Latvia, Lithuania, Poland, Slovakia and Slovenia), the three EU Accession countries (Bulgaria, Croatia and Romania), as well as Albania, Bosnia and Herzegovina, FYR Macedonia, Serbia and Montenegro, and Moldova.
- *Commonwealth of Independent States (CIS)*, which includes Russia and all other countries of the former Soviet Union, with the exception of the Baltic states, which are included in CSEE.
- *Additional country clusters*, which are outlined on p. 157.

## Private equity: Facts and figures

### CSEE

According to EBRD estimates, over €8bn of funding has been raised by CSEE-dedicated private equity funds since 1990. Of that, approximately €1bn was raised in 2005 alone, a record amount for the region. The significant increase in private equity fund-raising is attributed to a heightened interest from institutional investors in the new European Union (EU) and the second wave accession countries.

### CIS

Total capitalisation of funds raised for Russia/CIS over the last decade are estimated to be in excess of US$4bn, of which approximately US$1bn was raised in 2004 alone. Despite positive economic and political developments, and when compared to other markets, eastern Europe is still underserved with long-term capital. This is evidenced by the emerging economies' relatively small proportion of private equity investment as a percentage of GDP (see Exhibit 11.1). However, given that private equity in the region was non-existent until the early 1990s, substantial progress has been made since 2000.

Exhibit 11.1
**Private equity investment by country as a percentage of GDP, 2004**

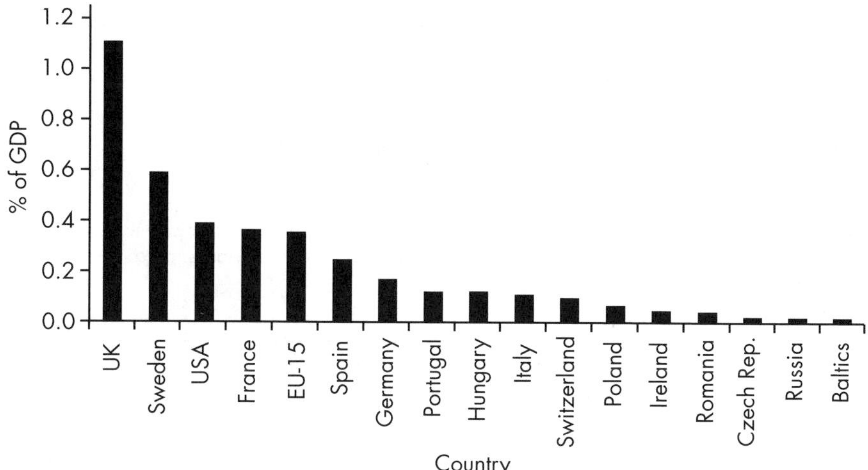


*Source*: Thomson Financial.

## The EBRD's role

Established in 1991 in London following the fall of the Berlin Wall, the European Bank for Reconstruction and Development (EBRD) is an international financial institution created predominantly by OECD[1] nations and former Comecon[2] countries. Its primary objective is to help central and eastern Europe and ex-Soviet countries develop and build a new private sector within a democratic framework. It is committed to supporting transition from state-controlled to market economy as well as promoting western-style business practices.

The EBRD launched its regional private equity strategy in the early 1990s and currently manages the largest funds investment programme dedicated to CSEE and CIS. Total cumulative commitments since 1992 are approximately €1.5bn spread between 90 funds and 60 managers. As of the end of 2004, 800 investments had been made by these funds, of which over half were realised. As reporting by the fund managers is obligatory and there is no survivor bias, it is believed that this portfolio represents the best available sample of private equity performance in the region and serves as a proxy for other investors seeking to enter the region.

Over half of all investments made by EBRD-invested private equity funds were in the new EU member states, whereas Russia represents around one-fifth of total investments to date. Looking at CSEE in more detail, Poland has been by far the largest single recipient, attracting over 40 per cent of all investments made by private equity funds in CSEE up to the end of 2004. Hungary, the second largest recipient, received less than 20 per cent, followed by Romania, the Czech Republic, Bulgaria and Slovakia (see Exhibit 11.2). Investment activity in south-eastern Europe has been steadily increasing, and this trend is expected to continue with the momentum created by the accession wave.

Exhibit 11.2

**Investments by EBRD-invested private equity funds per country, 1992–2004**

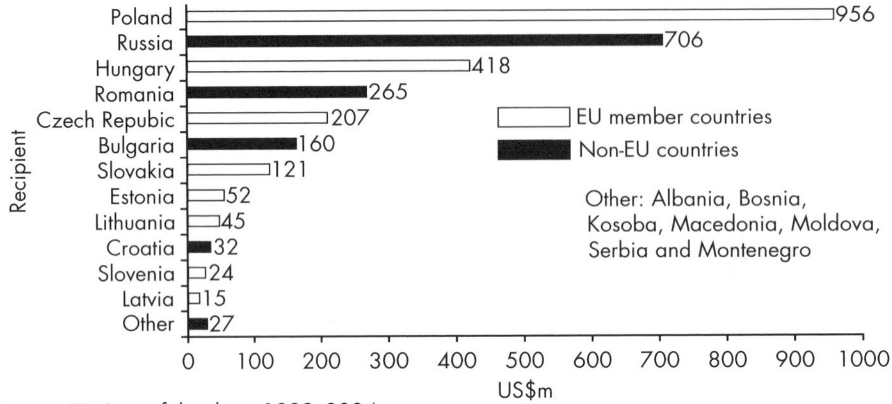


*Source*: EBRD portfolio data, 1992–2004.

## Sector focus

Approximately one-third of all investments made by funds in CSEE focused on the telecommunications, informatics and media (TIM) sector (see Exhibit 11.3). Other significant recipients were the services, consumer and retail sectors. The low level of investment activity in the manufacturing sector stands out, especially when compared to western Europe (manufacturing represented 20 per cent of investment cost in 2004 according to EVCA).

The sector breakdown for the CIS shows a slightly different picture. The TIM sector is less dominant than in the CSEE region, representing less than a quarter of total investments made by EBRD-invested private equity funds. The consumer sector was the largest recipient, representing one-quarter of total investments. Services, primary and energy and manufacturing each represent between 11 and 13 per cent of investments, whereas investment in the retail sector has been insignificant at only 3 per cent.

The developments experienced by the EBRD's portfolio of private equity funds show that, after a slow start, there has been a steady increase both in the investment pace as well as an improvement in the exit environment and, consequently, distributions. The performance of realisations is good, with the surviving funds investing in CSEE (that is, those fund managers who have successfully raised follow-funds) achieving on average a 26 per cent gross IRR and 2.2 × money on realisations, including write-offs. Since 2002 distributions have accelerated and record amounts have been returned to investors, thus endorsing continued interest in the region.

Exhibit 11.4 demonstrates that private equity in eastern Europe has not only outperformed other emerging markets, but, with a spectacular 52.2 per cent year-on-year return, outperformed all other private equity markets in 2004–05. Eastern European returns over three and five-year periods are very strong as well, ranking just behind the western Europe Private Equity Index and outperforming all other emerging markets.

Exhibit 11.3

**Investments by EBRD-invested private equity funds in CSEE per sector, 1992–2004**

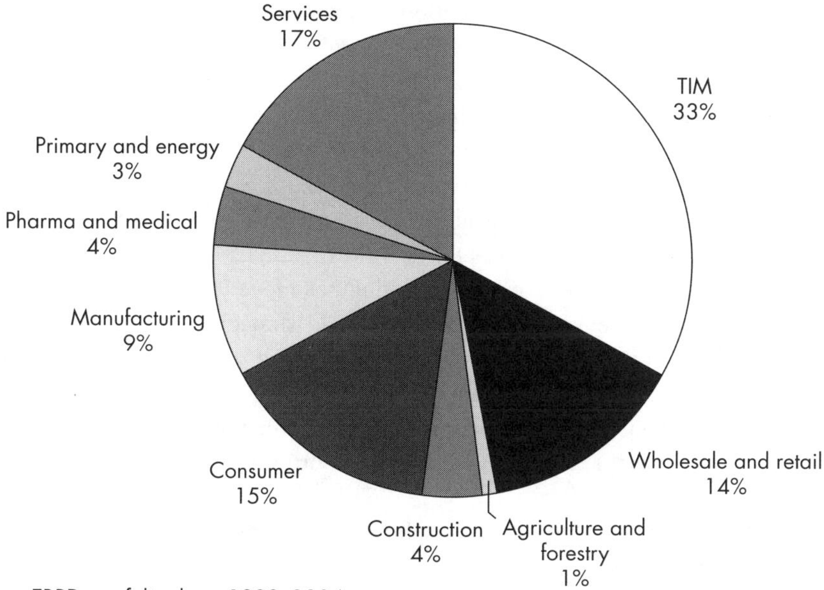


*Source*: EBRD portfolio data, 1992–2004.

Exhibit 11.4

**Emerging Market Private Equity Index, as of 31 March 2005**

| | 1 year | 3 year | 5 year | 10 year |
|---|---|---|---|---|
| EM VC & PE Index | 18.0 | 6.7 | 0.2 | 1.8 |
| Asian PE Index | 10.6 | 5.5 | 0.1 | 1.8 |
| CEE Russia PE Index | 52.2 | 22.2 | 12.6 | 9.0 |
| Latin American PE Index | 16.1 | –2.8 | –8.9 | –5.5 |
| US PE Index 31 Dec 2004 | 23.5 | 12.3 | 5.0 | 12.3 |
| W. Europe PE Index 31 Dec 2004 | 31.2 | 27.0 | 17.9 | 19.2 |
| MSCI EM Index | 17.0 | 19.2 | 4.5 | 4.9 |
| S&P 500 | 6.7 | 2.8 | –3.2 | 10.8 |

*Source*: Cambridge Associates 2005.

## Evolution of private equity investing

The types of private equity investments have evolved over time, adapting to the continuously changing market environment. As the economies in the region developed, the types and range of deals evolved and expanded as well. In the early 1990s, the main sources of deals were privatisations and start-ups, both considered to be highly risky investment types. Privatisations of state-owned enterprises were slow and opaque processes. Privatised companies suffered from weak and inexperienced management, lack of transparency and flawed business models requiring radical restructuring. Workforce reduction was met with fierce political and social resistance. Start-up companies built on imported 'Western' models often faced a number of hurdles such as scarcity of experienced management talent and market volatility.

Over the course of the 1990s, deal types gradually evolved, with expansion capital becoming the dominant type of private equity investment. As the market and economy began to mature, other deal types began to emerge, including buyouts, spin-offs of non-core business units and consolidation plays. Privatised companies in need of a restructuring and businesses that had grown from start-ups became the main sources for deal flow.

In recent years, the focus of private equity investing has moved to later stage expansion financing for mid-sized businesses as well as buy-and-build strategies. Private equity funds typically target profitable, growing businesses managed by their founders or local managers who have acquired the necessary management skills and Western experience.

Professionalisation of management as well as the development and stabilisation of markets have set the scene for a wider range of investment opportunities.

- Buy-and-build investments involving the consolidation of fragmented industries to build national/regional leaders.
- Divestments resulting from the rationalisation of large groups selling off non-core assets or entrepreneurs wishing to cash in.
- Spin-offs by large international corporates seeking to sell the unwanted parts of their operations in the region. This can be driven by the groups' own considerations (financial or strategic).
- Growth and expansion capital as a large number of companies experiencing strong growth rates are seeking to finance their expansions.
- Public-to-private transactions for companies with limited free float, with the objective to streamline the company's focus.

The increasing availability of leverage has been another important development for private equity activity in the region since 2002. This has provided fund managers with additional instruments to structure investments and has led to a sharp increase in buyout transactions, representing today the main private equity investment type. In 2004, buyouts represented about 60 per cent of all investments by value made by funds in the EBRD's portfolio, a level comparable to western Europe where, according to the EVCA, 70 per cent of all investments by value were buyouts. The most developed markets in the region in terms of buyout transactions are Poland, the Czech Republic and Hungary, although a couple of landmark transactions took place in Bulgaria in 2004.

Although there has been a continuous increase in the size of investments since the late 1990s, deals are still relatively small when compared to the western European market. Excluding some of the telecom deals, investments above €30m are still considered large. This reflects both the size of the funds operating in the region and the average size of the companies in the CSEE countries. The larger telecom transactions mentioned above were far too large for any one of the CSEE funds to invest in, and were therefore financed by a syndicate comprising a handful of private equity funds.

Private equity investments in eastern Europe have significantly matured since the early 1990s. Privatisations and start-up investments evolved into expansion capital transactions over the 1990s. However, as the market environment matured, buyouts began to dominate the private equity market, representing two-thirds of total private equity investment. The remaining one-third is allocated to expansion capital transactions.

## Venture capital

Start-ups and seed capital constitute a very small proportion of deals. Domestic funding for this type of investment is still limited. There is at present no culture of angels or venture capitalists. However, successful exits that generate wealth for local entrepreneurs could lead to the creation of a new class of domestic angel/venture capital investors in the near future.

## Key elements for a successful private equity environment

### Legal infrastructure and taxes

The eight countries that joined the EU in May 2004 have largely completed the process of adapting their legal codes to the EU requirements, subject to a few exceptions (such as environmental issues). These changes have benefited private equity investors and have led to increased confidence in transaction execution in the region.

Implementation of structural reforms is more challenging in the countries of south-eastern Europe, but EU admission criteria include steps to improve both administrative and judicial infrastructure, which should significantly improve the investment environment for foreign investors. In all instances, progress is being made in this area, even if the pace of reforms differs from country to country.

The continual harmonisation of the tax regime with EU rules is creating an increasingly positive environment for investment and private equity. The majority of countries significantly reduced both personal and corporate tax rates, thus encouraging owners to realise their existing wealth and reinvest domestically to create new wealth.

### Banking sector development

In the early 1990s, lack of credit-lending skills and experience led to arbitrary lending and distortion of financial markets, resulting in many banks accumulating large portfolios of non-performing loans. The privatisation of the banking sector dramatically changed the banking landscape as foreign strategic investors became owners of many key local banks in the region. Foreign ownership represents between 60 per cent and 90 per cent of bank assets in Poland, Hungary and the Czech Republic. This, in turn, has led to a marked improvement in lending practices, with a gradual willingness to provide debt to corporations as well as private equity-backed companies. During the 1990s, the absence of cash flow-based lending, extensive security requirements and other stringent prerequisites hindered the development of new and growing businesses. This positive development, followed by a decade of long-term debt scarcity as well as limited and expensive short-term financing, indicates an increasing degree of market maturity and sophistication.

Foreign ownership of the privatised banks, reduced inflation and interest rates, and the improved legal and regulatory framework resulting from the EU accession, all contributed to the increased availability of specialised leveraged finance capabilities. These recent development have played a key role in the development of the private equity market in the region, encouraging the growth of leveraged buyout transactions (LBOs). Another important aspect of the banking sector maturation is the recent process of institutionalisation and Westernisation of lending practices, relative to the ad hoc lending so characteristic of the 1990s.

### Management professionals

Up until the late 1990s, the brightest and most dynamic talents would leave the region to study abroad, often opting to stay abroad to acquire experience. One of the main challenges facing private equity investors had been a pronounced scarcity of local management talent. However, the recent positive economic and political developments have played a key role in encouraging 'reverse immigration' in the region. Many of those who left eastern Europe in the wake of the uncertainties of the 1990s are now returning and, with their education and experience, are helping to build up a new class of sophisticated entrepreneurs and professional managers. Furthermore, there is a recognition that the average standard of living is rising, and that real career opportunities and prospects exist in the region.

In parallel, western companies have trained numerous locally hired mid-level managers according to western commercial principles, creating strong candidates to run stand-alone businesses backed by private equity funds.

These important developments have contributed to the improving quality and quantity of the local managerial talent pool, which is undoubtedly the cornerstone to a successful private equity industry.

### Liquidity

One of the most noteworthy developments since early 2000 in the private equity landscape is the improving exit situation. In the past, concerns over exit routes were often quoted as one of the main risks associated with private equity investment in the region.

While trade sales used to constitute the most frequent, if not the only, path to liquidity for private equity funds, there has recently been an emergence of alternative liquidity alternatives, such as public market offerings, secondary sales and management buyouts. Looking at the EBRD investee funds' portfolio company exits realised in 2004, over one-third of exit proceeds were generated from trade sales, another one-third from initial public offerings, with the balance being evenly split between management buyouts and secondary sales.

The larger proportion of management buyouts is a reflection of the increased availability of leverage coupled with the overall improved quality of the management teams and a testament to the increasing market maturation. The recent emergence of secondary sales is a sign of the heightened interest from western European buyout funds looking at investments in the region. This interest tends to be limited to large investments (typically in excess of €100m) as well as to selected sectors, such as telecommunications or media. There has also been some secondary activity taking place among the funds operating in the region, with instances of smaller country funds selling investments to larger regional funds, or funds nearing the end of their life becoming motivated to exit.

Although public markets in the region are still underdeveloped, initial public offerings are becoming a viable route to liquidity for private equity funds. In 2005, the Warsaw Stock Exchange was one of the most active national stock exchanges for initial public offerings in Europe, with a record 35 offerings. The Warsaw Stock Exchange is also the largest market in the region as measured by market capitalisation and is of a comparable size to the Vienna Stock Exchange. This positive development is largely a consequence of the domestic capital supply from Polish pension funds, which have to invest the bulk of their assets in listed domestic securities. As of 2005 year-end, Polish pension funds managed €22.35bn, of which some 40 per cent is invested in equities. Furthermore, approximately PLN10bn (€2.6bn) of new capital has been invested into Polish pension funds.

## Private equity in Russia: A case study

Russia, by its economic size and political significance, sets itself apart from the other European emerging economies. This case study looks at Russia and its fast growing private equity market.

### Macro context

With a population of 142 million and 2004 purchasing power parity GDP per capita of US$9700,[3] Russia is by far the largest of the European emerging economies. It has enormous reserves of natural resources, a highly literate and educated population, a large industrial base and considerable infrastructure. The year 2005 marked the seventh consecutive year of solid GDP growth, estimated at 6.7 per cent average over the period 2000–05. Russia's GDP per capita, highest of the BRIC countries, has shown compounded annual growth of 7.0 per cent in the period 2000–04, well ahead of Brazil and India and only marginally behind China (7.4 per cent). Private consumption grew 11.3 per cent in 2004, gross fixed capital formation grew 10.8 per cent and industrial gross output grew 7.3 per cent. Unemployment stood at 8.5 per cent and 2005 end-year inflation was 11 per cent, down every year since 1999. Russia's 2005 trade balance showed a US$112bn surplus. As of the end of 2004, the mobile phone penetration rate was 51.6 per 100 inhabitants.

On the fiscal side, Russia's federal budget ran a large overall surplus for the fifth consecutive year in 2004. The exchange rate remains firm, Russia has been given an investment grade rating by the three commercial rating institutions, and Russian companies and banks increasingly have access to international capital markets. Substantial reforms have been made in the banking sector, which, after a slow-down in 2004, resumed its rapid expansion in terms of assets, deposits, capital and loans to the private sector. Acceptance of IFR standards has become obligatory for banks from 2005, though full compliance has not yet been achieved. New legislation affecting the banking sector that has been adopted or is under parliamentary consideration includes a law on credit bureaus, a law on consolidated reporting, syndication, mergers and acquisitions, and a law governing the transparency of ownership of banks. Among Europe's emerging economies, Russia is among the leaders in privatisation, price liberalisation, trade and foreign exchange system reform, competition policy and laws on corporate governance.

At the same time, however, challenges remain. To complete its integration into the world economy, Russia must continue to modernise, restructure and diversify its economy and keep on track the reform of its public institutions, clarifying the role of the state and the framework for private businesses. Such structural and institutional reforms are ongoing, with progress on tax and fiscal reforms, trade and currency liberalisation, advances in creating a new pension system, initial stage reform of the banking sector, public administration, restructuring of the power and railway sectors and improving the regulatory framework for SMEs. In terms of transparency of Russia's government and regulatory agencies, the 2004 Kurtzman Group Opacity Index placed the country essentially even with China and India in terms of corruption, and gave it an overall Opacity Score of 46, between Brazil at 40, India at 48 and China at 50. For reference, the US score was 21.

## Investment environment

In the atmosphere of growing prosperity, 80 per cent of respondents in the September 2005 Monitor Group Russian Attitudes and Beliefs Survey stated their agreement that 'Free markets are the most likely way for an economy to succeed'. While the majority of Russians are employed by larger firms, most new jobs are being created by medium-sized enterprises. Since the early 1990s, a dramatic shift has occurred towards a 'new economy' of smaller, entrepreneurial companies. There is now a critical mass of companies grossing US$50–100m in annual sales. The political combativeness observed in large natural resource-type deals is unlikely to extend to Russia's middle market. Meanwhile, there is a very obvious reverse diaspora as young Russians flock back with their Western education and skills to join the new class of professional entrepreneurs and managers.

At the end of 2004 PE investment in Russia as a percentage of GDP stood at 0.014 per cent, compared with 0.07 per cent in Poland, 0.4 per cent in the United States and 1.1 per cent in the United Kingdom. The lending system is still inefficient, and most loans are short term. Capital scarcity is a real issue for most Russian companies. The current PE market may be underserved.

## Private equity market

The Russian PE industry grew rapidly during the years 2004–05. By various estimates, funds under management reached US$4bn. The EBRD, by far the largest fund-of-funds for central and eastern Europe, reports that one-third of its fund commitments and 22 per cent of all underlying investments in its portfolio funds are in Russia.

The growth in fund formation and capital under management is spurred by emerging fund success stories: recently closed new funds have ranged up to US$400m in size. Over one-third of the capital committed to new funds in 2004 came from institutional investors, with another 15 per cent from corporates. Only 10 per cent of the capital raised was of Russian origin.

The industry is maturing, with a number of established management groups running multiple funds. In the EBRD's portfolio, multiple fund managers control twice as much capital as single fund managers. The investment professionals in the industry tend to have

Western education and experience. All managers with funds of over US$150m are of Western origin.

**Deal flow**

Historically, PE investment in Russia has flowed into telecommunications, computer, media, energy and the food and beverage industries. However, over the past two to three years the emphasis has shifted towards consumer products and services. According to RVCA, 2004 consumer-related deals accounted for 26 per cent of total investment by value, with computer-related at 27 per cent and communications and financial services at 11 per cent each.

In terms of investment stage, buyouts are just beginning to make an appearance as leverage is still scarce. Most investment is in expansion-stage companies. In 2003–04, 70 per cent of the money invested was in this category, with buyouts accounting for 20 per cent and later-stage deals 10 per cent. Average deal size is growing: in expansion-stage deals it was US$8.9m in 2003–04. Top-quartile performing funds in Russia make average investments 33 per cent larger than the same group in CEE/SEE. It should also be noted that Russia's regions are a substantial source of deals for the PE industry.

**Exits and performance**

The past three years have seen a steady flow of exits in Russian PE portfolios. Trade sales and management buyouts and buyins dominate by number of transactions; however, it is trade sales and IPOs that dominate by value. Many of the strategic buyers are local.

The performance has been strong: in the EBRD's portfolio, 2004 exits from post-1998 investments averaged a 2.8 × multiple of cost. Across its overall portfolio since inception, over half of the underlying investments have been exited, and fully and partially realised investments have returned 30.3 per cent gross IRR and 2.8 × investment cost. 'Survivor' managers' (those who have raised follow-on funds) results are even stronger: fully and partially realised investments have returned 35.1 per cent gross IRR and 2.5 × investment cost. With write-offs taken into account, the numbers become 23.3 per cent (2.4 ×) and 30.3 per cent (2.2 ×), respectively. Significantly, the overall returns of EBRD portfolio funds in Russia have been 29 per cent higher than in CEE/SEE.

## Regional macroeconomic environment

### Central European and Baltic states (CEB)

The CEB countries include the eight new EU member states from central Europe – namely the Czech Republic, Estonia, Hungary, Latvia, Lithuania, Poland, the Slovak Republic and Slovenia.

Two significant events shaped the macroeconomic environment for CEB countries in 2004.

- In May 2004 the CEB countries, together with Malta and Cyprus, joined the European Union.
- Since then, several countries have also joined the exchange rate mechanism II (ERM II) as a first step towards adoption of the euro.

A favourable external macroeconomic environment, abundant international liquidity, and advantages of EU accession and ERM participation for some of the smaller countries triggered a surge in CEB investment, exports and economic growth. With average real GDP growth of 5.2 per cent for 2004, the new CEB EU member states experienced the highest growth rate since 1995. This growth decelerated in 2005 to an estimated 4.3 per cent across the region; however, it is still robust in comparison to average GDP growth for the original EU-15 countries.

Following the rise in inflation associated with EU accession (mainly due to alignments in excise taxes on fuel and alcohol and VAT), price increases have eased across the region, apart from in the Baltic states. Despite rising oil prices, it is estimated that average CEB consumer price inflation will fall to 3.3 per cent in 2005 from 4.3 per cent in 2004. This largely reflects recent tighter monetary policies and lower interest rates in central Europe. Inflation remains high in the Baltic states partly due to rapid credit growth, rising wages and prices, as well as the oil price boom and the recent euro depreciation against the US dollar. Failure to control inflation may jeopardise plans for the adoption of the euro, planned for early 2007 in Estonia and Lithuania, and 2008 in Latvia.

International liquidity and EU accession seem to have attracted further inflows of foreign direct investment (FDI) into the CEB economies. Net FDI inflows increased by two-thirds over 2003 to US$22.7bn in 2004, while 2005 estimates point to another increase to US$26.5bn. These numbers are a little misleading, however, considering that the sharp increase in net FDI inflows into certain countries in 2004 was due largely to the one-off privatisations of large state-owned companies.

In general, the countries of the CEB region have made considerable progress on the road to complete harmonisation with the EU, with the goal of one day entering the euro-zone. The business environment improved dramatically due to a reduction in bureaucratic obstacles to doing business, improved market mechanisms, and enhanced regulations and protection for enterprises. As a result, there has been a strong market response in many CEB countries, with higher levels of investment activity and greater access to international capital markets.

## South-eastern Europe (SEE)

With their goals set on EU accession in the coming decade, the SEE countries have been making good progress in the transition process. EU accession for the SEE-3 (first Bulgaria and Romania, then later Croatia) is expected in 2007–10. Growth in Bulgaria and Romania has been driven mainly by increased private consumption, while investment continues to be boosted by the prospect of EU accession and ongoing privatisations. Croatia has made considerable progress in improving its business environment, but it is still behind Bulgaria and Romania. Croatia's main challenge remains the reforming of its judiciary and civil service. The countries of the SEE-4 (Albania, Bosnia and Herzegovina, FYR Macedonia, and Serbia and Montenegro) have also made some limited progress with structural reforms, which has helped to sustain economic performance. Nevertheless, it is estimated that average GDP growth in the SEE region decelerated from 6.5 per cent in 2004 to 4.6 per cent in 2005.

Average inflation in the SEE region is estimated to have risen from 5.4 per cent in 2004 to 6.1 per cent in 2005, pushed up by Serbia's expected acceleration reflecting strong wage growth, increases in administered prices and high oil prices. The rate of inflation is falling in all other SEE countries except Croatia (where inflation is already low).

Net FDI inflows into the SEE region increased to a record US$9.2bn in 2004 and estimates point towards a further increase to US$11.8bn in 2005. These inflows remain concentrated in the SEE-3, where they cover more than half of the current account deficits. Serbia and Montenegro is also becoming an important recipient of FDI, but, in common with other countries of SEE-4, it relies to a significant degree on grants and loans from international financial institutions and other countries as well as remittances from workers living abroad.

The business climate in the SEE region as a whole has improved over the past three years, but obstacles to doing business typically remain higher than in central Europe. The levels of bribes paid to public officials have fallen significantly across the region, but businesses are still concerned about how certain laws are applied and implemented, as well as the quality of the judiciary. Many businesses, especially in the western Balkans, are still forced to spend a considerable amount of time dealing with public officials.

## Commonwealth of Independent States (CIS)

Growth in the CIS region as a whole has continued at a strong pace on the back of high commodity prices (oil and gas, metals and agricultural products) and strong domestic demand. After four years of strong average GDP growth peaking at 8 per cent in 2004, GDP growth decelerated to an estimated to 6.4 per cent in 2005. Nevertheless, the outlook remains generally favourable due to the continued strength of oil prices and increased consumption. The most striking slow-down occurred in Ukraine, where GDP growth dropped (from 12.1 per cent in 2004 to an estimated 2.4 per cent in 2005) due to a sharp decline in external demand for its steel output and a decrease in investment caused by the continuing uncertainty over the country's business and political environment. In Russia, GDP growth fell from 7.1 per cent in 2004 to an estimated 6.1 per cent in 2005, due to a slow-down in oil production growth and domestic investment. In Kazakhstan, GDP growth has remained stable over the past two years at an estimated 9.4 per cent.

Large inflows of foreign currency from booming commodity exports have led to substantial increases in foreign exchange reserves across the region. The increased liquidity in the banking system has led to a sharp credit expansion and a rise in inflation, averaging 9.1 per cent in 2005 for the CIS region, up from 8.9 per cent in 2004. Monetary policy and banking supervision in many of the CIS countries need to take into account the challenges of rapid credit growth.

Current account deficits in the CIS region of around 2.4 per cent of GDP in 2004 have improved to an estimated surplus of 0.3 per cent in 2005. Kazakhstan, Russia and Ukraine should record current account surpluses on the back of high commodity exports. In addition, gross FDI inflows increased by more than three-fold in 2005 over 2004 for Russia and Ukraine, while decreasing almost five-fold for Kazakhstan. It is estimated that FDI inflows for the CIS region as a whole reached a record US$17.7bn in 2005. These strong inflows have contributed to an almost halving of net private capital outflows.

Under the new leadership elected at the end of 2004, Ukraine has built on the previous government's reforms and affirmed its commitment to the democratic and market reforms as well as European integration. It has reached several milestones on the way towards achieving membership of the World Trade Organisation. In the banking sector, Ukraine repealed the burdensome regulations that required all investments to be made only in local currency and through local bank accounts. An improved regulatory framework has led to increased foreign investment and growth in lending to the private sector. Despite these achievements, progress in other reform areas has been slower than expected.

In Russia, the economy has continued to grow strongly, with strong FDI and foreign reserve indicators. Importantly, Russia has been assigned an investment grade rating by the three leading credit rating agencies (Moody's, S&P and Fitch), and Russian companies and banks increasingly have access to international capital markets. In some strategic sectors, notably natural resources, the state has sought to regain control of some large companies, but this has not diminished the growth of the private sector or foreign investment into the country. The majority of the country's oil revenues have been allocated to the Stabilization Fund, which has largely been utilised to reduce the country's foreign debt and finance social welfare programs.

Exhibit 11.5

## Macroeconomic indicators by country

| | Real GDP growth (%) | | | GDP per capita (US$) | | Inflation (%) | | | Net FDI inflows (US$m) | | | Net FDI per capita (US$) | | Unemployment (% labour force) | | Trade balance (US$m) | | Population (m) |
|---|---|---|---|---|---|---|---|---|---|---|---|---|---|---|---|---|---|---|
| | 2004 | 2005E | 2006F | 2004 | 2005E | 2004 | 2005E | 2006F | 2004 | 2005E | 2006F | 2004 | 2005E | 2004 | 2005E | 2004 | 2005E | 2005 |
| **CEE and Baltics** | | | | | | | | | | | | | | | | | | |
| Czech Republic | 4.7 | 5.0 | 4.2 | 10,537 | 12,116 | 2.8 | 1.9 | 1.9 | 3,917 | 8,500 | 4,500 | 383 | 832 | 8.3 | na | 869 | 1,500 | 10.2 |
| Estonia | 7.8 | 8.0 | 6.8 | 8,314 | 9,547 | 3.0 | 4.1 | 3.3 | 781 | 2,882 | 1,200 | 578 | 2,140 | 9.7 | na | 1,966 | 1,942 | 1.4 |
| Hungary | 4.6 | 4.2 | 4.2 | 9,971 | 10,911 | 6.8 | 3.6 | 1.9 | 3,542 | 3,500 | 3,500 | 351 | 347 | 6.3 | na | 3,038 | 3,500 | 10.1 |
| Latvia | 8.3 | 9.1 | 7.7 | 5,854 | 6,552 | 6.2 | 6.7 | 6.0 | 596 | 622 | 740 | 257 | 270 | 10.4 | na | 2,781 | 3,110 | 2.3 |
| Lithuania | 7.0 | 7.3 | 6.2 | 6,518 | 7,568 | 1.2 | 2.7 | 2.8 | 510 | 655 | 667 | 148 | 191 | 11.4 | na | 2,382 | 2,421 | 3.4 |
| Poland | 5.3 | 3.2 | 4.5 | 6,609 | 7,809 | 3.5 | 2.1 | 1.3 | 11,826 | 8,177 | 8,400 | 310 | 214 | 19.1 | na | 5,622 | 3,096 | 38.2 |
| Slovakia | 5.5 | 5.5 | 6.0 | 7,639 | 8,629 | 7.5 | 2.5 | 3.2 | 1,259 | 1,800 | 2,000 | 234 | 335 | 17.5 | na | 1,456 | 2,895 | 5.4 |
| Slovenia | 4.2 | 3.9 | 4.0 | 16,329 | 17,337 | 3.6 | 2.5 | 2.5 | 277 | 346 | 470 | 139 | 174 | 6.8 | na | 1,258 | 1,100 | 2.0 |
| *Average* | *5.2* | *4.3* | *4.7* | | | *4.3* | *3.3* | *2.9* | | | | | | | | | | |
| **SEE-3** | | | | | | | | | | | | | | | | | | |
| Bulgaria | 5.6 | 5.8 | 5.5 | 3,109 | 3,381 | 6.1 | 5.0 | 3.5 | 1,232 | 1,991 | 2,356 | 159 | 257 | 12.0 | na | 3,366 | 5,044 | 7.8 |
| Croatia | 3.8 | 4.0 | 3.8 | 7,721 | 8,426 | 2.1 | 3.3 | 3.0 | 899 | 2,000 | 1,200 | 203 | 450 | 13.8 | na | 8,350 | 8,546 | 4.4 |
| Romania | 8.3 | 4.0 | 5.0 | 3,376 | 4,295 | 11.9 | 9.5 | 7.5 | 5,020 | 5,230 | 4,480 | 232 | 241 | 6.3 | na | 6,612 | 9,873 | 21.7 |
| **SEE-4** | | | | | | | | | | | | | | | | | | |
| Albania | 5.9 | 5.5 | 5.0 | 2,372 | 2,730 | 2.9 | 2.3 | 3.0 | 343 | 288 | 339 | 107 | 90 | 14.5 | na | 1,579 | 1,933 | 3.2 |
| Bosnia & Herzeg. | 6.0 | 5.0 | 5.0 | 2,172 | 2,353 | –0.3 | 0.1 | 2.0 | 490 | 540 | 570 | 129 | 142 | 41.0 | na | 2,832 | 3,123 | 3.8 |
| Macedonia | 4.1 | 3.6 | 4.0 | 2,653 | 2,839 | 9.5 | 16.2 | 12.0 | 156 | 150 | 200 | 78 | 75 | 37.2 | na | 1,112 | 1,100 | 2.0 |
| Serbia & Monten. | 7.2 | 6.0 | 4.0 | 2,864 | 3,126 | 9.5 | 16.2 | 12.0 | 1,028 | 1,600 | 2,000 | 123 | 192 | 31.7 | na | 7,434 | 7,065 | 8.3 |
| *Average* | *6.5* | *4.6* | *4.7* | | | *5.4* | *6.1* | *5.2* | | | | | | | | | | |
| Russia | *7.1* | *6.1* | 5.5 | 4,012 | 4,926 | *11.0* | 12.8 | 9.8 | 2,132 | 7,000 | na | 15 | 49 | 8.5 | na | 87,145 | 123,700 | 144.9 |
| Ukraine | 12.1 | 2.4 | 1.5 | 1,374 | 1,668 | 9.0 | 13.5 | 9.8 | 1,711 | 6,500 | 1,800 | 36 | 138 | 3.5 | na | 3,741 | 1,576 | 47.3 |
| Kazakhstan | 9.4 | 9.4 | 8.5 | 2,703 | 3,250 | 6.9 | 7.6 | 7.7 | 5,548 | 1,000 | 2,500 | 368 | 66 | 8.4 | na | 6,786 | 11,912 | 15.1 |

*Source*: EBRD Transition Report 2005, updated to 31 January 2006.

*Note*: Data for 1994–2004 represent the most recent official estimates of outturns as reflected in publications from the national authorities, as well as the IMF, the World Bank and Eurostat. Data for 2005 are preliminary actuals, mostly official government estimates. Data for 2006 represent EBRD projections.

## Conclusion

Professional expertise in the PE industry has improved considerably since the early 1990s. The industry has undergone a steep learning curve and is consolidating and maturing. The bulk of the first funds were raised with government support (for example, US sponsored 'Enterprise Funds' and EBRD), and fund managers employing mainly expatriates would transfer know-how and technology to these new markets.

Today, teams and individuals can display track records which in certain instances exceed ten years. With the availability of track records: investors no longer need to choose between a local manager with no private equity background and an experienced private equity practitioner with no local knowledge. This and the more conducive environment for private equity has contributed to the fact that the profile of limited partners has evolved considerably, with blue chip institutional investors representing an increasing share of the funds' capital, especially for the larger regional funds. Funds investing in CSEE, especially the new EU members, are attracting much more interest from investors, and this is reflected in the amounts raised for the region. Furthermore, there is a growing realisation among western European businesses that eastern Europe represents significant cost advantages for production and to a lesser extent services.

Despite the remarkable developments of private equity funds over the past 15 years, the region still suffers from capital scarcity. The need for growth and development generates a demand for equity capital which is not fulfilled. There are still ample opportunities for private equity investment. To put things back in perspective, the largest fund raised to date for eastern Europe region is €650m, which is a far cry from the amounts being raised in the more developed markets.

Although these emerging economies will converge economically and politically with western Europe over many years, today private equity investors are applying the same stringent criteria to the fund manager selection process in eastern Europe as in western Europe. There is an organic private equity market across eastern Europe which has produced high returns for investors and is growing on size and maturity.

---

1 Organisation for Economic Cooperation and Development.

2 Economic organisation from 1949 to 1991, linking the USSR with Bulgaria, Czechoslovakia, Hungary, Poland, Romania, East Germany (1950–90), Mongolia (from 1962), Cuba (from 1972) and Vietnam (from 1978), with Yugoslavia as an associated member. Albania also belonged between 1949 and 1961. Comecon was formally disbanded in June 1991.

3 Sources for the Russia section include EBRD and the Russian Private Equity and Venture Capital Association (RVCA).

Chapter 12

# The rise of venture philanthropy: Private capital and public benefit

Rob John
*The Skoll Centre for Social Entrepreneurship, Saïd Business School, University of Oxford*

## Introduction

Private equity funds exist to yield financial returns to investors and to create commercial value by selecting companies with the highest growth potential, or knowing how to turn poorly performing firms around; by selecting the best management team for the job; and by bringing to the table knowledge, expertise and networks. When all goes well, investors reap substantial rewards. Along the way, broader society benefits – from more efficiently run businesses, bigger markets and better access to lower priced goods. What if the 'art' of the private equity industry was more directly applied to organisations whose primary purpose is social or charitable, rather than commercial? Are there ways of 'investing' in nonprofit organisations that create greater organisational value, and thus assist more beneficiaries more efficiently? Are such investments purely philanthropic gifts or are there ways in which capital can be loaned or can generate financial returns?

This chapter explores three innovations in social investment that trace their roots to the practices of the private equity and venture capital community.

- A venture capital fund that combines government and private capital, which is invested in socially deprived locations – generating financial returns to its investors and directly benefiting poor communities through local employment.
- A mezzanine fund tailored to nonprofits, employing unsecured risk lending coupled with strategic financial advice. Philanthropic capital is recycled many times, with some investments giving the potential for sharing in the upside of the business.
- Venture philanthropy – a model of supporting a portfolio of high-potential, nonprofit organisations with long-term development funding and business-like advice.

The chapter argues that the skills and thinking associated with private equity have a valuable role to play in growing the social value of charitable organisations or businesses with clear social purpose. On occasion there may be opportunity too for using private capital, with the potential for a 'blended' financial and social return.

## Engaged philanthropy

The foundation created by the legendary 'cereal entrepreneur' W. K. Kellogg defines philanthropy as 'the giving of time, money and know-how to advance the common good'.[1] Kellogg amassed a fortune by combining vision, shrewd business practice and low tax rates to subsequently become one of America's most innovative and generous philanthropists. Three-quarters of a century later, foundations, individual philanthropists and other social investors are still searching for ways to maximise their effectiveness by donating time and know-how in addition to money. The nonprofit capital market, where charitable ventures compete for philanthropic capital, is not as diverse or efficient as its for-profit counterpart. The Kingston matrix (see Exhibit 12.1) illustrates the overall market-place viewed through two metrics: first, social or financial return on investment; and, secondly, how engaged the capital provider is in the venture being funded.[2]

Relatively high engagement financing for business enterprises flows from the venture capital/private equity industry, where investors build the commercial value of a portfolio company through direct involvement at board and management levels, coupled with access to networks and co-investors. This is traditionally an unfamiliar concept in nonprofit financing, where low engagement models predominate. Nonprofits expect to receive little in the way of involvement from the foundations or individuals who fund them. Foundations are seldom equipped to provide tailored advice or work at all with a small portfolio of nonprofit organisations, preferring instead to provide small sums to a large number of grantees.

The paucity of engaged capital providers is further hampered by a lack of financing instruments to meet the needs of small, but high-potential, nonprofit organisations. Most nonprofit funding is in the form of grants – non-returnable, cash gifts that pay for services delivered to the beneficiaries of a charitable venture (such as children educated and homeless people employed). Not uncommonly, such project- or service-based funding does not help a charity recover the full and real cost of developing and delivering its social mission. New Philanthropy Capital, a

Exhibit 12.1
**Kingston matrix**

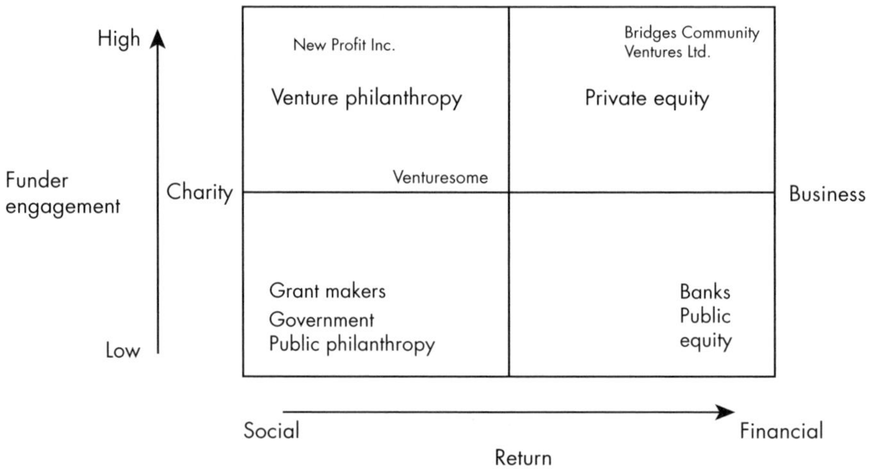


*Sources*: Adapted from *New Approaches to Funding Not-for-Profit Organisations*, M. Bolton and J. Kingston, 2004 available at www.venturesome.org.

nonprofit research and advisory organisation, has developed a guide and toolkit on cost allocation to help nonprofits recover the true cost of delivering social mission.[3] The nonprofit sector remains, however, starved of the development capital needed to research and develop ideas, pilot new programmes or take small but promising nonprofits to a scale of operations where they have significant social impact by reaching more beneficiaries with better services.

Countries in Europe vary greatly in their generosity to charitable causes and attitudes to giving. While private giving in the United States is a higher percentage of GDP than any European country, when volunteering of time is factored in, five European countries fare better than the United States, as shown in Exhibit 12.2. Increasingly, individual donors, seeking to have personal impact in the social sector, look to some degree of engagement with nonprofits, which draws in their skills, networks and energy, in addition to their donations.

## Returns on social investing

The driving force in commercial investment is to make a financial return on capital. The benefits to society at large of creating better performing businesses are important, but incidental – jobs are made or secured, lower priced goods or services are available to a wider public. In reality, any commercially driven investment in a for-profit company results in a blend of financial, environmental and social returns. Investors may make one investment decision over another because they prefer the environmental position or social profile of a particular company – a decision that could impact on financial return. There has been considerable development of thinking in this field by Jed Emerson and others, resulting in propositions like 'social return on investment'[4] or 'blended value'.[5]

Exhibit 12.2

**Private philanthropy (volunteering and financial) as a percentage of GDP**

| Country | Volunteering and giving as a % of GDP | Giving only as a % of GDP |
|---|---|---|
| Netherlands | 4.49 | 0.37 |
| Sweden | 4.41 | 0.40 |
| Norway | 3.01 | 0.26 |
| France | 2.93 | 0.28 |
| United Kingdom | 2.57 | 0.62 |
| United States | 2.47 | 1.01 |
| Finland | 2.36 | 0.28 |
| Spain | 2.10 | 0.87 |
| Germany | 2.10 | 0.13 |
| Belgium | 1.97 | 0.44 |
| Ireland | 1.67 | 0.55 |
| Italy | 0.80 | 0.09 |

*Note*: Does not include donations to religious organisations. Giving includes cash or in-kind gifts by individuals, corporations and foundations.

*Source*: Salamon L., S. Sokolowski and associates (2004), *Global Civil Society: Dimensions of the Nonprofit Sector, Volume 2*, Kumarian Press, as adapted in *Giving More for Research in Europe*, European Commission Director-General for Research, 2005.

The mission objective of a nonprofit organisation is to provide a public benefit – education, health, social services, art, solutions to poverty, homelessness or marginalisation; whether to society at large or to some particular group. Charities generally provide services at break-even and, if they generate revenue through trading, surpluses are not distributed for personal benefit but are ploughed back into mission. Social enterprises are businesses with clear social objectives – for example, they may employ vulnerable people, trade in recycled furniture for low-income families, run community-owned, environmentally friendly wind power turbines; their number and diversity are endless.

Most charities and social enterprises are legally constituted so that their ownership is in some form of public trust, not held privately, so a potential investor cannot take an equity position in a nonprofit. A socially motivated investor may gift capital to the nonprofit (grant-making) or use a variety of debt instruments, and for the majority of such transactions the investor is seeking an environmental or social return. This 'return' is the value created through some environmental or social benefit, and, while the investor sees this value intuitively, measuring it is far more difficult – often leading to a disconnect between funding and results in the nonprofit sector. In a world of perfect information, social investors could, in theory, track performance across a range of nonprofit organisations and make philanthropic decisions accordingly.

New Philanthropy Capital (NPC), mentioned earlier, advises donors and funders how to give more effectively, and has its origins in the world of commercial investment analysis and advice. NPC does not seek to replace the passions and personal motivations that direct people's philanthropy, but to provide a level of research and analysis that complements and strengthens intelligent giving. NPC's approach is a framework for measuring social value creation at four levels – the individual affected, their community and family, the services available to them and, finally, wider society. NPC argues that, for social or environmental benefit to be sustained, funding should be allocated across a 'balanced portfolio'[6] of activities that touches all four levels. In the sector that aims, for example, to combat poverty among the elderly, there will be nonprofits working at all levels – directly with elderly individuals; with the local communities where they live; and advocating government policy changes nationally. The social returns at the individual level may be increases in low-income benefits; at community level the outcomes might be greater participation by older people in local decision-making. At national level, a social return may be changes in legislation that directly impact on the well-being of the elderly. NPC has developed tools to identify a charity's activities and the resulting longer-term outcomes. The social value created is categorised into 'depth' (how significant are the results for each person affected?); 'breadth' (how many people does each activity reach?); and 'change' (are fundamental issues being positively addressed?).

## Three innovations in social investment

This section draws on three ground-breaking examples of how private capital can return a direct public benefit. Venturesome (a specialist financing unit within Charities Aid Foundation) provides mezzanine funding to charities – usually bridging finance or working capital – well known in commercial finance but virtually unknown in the nonprofit sector. This is a powerful adaptation of business principles that is beginning to influence the practices of other capital providers.

New Profit Inc. is a US-based venture philanthropy fund that clearly demonstrates the potential of a relatively pure portfolio model – a philanthropic fund raised from private investors; an expertise in selecting scaleable nonprofits with entrepreneurial leaders; a means of delivering high-quality consulting to the portfolio; and well thought through performance metrics.

First, however, is an example of a venture capital fund that invests in commercial enterprises located in economically deprived areas. Established in the United Kingdom by leading figures in European private equity, it exemplifies how a US model can be adapted to fit a European context – most noticeably its partnership with government.

These three examples are all pioneers in helping create a more diverse and performance-driven nonprofit capital market-place. Together, they represent an investing spectrum from commercial to philanthropic.

## Community development venture capital: Bridges Community Ventures Ltd.

Bridges Community Ventures Ltd. is the first European example of a well-established American model – community development venture capital (CDVC) funds – which invest in businesses in low-income, under-invested communities. Like traditional venture capital funds they seek high-growth opportunities, excellent business ideas and strong management teams. However, in needing to balance social and financial returns, they tend to make smaller equity investments (US$50,000 to US$1.5m) in businesses that most readily provide employment for low-skilled, entry-level workers – in manufacturing, service or retail industries. There are over 60 such funds in the United States, managing US$870m.[7]

Bridges was established in 2002 by two of the UK's leading private equity firms, Apax Partners and 3i, and the business entrepreneur Tom Singh, founder of New Look. Two years earlier, Sir Ronald Cohen (then executive chairman of Apax Partners) chaired the UK Treasury's Social Investment Task Force, from which emerged a string of policy recommendations aimed at sustainable investments in deprived areas, including CDVC funds. Cohen went on to chair Bridges, which is today a fund of €58m, half from private investors and half from government.

Bridges is a private sector, mission-driven company offering its investors a combination of attractive financial returns and strong social impact. It aims to bring the best of venture capital investment – a long-term outlook, hands-on support and an understanding of the issues that growth brings – to businesses that benefit under-invested or deprived areas in England. The initial capital of €58m was raised by September 2002, with the first investment made the following month. Private sector investors committed half of this capital. They include the founder investors – Sir Ronald Cohen of Apax partners, 3i and Tom Singh – along with Doughty Hanson, HSBC, The Royal Bank of Scotland, Lloyds TSB Scotland, Railways Pension Trustee Company, West Midlands Pension Fund, South Yorkshire Pensions Authority, Lehman Brothers, Merrill Lynch and Citigroup. This was matched by €29m of UK government investment, subordinated in part to the private sector capital.

Bridges' vision was founded on the belief that market forces and entrepreneurship can be harnessed to bring social benefits as well as make financial returns, aiming to show that thriving businesses can be created and developed in deprived communities. It exists to:

- invest in entrepreneurial businesses with growth potential in the most under-invested areas in England;
- provide hands-on support to help these businesses grow;
- make a financial return on investment that will attract private sector investors into future funds of this type; and
- make a difference in deprived areas by creating jobs, stimulating economic dynamism and fostering entrepreneurs who can become role models for business success.

The company has been investing for three years and is beginning to demonstrate results in terms of financial return on investment as well as social impact.

Bridges invests from €215,000 to €2.9m in each portfolio company. By September 2005 it had invested or committed €22m in target geographical areas – 18 initial investments and 26 following on – balancing its portfolio between early-stage (38 per cent), MBOs (30 per cent) and property-backed ventures (32 per cent). Its first exit was achieved in May 2005 when specialist label printer Harlands of Hull was sold for €12.2m, representing a multiple of 3.3 times for the fund and an IRR of 84 per cent. The social impact, in one of England's most deprived districts, was realised by saving 50 jobs through turnaround of the company and creating five more after investment. More jobs may be created if the acquirer integrates its own label printing operations into Hull.

To guarantee its strong social mission, Bridges seeks to invest in ambitious businesses that have a strong economic connection with deprived communities. These businesses must be based in electoral wards in England that fall within the most deprived quartile,[8] and linked economically to deprived areas through creation of jobs for staff living there, spending on suppliers in those areas or serving those areas as a core market.

The Bridges team has developed an expertise in terms of finding opportunities in under-invested areas, building upon existing executive teams and then managing investments to help produce growth. Additionally, Bridges has set up the Bridges Entrepreneurs' Club, comprising over 20 successful entrepreneurs and business people across England, to provide guidance, support and experience to the companies in which it invests. Each member of the Club has invested in Bridges' funds.

The following three investments illustrate each of the fund's target stages.

- *Early-stage: SimplySwitch*. Backed by Bridges in 2002 as a start-up company, the firm provides a price comparison service for energy consumers as well as for fixed-line telecoms, broadband and a range of financial products. Bridges initially invested €180,000 as sole funder, enabling SimplySwitch to relocate to a deprived ward in London. The business grew extremely rapidly and is today number two in its market. In terms of social impact, it created 67 new jobs and raised over €580,000 for charities through affiliate marketing partnerships with organisations such as MIND, Barnado's and the Woodland Trust. Bridges' investment in the company now stands at €497,000.
- *MBO: Harlands of Hull*. Harlands Labels was established in 1832 and was a family-run business until the mid-1990s. The company produces specialised high quality self-adhesive labels for leading manufacturers in the toiletries, personal care and cosmetics, beverages and pharmaceutical markets, serving brands like The Body Shop, Avon and Marks & Spencer.

Bridges invested in a management buyout with a minority stake of €1.08m, as a co-investment with Yorkshire Fund Managers resulting in a total funding round of €5.8m. A member of the Bridges Entrepreneurs Club was appointed to the board. In a first exit for Bridges, in June 2005 Harlands was sold to the Clondalkin Group for €12.2m, producing an IRR of 84 per cent, being a 3.3 multiple of capital for the fund. The investment had a positive social and economic impact on the area and provided Harlands with a platform for future growth with the Clondalkin Group. Clondalkin will maintain and develop the Harlands brand and open a printing operation with Harlands in Poland to serve mainland Europe.

- *Property-backed: The Office*. This business acquires and renovates run-down buildings in deprived areas and manages them to provide 'easy-in', 'easy-out' managed offices to suit small businesses. Bridges created the business in 2003 and was the sole venture capital investor, investing €880,000 in a total funding round of €1.9m. To date, The Office has acquired three buildings in deprived wards in London totalling some 30,000 square feet and has achieved full occupancy. The Office currently houses around 40 businesses and this is set to double once its most recent building is renovated. The early buildings are generating gross ungeared yields of 18 per cent. In terms of social impact, The Office creates a multiplier effect by attracting small businesses to do business and spend money in those areas. The company is also working with the charity Global Generation to develop 'green roofs' on their buildings created by children from the local community.

## Mezzanine risk funding: Venturesome

Like several of those behind the start up of Bridges, Venturesome was founded by an individual whose background was the venture capital industry. John Kingston spent his early career with the Industrial and Commercial Finance Corporation (later to become 3i) before moving to the large UK charity, Save the Children Fund. Housed institutionally within Charities Aid Foundation (CAF), Venturesome was launched in 2002 to pilot the provision of risk or 'mezzanine' finance to the UK charity sector to fill a gap between grants and bank loans. Providing customised financial advice to the client charity, in addition to risk capital, makes Venturesome a much more engaged financing partner than, for example, a high street bank.

As a risk fund, Venturesome seeks to support charities that find it difficult to raise funds from more traditional sources, such as grants or bank borrowing. This may be because the application falls outside of traditional grant-makers' criteria, is not project specific, has too great a commercial characteristic or because competition for funding in the sector is intense. In addition, some charities actively seek debt as part of a longer-term funding strategy. Venturesome concentrates on underwriting and unsecured lending products; on occasion, a stake in the performance of the organisation may be part of the investment ('quasi-equity'). The primary target market is small and medium-sized charities; Venturesome has also worked with social enterprises with a clearly defined charitable purpose. The heart of the Venturesome model is to balance financial risk with potential social impact; the key concepts in Venturesome's approach are recycling and social return.

Venturesome is not a grant-maker, and therefore there is a strong expectation that investments will be paid back or 'recycled'. Venturesome is able to assume higher financial risk than a conventional bank lender, for whom, in the absence of security, the charity or project could be assessed as too risky or as having too high an appraisal and monitoring cost. As a result, recycling rates are projected to be lower – a bank lender would project recycling rates of greater than 98 per cent, whereas Venturesome projects an average recycling range of 75–80 per cent. This rate of recycling means that the funds invested in the voluntary sector via Venturesome work hard, perhaps being recycled four to five times. This contrasts with both the commercial banking sector (recycled many times against security) and the one-off donation of a traditional grant-maker (never recycled).

While risk capital funds such as Venturesome do not necessarily expect a higher financial return for this increased risk, they expect and monitor social returns on their investments. The total return is therefore made up of both financial and social elements. This enables risk capital funds to invest where the pure financial return is not commensurate with the level of risk.

Venturesome provides three types of finance:

- pre-funding of capital fund-raising: bridging finance;
- working capital: underpinning cash flow/financial stabilisation; and
- development capital: building new streams of income generation.

Venturesome knowingly assumes higher financial risk, which is reflected by a combination of social and financial return, and works to reduce the risk taken on through value-added, high-engagement, customised advice and financing:

- engagement with the charity, through a personal, two-way relationship;
- provision of advice and support;
- variety of financial products, customised to each situation;
- links to professional and funding networks; and
- faster access to funding than traditional grants.

Venturesome's pilot and subsequent development phases have been successful: the fund currently stands at €7.2m, and since inception Venturesome has offered facilities to over 100 clients worth €8.7m; €3.5m is currently outstanding across a portfolio of 43 deals. Venturesome was launched with an initial capital injection from Charities Aid Foundation, and has since raised funds from grant making trusts and individual donors.

## Venture philanthropy: New Profit Inc.

For some the term 'venture philanthropy' is an oxymoron – inherently a contradiction between philanthropy (from the Greek for 'love of humankind') and commercially driven, for-profit ventures seeking personal financial reward. While it was probably first coined by John D. Rockefeller III back in 1969,[9] its modern usage stems from the Harvard Business School in 1997,[10] which challenged US foundations to 'invest' in nonprofit organisations, employing tools from venture capital to create stronger, better performing institutions. At this time the dot-com boom spawned bold entrepreneurs with ambitions to become a generation of new economy philanthropists; several embraced venture philanthropy, but the aggressive approach to the social sector by some entrepreneurs was not always viewed positively.[11] Despite this early controversy, several funds were launched in the United States, whose high level of engagement with a portfolio of nonprofits distinguished them from more traditional forms of grant-making.

### Case study
### Venturesome client

A client develops and supports workshop projects in prisons. Offenders work voluntarily to provide goods and services for the benefit of other people. This 'restorative' work helps them to build their confidence and self-esteem. Offenders gain skills and qualifications that help them to secure a job on release, and to lead law-abiding and constructive lives. The client's work makes an important contribution to the criminal justice system in the United Kingdom, both through its direct work and indirectly through advocacy.

The newly appointed director at the client contacted Venturesome in summer 2004. Difficulties with a major contract had led to a funding crisis. Venturesome and the director agreed that the charity required both development capital to underpin reserves and working capital to assist cash flows. Venturesome provided €50,000 in development capital, as an unsecured, medium-term loan, with repayment linked to the level of reserves over five years, and a €94,000 working capital facility, repayable from cash flow.

It would be unwise to push too far the analogy between venture capital and venture philanthropy, but language, tools and practices are recognisably similar. As a rule of thumb, venture philanthropists seek out a portfolio of small, well-performing, entrepreneurial nonprofit organisations with growth potential led by an excellent management team. After a prolonged period of due diligence, they provide performance-based development capital[12] coupled with strategic management advice and executive coaching. They bring to the table problem-solving skills, access to networks and co-funders. They agree performance metrics and hold management to account for reaching milestones. Naturally enough, they seek an exit after three to five years, although, in the nonprofit world of public benefit and ownership 'in trust', this can be elusive.

Venture philanthropy is fundamentally a charitable activity – focused investments of money, time and skills to help nonprofits deliver more mission, more effectively to more people by deploying and adapting the tools usually associated with venture capital.

From the perspective of a nonprofit seeking venture philanthropy investment, it represents an opportunity for development capital plus access to a skill set not normally available to most small charities. It is very difficult for small nonprofits to finance their growth and development. Younger, less well-known organisations struggle in a highly competitive market for philanthropic capital. With little access to information about performance and real social impact, giving by individuals flows most readily to well-known charity 'brands', while many good nonprofits fall beneath public radar.[13] Even when funds are raised, they seldom do more than cover the cost of fund-raising (which can be as much as 30 per cent) and administration, in addition to delivering the particular social service. It can take decades before a charity builds unrestricted reserves sufficient to fuel growth or product development. Venture philanthropy gives a nonprofit access to development capital and a host of advisory services to make those funds work more effectively.

**History and operations**

New Profit Inc., located in Boston, was founded in 1998 by social entrepreneurs frustrated with the structure of the US nonprofit sector – a market characterised by fragmentation, subscale operations and donors unable to readily measure the impact of the organisations they fund. Though there are over 1.5 million nonprofit organisations in the United States, 91 per cent report annual revenues of less than US$1m. Solutions to the same problems are being invented over and over again by multiple organisations with no mechanism to float the best ideas to the top. The short-term and fickle nature of funding streams demands that nonprofit executives spend inordinate amounts of time chasing revenue opportunities with little money or time to build stronger and more sustainable organisations. Thus, despite rapidly growing numbers of nonprofits and increased funding to the sector (US$250bn in the United States in 2004), solutions do not keep pace with the growth of social challenges.

New Profit Inc. provides multi-year financial and strategic support to a portfolio of nonprofit organisations that are focused on a range of issues including education and child development, workforce and economic development and civic engagement. The fund brings together financial and intellectual capital from individual investors (donors) with a unique set of strategic resources from the Monitor Group global strategy consulting firm and other partners, to help its portfolio organisations scale up and increase their social impact. New Profit invests mostly in mezzanine-level and early-stage organisations that have under US$5–10m in annual income. New Profit's level of engagement and use of rigorous performance metrics helps to ensure the impact of investors' commitments. Since 1998, New Profit has made 14 investments in leading social entrepreneurs and their organisations, and has raised more than US$20m, mostly from individuals – many from the private equity industry.

After more than five years of operation, and having 'graduated' its first three investments, New Profit's approach is starting to demonstrate results. Its portfolio organisations measure social impact, revenue growth, number of people benefited ('lives touched'), and other key dimensions of their performance. In 2005, New Profit's portfolio includes some of the fastest growing nonprofits in the United States. Selected investments include 'Teach For America,' 'College Summit,' 'New Leaders for New Schools,' 'Year Up,' 'Jumpstart,' 'KickStart' and 'Right To Play.' Overall, the portfolio has demonstrated compound annual growth in the number of 'lives touched' of 45 per cent, and compound annual revenue growth of 31 per cent, compared to 4 per cent compound annual revenue growth across all service-delivery nonprofits. Two-thirds of New Profit's portfolio organisations have increased (and the other one-third maintained) their impact per life touched, demonstrating that, if done right, scaling up has a positive effect on quality. Even benchmarking against other nationally recognised nonprofits, New Profit's portfolio appears to have demonstrated superior growth and impact, indicating that its mix of financial and nonfinancial resources, applied systematically, yields significant benefit.

**Investment procedures**

New Profit reviews over 300 potential investments each year, and, on average, selects 50 'deals' to undergo initial due diligence. In due diligence, organisations are assessed against five criteria: potential for social impact; strength of the entrepreneur and leadership team; the organisation's performance to date; capacity for growth; and, finally, the potential for New Profit to add value (or 'fit'). Among these five criteria, the social entrepreneur and the social impact potential are the most important, followed closely by fit with New Profit's competencies and approach. When assessing an organisation's leadership, New Profit looks for founding social entrepreneurs with exemplary knowledge, skills, personal qualities and ability to mobilise resources. In examining social impact, it looks at the importance, size and urgency of the need being addressed; the organisation's model for addressing that need (both its direct impact and power to change the sector); as well as previous performance. Of the initial 50 organisations that enter preliminary due diligence, only two to four deals will be considered by the investment committee, and, by the time a new investment is approved, New Profit will have already spent 100 to 200 hours with the organisation. The same five criteria are continually assessed as New Profit gets to know an organisation better, from an initial hypothesis to a highly developed theory of the engagement.

With due diligence completed, New Profit sets the baseline for an organisation's effectiveness, efficiency and sustainability so that incremental improvement can be assessed. Portfolio organisations receive continued financial commitments contingent upon their results, measured in terms of agreed-upon growth metrics. New Profit monitors the organisation's capacity building – its work to build the infrastructure, human resources and systems – towards sustainability, helping each portfolio organisation identify and cultivate long-term reliable funding.

New Profit's portfolio managers, together with the strategic consultants they deploy, typically spend 2000 to 5000 hours working with each portfolio organisation over the course of a four-year investment. These managers act as resource brokers, help organisations recruit and develop management talent, co-fundraise with the organisation, and plan for growth. They also take a seat on the portfolio's board of directors.[14] Typically, New Profit's managers are social entrepreneurs or nonprofit leaders themselves who engage well with the portfolio organisation's management team. Portfolio managers also coordinate pro-bono strategy projects delivered by New Profit's partner, Monitor Group. Key projects typically include developing an organisation's theory of change, and creating and supporting an enterprise-wide growth plan. Depending on the organisation's needs, consulting teams may also work on detailed financial plans, HR strategies, board development, evaluation approaches and brand building. Executive coaching from senior Monitor consultants is another key strategic contribution leveraged by New Profit. Social entrepreneurs clearly value these forms of support; in fact, the first set of New Profit organisations say that the intellectual resources they received were far more valuable to their growth than the financial resources New Profit provided.

As part of its investment terms, New Profit requires that each portfolio organisation develop a Balanced Scorecard™ (BSc) or equally robust performance tool. The BSc captures and measures a holistic view of an organisation's performance, complementing bottom-line/financial measures with an additional four perspectives: social impact, constituent satisfaction, internal business operations and capacity. Progress is monitored on a quarterly basis, with new BSc goals being set each year. New Profit requires that the scorecard be implemented at the enterprise level, but also recommends that each organisation expands the BSc to incorporate goals for all sites/affiliates. New Profit also develops a BSc for itself, and ties its own performance to that of its portfolio organisations. New Profit reports quarterly to its investors and board on progress against its own BSc goals as well as the BSc for each of its portfolio organisations. Reporting enables New Profit investors to track portfolio performance and lends quantitative data to support anecdotal evidence of success.

## Is exit possible?

Exiting a venture philanthropy investment is a concept that defies any facile adaptation from the practices of commercial venture capital. 'B' round investors, sales to third parties or IPOs, while well understood exit strategies in the for-profit world, have no direct counterparts in the nonprofit capital market. Venture philanthropy funds all struggle with the concept and practice of how an organisation exits from a portfolio.[15] Generally the nonprofit market cannot provide a segmented supply of capital meeting the needs of growing nonprofit organisations at different stages of their development (seed, start-up and scale-up). As yet there is no nonprofit stock market, and ownership issues prevent most forms of public offering. Even though exits, when viewed through a commercial lens, are severely limited or non-existent, the concept is a vital component of good venture philanthropy practice. Discussion of exit even before an investment is agreed helps shape the investor's strategy for creating a viable and robust nonprofit; it helps the investor tailor a range of financial instruments as the nonprofit develops.[16] For example, the Sutton Trust, in the United Kingdom, founded by the business entrepreneur, Sir Peter Lampl, to increase access to the country's top universities by children from disadvantaged communities, funds pilot projects grounded in research, and finds a natural exit to government and other public funders.[17]

Maintaining a portfolio organisation's current size is not the challenge; rather, it is finding growth funding to achieve continued 30 per cent annual growth. Additionally, because there is no financial return to the funder of a nonprofit venture, at the point of exit there is a much higher premium placed on the continued success of the organisation. Any failure of a portfolio organisation, even after exit, will affect the reputation of the venture philanthropy fund. For these reasons, New Profit has had to adapt the notion of exit to the nonprofit context, and, in 2005, comfortably exited its first three investments: 'Working Today,' 'Jumpstart' and 'Citizen Schools'.

In preparing an organisation for graduation (funding exit), New Profit has a checklist against which it assesses the organisation on a quarterly basis; work with the organisation focuses on areas of greatest need. This checklist includes metrics in the categories of: mission and social impact; organisational competencies; and financial sustainability. Achieving financial sustainability is arguably the greatest challenge for the growth-focused nonprofit organisation. New Profit helps its portfolio organisations to develop diversified funding – with an appropriate mix of government contracts, corporate sponsorship, individual donations, foundation grants and fees for service.

In order to understand the progress New Profit's portfolio organisations make towards financial sustainability, it helps to consider the following examples. 'Working Today' received its start-up capital from individuals and foundations; with New Profit's guidance it evolved its fee-for-service model and has recently achieved financial break-even with this earned income. Moreover, 'Working Today' developed such extensive expertise in an under-served market that it is now creating its own for-profit social purpose insurance company. For 'Jumpstart', financial sustainability has come through a balanced mix of national corporate sponsors, such as Starbucks, university partnerships and government funding for tutors through the AmeriCorps programme. 'Citizen Schools,' on the other hand, has created a highly diversified funding stream, with income from across all categories: foundations, individuals, corporations, government and fee-for-service.

New Profit is currently working with partners to develop the pool of later-stage growth funding available for graduating organisations. Meanwhile, as nonprofit capital markets develop, New Profit aims to keep its graduate organisations within the New Profit network, so that they can continue to benefit from its web of contacts, information and resources.

New Profit is a small fund, but it has successfully brokered a co-funding arrangement with a large established US grant-making foundation, and, more recently, New Profit has formed a partnership with the One Foundation, a young foundation in Ireland employing a high-engagement approach. The One Foundation sought out New Profit as a partner to ramp up its capacity to operate the first fund of this kind in Ireland. Several learning sessions and staff internships have given the One Foundation a knowledge base that they have customised for the unique Irish landscape.

## The European dimension

While venture philanthropy's modern origins are clearly American, with New Profit demonstrating a powerful and focused model, it is taking root throughout Europe. In 2004, five European private equity professionals, who had long wrestled with how to make their own personal philanthropy more effective, set up the European Venture Philanthropy Association (EVPA)[18] with initial sponsorship from 3i, Barclays Capital and KPMG, to encourage the expansion of venture philanthropy across Europe. The EVPA was quickly endorsed by both the European Private Equity and Venture Capital Association (EVCA) and the European Foundation Centre (EFC), and within 12 months had gained 26 members in nine countries. These included full, practising venture philanthropy funds but also associates with an interest in the field, including two leading private equity houses and four major grant-making foundations. The EVPA is a rapidly growing network, which sees itself as a catalyst bringing together players from the private equity community, grant-making foundations, public funders and entrepreneurial nonprofits.

A baseline mapping exercise recently completed by the EVPA[19] identified some 26 organisations in 10 European countries practising some form of venture philanthropy, in its broadest interpretation. These figures are probably a conservative estimate; the number of operations and countries is likely to grow significantly over the next 10 years.

Over the past five years venture philanthropy and related funds have emerged from individuals connected with the European private equity, venture capital or investment communities, and business entrepreneurs, including: Impetus Trust (UK); BonVenture (Germany); Fondazione Oltre (Italy); Venturesome (UK); Venture Partners Foundation (UK); Sutton Trust (UK); Noaber Group (Netherlands); and Invest for Children (Spain).

Exhibit 12.3

**Venture philanthropy compared to overall Private Foundation spending**

| Private grant-making and operational foundations | Total annual expenditure €m | Estimated annual expenditure on venture philanthropy m |
|---|---|---|
| US private foundations | 23,000 | 41.5 |
| UK private foundations | 3,300 | 12.3 |
| European private foundations | 51,000 | unknown |

*Sources: Venture Philanthropy 2002,* Venture Philanthropy Partners & Community Wealth Ventures Inc.; Association of Charitable Foundations; *Foundation Facts & Figures Across the EU,* European Foundation Centre; UK estimates are based on unpublished research and are for England and Wales only.

The three examples in this chapter of applying an investment approach to social sector organisations illustrate how the private equity/venture capital community can realistically and usefully engage with the nonprofit sector, beyond passive forms of philanthropy or corporate social responsibility.

Venture philanthropy in the United States and Europe is a small, niche, philanthropic market (see Exhibit 12.3). Compared to spending by foundations alone, venture philanthropy in the United States accounts for less than 0.2 per cent of the volume of grants made (2000 figures). In the United Kingdom the figure is proportionally higher at 0.3 per cent when applying the broadest possible definition of venture philanthropy. There is no research yet estimating the scale of venture philanthropy funding across Europe as a whole, but if it reached UK proportions it would represent a market of €200m. Where will this growth come from? It is likely that a small number of foundations currently practising fairly traditional grant-making will set aside proportions of their income towards a high-engagement portfolio; new players will emerge with the roots (and wealth) in private equity and venture capital; governments, too, see the logic of helping to build their nonprofit sector through a mix of traditional and venture funding.

Just as private equity is relatively limited compared to the volume of the public equity markets, so venture philanthropy will not grow to dominate the funding of nonprofits, but will be a small and effective tool in the social sector. The intellectual capital and tools of private equity, when adapted and applied with sensitivity, can be powerful agents of change in the mission-driven world of social purpose organisations.

The author gratefully acknowledges the cooperation of organisations used as case studies in this chapter. In particular, helpful background material and data were provided by Michele Giddens (Bridges Community Ventures), John Kingston (Venturesome) and Heiner Baumann (New Profit Inc.). Further information about these organisations can be found at: www.bridgescentures.com; www.venturesome.org; www.newprofit.com.

---

[1] *Unleashing Resources*, Program Strategy Fact Sheet (www.wkkf.org).

[2] After John Kingston, Venturesome (www.venturesome.org).

[3] *Full Cost Recovery: A Guide and Toolkit on Cost Allocation*, Caroline Fiennes, Cathy Langerman and Jeni Vlahovic, NPC & ACEVO (www.philanthropycapital.org).

[4] See New Economics Foundation work on SROI at http://sroi.london.edu.

[5] See Jed Emerson's work on the blended value concept (www.blendedvalue.org).

[6] Lumley, T., C. Langerman and M. Brookes *Funding Success: NPC's Approach to Analysing Charities* (London: New Philanthropy Capital, 2005).

[7] For a history of the community development venture capital industry in the United States and the current situation, see their website (www.cdvca.org).

[8] As defined by the Index of Multiple Deprivation, which combines indicators on Income, Employment, Health Deprivation and Disability, Education, Skills and Training, Housing and Geographical Access to Services into a single deprivation score for each location.

[9] At a hearing before a US Congressional Committee, which led to the Tax Reform Act (1969).

[10] See 'Virtuous Capital: What Foundations Can Learn from Venture Capitalists', Christine Letts, William Ryan and Allen Grossman, published in the *Harvard Business Review* (1997) HBR97207.

[11] For an early critique of venture philanthropy see *If Pigs Had Wings: The Appeals and Limits of Venture Philanthropy* by Bruce Sievers (2001) (available at www.philanthropyuk.org).

[12] Usually non-returnable grants, and sometimes a mix of grant and sub-market loans.

[13] See *Funding Success*, New Philanthropy Capital, December 2005.

[14] New Profit employs a ratio of one portfolio manager for every four organisations, rather than the 1:30 ratio that is typical of many large charitable foundations.

[15] For a thought-provoking discussion by three venture philanthropy funds, see *When Is It Time to Say Goodbye?*, by Kim Alter, Paul Shoemaker, Melinda Tuan and Jed Emerson, 2001 (available at www.redf.org).

[16] A very early example of venture philanthropy in the United Kingdom, World in Need (now renamed ACT), would taper its annual grants and graduate an investee to underwriting or long-term debt.

[17] See www.suttontrust.com.

[18] A membership organisation registered in England as a charity (see www.evpa.eu.com).

[19] *Venture Philanthropy in Europe: Obstacles and Opportunities*, P. M. Grenier (see www.evpa.eu.com).